Fred Schepisi: Interviews

Conversations with Filmmakers Series
Gerald Peary, General Editor

Fred Schepisi
INTERVIEWS

Edited by Tom Ryan

University Press of Mississippi / Jackson

www.upress.state.ms.us

The University Press of Mississippi is a member of the Association of American University Presses.

Copyright © 2017 by University Press of Mississippi
All rights reserved
Manufactured in the United States of America

First printing 2017

∞

Library of Congress Cataloging-in-Publication Data

Names: Schepisi, Fred author. | Ryan, Tom (Film writer) editor.
Title: Fred Schepisi : interviews / edited by Tom Ryan.
Description: Jackson : University Press of Mississippi, 2017. | Series: Conversations with filmmakers series | Includes bibliographical references and index. | Includes filmography.
Identifiers: LCCN 2016036166| ISBN 9781496811479 (cloth : alk. paper) | ISBN 9781496855688 (paperback : alk. paper) | ISBN 9781496811493 (epub institutional) | ISBN 9781496811509 (pdf single) | ISBN 9781496811516 (pdf institutional)
Subjects: LCSH: Schepisi, Fred—Interviews. | Motion picture producers and directors—Australia—Interviews.
Classification: LCC PN1998.3.S3465 A5 2017 | DDC 791.4302/33092 [B] —dc23 LC record available at https://lccn.loc.gov/2016036166

British Library Cataloging-in-Publication Data available

Contents

Foreword by Gillian Armstrong   viii

Introduction   xi

Chronology   xx

Filmography   xxiv

Fred Schepisi   3
   Sue Mathews / 1984

Devil's Playground: An Interview with Fred Schepisi   22
   Brian McFarlane / 2015

Playboy Interview: Fred Schepisi   27
   Rennie Ellis / 1982

Fred Schepisi: The Australian Director Talks about His New Controversial Film, *Barbarosa*   42
   Michael Sragow / 1982

Altered States in the Great White North   45
   James Verniere / 1983

Fred Schepisi: Taking Hollywood by Drizzle   48
   David Edelstein / 1984

Man of Plenty   52
   Brent Lewis / 1985

Man of Plenty   56
   David Stratton / 1986

Dialogue on Film: Fred Schepisi   61
    American Film / 1987

The Making of *Evil Angels*: Director Fred Schepisi Talks About Private Moments, Public Realities and Dingoes   67
    Philippa Hawker / 1988

The Man Meryl Streep Trusts   72
    Rennie Ellis / 1989

Fred Schepisi   79
    Peter Malone / 1998

Fred Schepisi: "Pushing the Boundaries"   86
    Scott Murray / 1990

A Cinematic Gallant   102
    Stephen Schiff / 1993

Last Orders: An Interview with Fred Schepisi   114
    Cynthia Fuchs / 2001

Fred Schepisi on *Last Orders*   120
    Tom Ryan / 2001

Fred Schepisi on *It Runs in the Family*   127
    Tom Ryan / 2003

Shooting Dialogue as Action—An Interview with Fred Schepisi   138
    Fincina Hopgood / 2011

All against One and One against All: Fred Schepisi's Outsiders   147
    Dan Callahan / 2014

Fred Schepisi on Making Movies—"What I'm Most Interested in—Always—Is the Humanity of the Piece"   153
    Tom Ryan / 2015

Appendices

    Planning and Problem-Solving: An Interview with Ian Baker   178
    Tom Ryan / 2016

    Key notes: an interview with Paul Grabowsky   183
    Tom Ryan / 2016

Additional Resources   189

Index   192

Foreword

Gillian Armstrong / 2016

I once tiptoed, head bowed, stumbling across terrifying cables and camera equipment, carrying coffee mugs to Mr. Schepisi and his cinematographer, Ian Baker. Four or five times a day for many days.
It was December 1971, I had just turned twenty-one, and Fred was shooting Tom Keneally's *The Priest*, as part of the feature, *Libido*. He was one of our final-year assessors at Swinburne Film School and had generously offered work to me and fellow student Roger Scholes, who was camera assistant.
Fred was a hotshot big-time commercials director who ran the production company, The Film House, which had given a break to past star students, like editor Jill Bilcock and cinematographer Ian Baker.
I was thrilled and terrified. I figured he must have liked my graduation film, *The Roof Needs Mowing*.
This was my first real grown-up film set with real, very real, very esteemed actors: Robin Nevin and Arthur Dignam . . . One black tea, one with sugar and milk.
What did I learn?
To be honest, I hid in the kitchen with the house-owner for most of the shoot. Fred was like the cliché of a movie director, so big, so loud, powerful and passionate.
Everything revolved around him and keeping him happy and focussed. I was sent to the local shops on an urgent life or death cigar-buying mission. I had to kangaroo jump Rhonda Finlayson's car. I couldn't get it out of second gear. He was the center of that world, and there were many intense, intimate discussions with the actors. God knows what was said. I tried to slide their cups into their hands without interrupting.
Looking back: it was a happy, busy, respectful set, and everyone was caught up in Fred's passion and devotion. He cared and they cared. He was a huge presence, and an inspiring one, a real leader, and his hearty, contagious laugh echoed through this tea-girl's kitchen walls.
I didn't become that loud bon vivant, red wine–drinking, cigar-smoking director

presence. But I am sure a nervous young intern was once sent post haste for my soy milk or tea bags!

I shared many Fred qualities: his passion for actors, for the craft of film, and for storytelling.

And his affirmation of my talent was an important brick on my own pathway. Two years later, I was proud to show him a cut of *One Hundred a Day*, the film I made at the Australian Film, Television, and Radio School (AFTVRS). I remember his input was thoughtful, positive, and, as always, encouraging.

And I felt equally proud of him in 1976 when I saw his first feature, *The Devil's Playground*, which is still one of my all-time favorite Australian films.

Years later in Los Angeles, he would invite me to his wonderful, noisy Sunday open barbies at the pink house in the Hollywood Hills. I remember Mary Steenburgen and Roy Scheider around his pool there, talking about how no one in America just says, "Roll up, bring a bottle, and stay all afternoon!" There, amongst the laughter, red wine, and chaos, I heard the very important stories about the Hollywood dance . . .

Advice about handling the studio system, fighting for the integrity of our scripts, our casts, and final cuts and, ultimately, just a properly budgeted release.

Wise guidance from the trenches. Not many directors would be so generous to up-and-coming young filmmakers. Yes, generous and inspiring.

I gained much from Mr. Schepisi, and I love his films.

The Devil's Playground: dark, beautiful, moving, compassionate. The winter family picnic by the Yarra with one figure in red is so Melbourne and brings back my own family memories. The strong simple visuals. Knowing when to take a risk and be brave. Arthur Dignam under water: I don't remember seeing anyone filmed like that under water before. A tough human personal story, told with insight and compassion. A brilliant cast and performances. A perfect film.

And *The Chant Of Jimmie Blacksmith*. Another brave story. Perhaps one of the first with an insight into an indigenous murderer. Fred takes a radical point of view, not the white man's. And so powerfully told. The crafting of the family massacre was bold, breakthrough filmmaking, and breathtaking. People walked out.

He also made so many other great films, many with big international stars, like Meryl Streep and Steve Martin, or stars to be, like young Will Smith. Actors, of course, adore him.

Plenty, Roxanne, Evil Angels, The Russia House, and *Six Degrees of Separation, Last Orders, The Eye of the Storm* . . . All styles, from romantic comedy to thriller and beyond, but with impeccable casts and performances

and powerful use of cinematography, music and editing.
Films that question and delve into the human condition.
Fred is forever working, tirelessly and passionately, fighting for great stories, human dramas, and great actors. Writing and fighting for the finance. All a tough ask.
He is one of the world's best directors, a master. Go back and take a look. His body of work is extraordinary; he has given back tirelessly and has inspired many—including this humble, non-cigar smoking ex-Swinburne filmmaker—to go out and fight for a career making movies that are from the heart. As he has.
He has given so much, and I thank him from the bottom of my own heart. How great there is now a book about him and his wonderful work. I might now learn something rather than foolishly hiding in the kitchen.

[Gillian Armstrong's first feature was *My Brilliant Career* (1979). Her other Australian credits include *Starstruck* (1982), *High Tide* (1987), *The Last Days of Chez Nous* (1992), *Oscar and Lucinda* (1997), and the *7-Up*-like documentary series about the lives of three women that began with her short film, *Smokes and Lollies* (1976). Her international work includes *Mrs. Soffel* (1983), *Fires Within* (1991), *Little Women* (1994), and *Death Defying Acts* (2007).]

Introduction

There are two Fred Schepisis. One is the easy-going guy who'll greet you at the door with a big smile, a firm handshake, and a hearty "G'day, mate." He's a fair dinkum Aussie bloke who likes to laugh and enjoys a drink or two. The kind of man who'll look you straight in the eye and tell you exactly how it is and who's of the firm belief that life wasn't meant to be easy. The other Schepisi emerges when he's working or talking about the movies he's made—as in this book—a filmmaker who's deadly serious about telling stories that matter and who invests his all in doing the best he can.

During the interviews I've done with him over the years and the informal conversations we've had in between, his excitement about films he's made and the cinema in general has always been infectious, just as his dismay about the projects he's been unable to get up is palpable. He talks about those a lot. As he tells Cynthia Fuchs in her interview with him about *Last Orders*, "If I do an autobiography, it'll be called *The Films I Didn't Get to Make*." A *Sight & Sound* subeditor's headline for an article about him offered a witty alternative: "Unmade Freds."[1]

But although the disappointments hurt and he's happy to tell you about them—the interview as therapy!—he'd rather get on with the next job than mope around worrying about the wide variety of ways in which circumstances seem to have conspired against him in the past. Intense, passionate, and focused, his hands constantly elaborating on his words, he'll talk in detail about the creative choices he's made in the films he *has* managed to shoot, enthuse about the collaborators who, he'll always insist, are crucial to his endeavors, and look back over previous achievements, sometimes with satisfaction, sometimes with bemusement. "One should learn these things before you do 'em," he observed ruefully to me regarding what he now sees as a miscalculation at the start of *It Runs in the Family*.

Schepisi is down-to-earth and totally unpretentious, and it's easy to see why so many young filmmakers over the years have turned to him for advice. He's willing to listen and generous with his time and has much sage advice to offer. But it's not only novices who look up to him; collaborators speak highly of his qualities as a team leader, and—although it wasn't always like this—peers express their admiration for both the role he played in the rebirth of the Australian film industry way back when, the so-called "renaissance" that took place during the 1970s, and for his ongoing commitment to its future.

In fact, it is virtually impossible to make sense of Schepisi's development as a filmmaker without some appreciation of the circumstances surrounding that renaissance. During the late 1950s, when he was beginning the career that led to an initial reputation, in Gillian Armstrong's words, as a "hotshot big-time commercials director," only a handful of feature films were made in Australia, most of them—like *The Shiralee* (1957) and *On the Beach* (1959)—by overseas production companies. There were filmmaking models pointing to possibilities—Schepisi notes several in the following interviews—but almost all of them came from Europe, Asia, and the US. Local film production, with a few notable exceptions (Ken G. Hall, Frank Thring Snr., Charles Chauvel, Cecil Holmes), was effectively squeezed out of existence by a distribution-exhibition duopoly driven by the priorities of its overseas owners. And for people like Fred Schepisi, there were few options.

It wasn't until the late 1960s that, first, federal and, then, state government funding initiatives began to turn the tide and, during the following decade, fresh new filmmaking careers were launched. They included Tim Burstall (with *Two Thousand Weeks* in 1969; *Stork*, 1971; and *Alvin Purple*, 1973); Peter Weir (*Homesdale*, 1971; *The Cars That Ate Paris*, 1974; and *Picnic at Hanging Rock*, 1975); Bruce Beresford (*The Adventures of Barry McKenzie*, 1972; *The Getting of Wisdom*, 1977; and "Breaker" Morant, 1980); John Duigan (*The Firm Man*, 1975; *The Trespassers*, 1976; and *Mouth to Mouth*, 1978); Richard Franklin (*The True Story of Eskimo Nell*, 1975, and *Patrick*, 1978); Paul Cox (*Illuminations*, 1976; *Inside Looking Out*, 1977; and *Kostas*, 1979); Philippe Mora (*Mad Dog Morgan*, 1976); Phillip Noyce (*Backroads*, 1977, and *Newsfront*, 1978); George Miller (*Mad Max*, 1979); and Gillian Armstrong (*The Singer and the Dancer*, 1977, and *My Brilliant Career*, 1979).

It was in that changing environment that Schepisi was able to embark on the kind of future that he could scarcely have imagined a decade earlier. Almost all of these filmmakers ended up pursuing their dreams overseas—their yellow brick roads generally leading from Oz to Hollywood—but periodically returning to make films Down Under.

In the interviews with Sue Mathews and Scott Murray and during my "On Making Movies" interview with him, Schepisi reflects on those times as a period of excitement and frustration in roughly equal measures. Building on a foundation of work on commercials and industrial documentaries, he shot a couple of shorts in the early 1970s with staff and students at the Swinburne Film and TV School before making his first fully professional film, *The Priest*, a twenty-seven-minute contribution to the portmanteau work, *Libido* (1973). The screenplay was by famed Australian novelist Thomas Keneally, a former student for the priesthood like Schepisi, whose literary credits include *Three Cheers for the Paraclete* (1968),

The Chant of Jimmie Blacksmith (1972), and *Schindler's Ark* (1982), and who also played—persuasively—a key supporting role for Schepisi in *The Devil's Playground*.

The financing was difficult—Schepisi paid for his portion of the film out of his own pocket—but *Libido* was acquired by B.E.F. Distributors (British Empire Films), which had also funded the blow-up from 16mm to 35mm, and received a limited release through the Greater Union Organisation's chain of cinemas, the company fifty percent owned by the Rank Organisation in the UK. However, the going was much more gruelling for Schepisi's first feature, *The Devil's Playground*, made three years later.

Eventually, with only limited government funds available for the film industry, about a third of the $A300,000 budget was provided by the Australian Film Development Corporation with Schepisi raising the rest. But it was only after the film had been finished that he began to feel the real weight of history pressing in on him. Without support from a foreign-owned distributor, access to the largely foreign-owned exhibition outlets became problematic. Schepisi ended up acting as his own distributor and only festivals and ostensibly "independent cinemas" agreed to exhibit the film. His major reward was the general acclaim it received and the significant place it has come to occupy in the history of the Australian film revival.

Any sense of achievement Schepisi had at the time was tempered by the fact that he still had to go knocking on doors to find backing for his next feature, *The Chant of Jimmie Blacksmith*. And the same was true for his peers, who begged and borrowed and did whatever they could to fund their films. However, these filmmakers didn't constitute a mutually supportive unit like France's *nouvelle vague*. For the most part, they operated independently of each other and effectively became rivals for whatever money was available. So, when the eventual budget for *Jimmie Blacksmith* turned out to be $1.2 million, the biggest ever for an Australian film at that time, the industry was watching, along with a media eager for controversy.

When *Jimmie Blacksmith* was released, it was positively reviewed for the most part but didn't do well at the box office. That provoked resentment from some of Schepisi's peers, fearful that the film's lackluster performance would make access to funding even more difficult for them. Beyond that, though, there was wider media criticism for the film's uncompromising tackling of the issue of racism in Australian films—it squarely identifies its half-caste outlaw protagonist as the product of historical forces—as well as for its cost.

In her evocative foreword to this book, fellow director Gillian Armstrong (who made her feature debut, *My Brilliant Career*, the following year) recalls the public response to Schepisi's film: "The crafting of the family massacre was bold, breakthrough filmmaking, breathtaking. People walked out."

For Schepisi, the experience was bewildering. In his interview with Murray, he sees what happened as a product of the so-called "tall poppy" syndrome: "Everybody seemed to want (the film) to fail," he says. "That is a disturbing trait in the Australian character: preferring people to fail rather than succeed. The only reason I mention this is because the otherwise good experience was tinged a little with bitterness." In his interview with *Films and Filming*'s Brent Lewis, his fury about what unfolded is palpable: "One Australian journalist wrote that 'Fred Schepisi's *Chant of Jimmie Blacksmith* maimed the fledgling Australian industry.' That's gobbledygook! The twerp!" And there is little doubt that his disillusionment with the local response to *The Chant of Jimmie Blacksmith* was an important factor in his subsequent shift to the US.

While that move also gave him the chance for a new start, further frustrations lay ahead, as the interviews in this book reveal. "You spend more time making deals than you do making the films," he tells Michael Sragow of his experiences in Tinsel Town. "You don't get to make many of the films you work on, and if you do, there are so many compromises along the way that the film you make is very different from the film you agreed to make. Fighting with the powers that be can be depleting for an artist." Yet, despite having to deal with the problems that confront any serious filmmaker in Hollywood, Schepisi still often managed to do things his own way.

His subsequent work was fuelled by a series of collaborations with fine writers from other mediums—including David Hare (*Plenty*), Steve Martin (*Roxanne*), John le Carré and Tom Stoppard (*The Russia House*), John Guare (*Six Degrees of Separation*), Graham Swift (*Last Orders*), and Richard Russo (*Empire Falls*)—and won him an international reputation. Stephen Schiff begins his comprehensive 1993 interview with Schepisi by describing him as "probably the least-known great director working in the mainstream American cinema—a master storyteller with a serenely muscular style that can make more flamboyant moviemakers look coarse and overweening."

It appears that the lessons that Schepisi had learned in Australia and his innate survival instinct were what enabled him to negotiate a path through the Hollywood minefield. In asides sprinkled throughout the following interviews, he openly acknowledges the mistakes he made along the way and that made life difficult for him. He also offers numerous and disarmingly frank observations about the film industry in the US. Asked about the Oscar ceremony in a 1984 interview by David Edelstein, Schepisi doesn't beat around the bush. "God, didn't they all puff themselves up?" he says. "That's pretty amazing for a place that ignores the most talented people in the business."

After *The Chant of Jimmie Blacksmith*, it was a decade before Schepisi made another feature in Australia, the equally controversial, *A Cry in the Dark* (shot as

Evil Angels). Based on an actual case, and starring Meryl Streep, it told the story of a woman whose baby had been killed by a dingo in 1980 but who was accused of her murder, ended up in prison, and was only finally exonerated of the perceived crime in 1988, the same year as the film was released.

After that, although Schepisi has regularly moved back and forth between Australia and the US, it took almost a quarter of a century before he got to make another film Down Under, his last to date. *Eye of the Storm*, shot in 2011, is adapted from a 1973 novel by Patrick White and stars Charlotte Rampling, Geoffrey Rush, and Judy Davis. Inexplicably, Schepisi still struggles to find funding for his projects in Australia, suggesting there's more than a little truth in the saying that "a prophet is not without honor save in his own country."

Taken as a whole, his features, of which there are currently seventeen, fall roughly into four groups, although the boundaries between them are frequently blurring:

(a) the social dramas: *The Devil's Playground*, *The Chant of Jimmie Blacksmith*, *Plenty*, *A Cry in the Dark*, *Last Orders*;
(b) the family dramas: *Six Degrees of Separation*, *Empire Falls*, *It Runs in the Family*, *The Eye of the Storm*;
(c) the romantic comedies: *Roxanne*, *I.Q.*, *Mr. Baseball*, *Words and Pictures* (maybe);
(d) the genre films: *Barbarosa*, *Iceman* (maybe), *The Russia House*, *Fierce Creatures* (a film in which Schepisi became involved only as a favor and to which he wishes he'd never attached his name).

As the interviews in this book indicate, Schepisi firmly resists the kinds of interpretation of his works that generally attach themselves to this kind of approach. He says that he's never gone looking for material of any particular kind; in fact, he generally prefers to tackle something he hasn't done before. And, while he's a little mellower about analyses of meaning in his work than he used to be, he's still hostile to any suggestion that he's adhering to anybody's rules other than his own. What Schepisi told *Films and Filming*'s Brent Lewis in their 1985 interview still applies: "I would never make formula, identikit films. You waste your life that way."

Nevertheless, critics have identified recurring features across his oeuvre (a word he'd mock if it was used in his presence). For David Stratton in his 1986 interview with the filmmaker, Schepisi's films to that point have been "about people trapped in a situation from which it's hard to escape, (not only) the Australian films, (but) his three American films too: Barbarosa, trapped in a pointless family feud; the Iceman, trapped in a strange and hostile world; Susan Traherne, trapped in a stifling postwar Britain that offers little of the 'plenty' she craves."

Dan Callahan, talking to Schepisi almost thirty years later, arrives at different but not contradictory conclusions, as noted in his article entitled "All against One and One against All: Fred Schepisi's Outsiders": "His interest in individuals facing off against a hostile world has been consistent across a wide range of genres, from the western (*Barbarosa*) to science fiction (*Iceman*), from romantic comedy (*Roxanne*) to espionage thriller (*The Russia House*) to high comedy of manners (*Six Degrees of Separation*)."

Stephen Schiff concurs with these views—"Usually, what grabs him are stories that pit a spirited outsider against a tiny-minded establishment"—but goes on to approach the films from a different angle. He argues, insightfully, that "Schepisi tells stories about storytelling," proposing that the central theme in his work is how fiction is both "the tie that binds . . . that glues a society together" and a force that oppresses.

Alongside this is Schepisi's ongoing interest in his characters' theatricality as a way of life. Crucial to *Barbarosa* is the to-and-fro flow between the title character's mythic dimension and his mortality. Both *Evil Angels* and *Plenty* revolve around women who put on fronts to keep the world at bay. The central characters of *The Russia House*, *I.Q.*, and *The Eye of the Storm* all pretend to be somebody they're not. *Roxanne*'s male protagonist engages the world according to the modus operandi of a stand-up comedian. We eventually see the surface serenity of the small town setting in *Empire Falls* as an illusion.

To these recurring elements one could add the cultural collisions and the attendant communication problems that become pivotal to *The Chant of Jimmie Blacksmith*, *A Cry in the Dark*, *Mr. Baseball*, *Six Degrees of Separation*, *I.Q.*, *The Russia House*, *The Eye of the Storm*, *Words and Pictures,* and the (hopefully) forthcoming *Andorra*.

Much of Schepisi's work also deals with communities under stress, even tearing themselves apart from within, as evident from early on in films such as *The Devil's Playground*, where the rules and the routines designed to bring order are also a force of destruction, and *A Cry in the Dark*, in which the media and the gossip-mongers in the general population become the human equivalents of the predatory dingo at the start. It's a concern that has been sustained throughout the director's career in films as various as *Six Degrees of Separation*, *Empire Falls,* and *Words and Pictures*.

Schepisi reluctantly concedes some of these points. When I asked him in 2016 about the politics that run through his work, he responded, "People have said that I'm attracted to outsiders. There's possibly some truth in that because it's a great way of looking at society in general because they're rubbing up against it." But he's less interested in pondering what his work might be taken to mean than in putting it together and allowing it to speak for itself in its own way. "What I'm most interested in—always—is the humanity of the piece," he insists. "What makes people behave the way they do."

He trusts his technique and his instincts to guide him. One can sense him nodding off-camera in furious agreement as *I.Q.*'s Albert Einstein (Walter Matthau) delivers a warning from his deathbed to the film's young lovers: "Don't let your brain interfere vit your heart." Discussing with Schiff the way he prepares a project, Schepisi himself puts it somewhat differently: "You can't cynically calculate what you want to get across. You just create the situation where it can happen, and then it just appears. I believe that . . . That's why I go on about all the technical stuff. Because if you do that stuff right, the spirit bubbles up through it."

And all "that stuff" is what matters most to him. The following interviews provide a goldmine of insights into Schepisi's filmmaking style, which is, as Schiff notes, very much his own. "Techniques like (his) aren't taught in film schools," he writes. "Most of them, in fact, belong to Schepisi alone. He seems to have made them up as he's gone along, inventing something new with every picture."

The stylistic adventurousness and the attention to detail that have characterized his career from the start might be unobtrusive, but they're crucial to his art. And they're evident in virtually all of his films, especially notably in the way, from *The Priest* onwards, they regularly usurp the customary chronological constraints that prevail in storytelling, simultaneously creating both what he has described as a "time mosaic"[2] and a crystal clear narrative momentum. In the interviews about *Last Orders*, he explains how and why this works, but what he has to say also makes sense of the convention-fracturing manipulations of time elsewhere in his work.

Much of his discussion about his work in what follows has to do with how he and his longtime cinematographer, Ian Baker, have gone about composing the films' imagery and choreographing the movement of their camera. "Fred's really good at working at what he wants a location to offer," Baker says in an interview in the appendix to this book. "Like me, he believes that locations should be an equal-billing character to the lead actors."

"With *Plenty*, [the setting] *where* something was being said was as important as *what* was being said," Schepisi tells Callahan. "Because it often belied what was being said, or it often exaggerated what was being said. Using the wide lens, again, without making a big deal out of it, you could show all that, you could show all the monumental things pressing in on Susan."

Schepisi believes in the importance of—as he puts it, citing William Hurt in Murray's interview—"filling in the corners" of a composition and a scene, creating a fully textured screen world by making the characters in the background just as important to the overall picture as those in the foreground. Referring to a public conversation session in which he'd participated during 2015 with an admiring

Quentin Tarantino, he says in the "On Making Movies" interview, "I really like the way he talked about how (in my films) everybody is so *there*. But it drives me nuts when they're *not*, because I'd like you to be able to look at the film again and again . . . (and) notice something that (you) didn't see before. You've got the front energy, but you've also got all this other stuff that's enriching it."

Schepisi's concern is always, as he puts it, "to get the camera where it needs to be,"[3] something which he explains is always going to be "dictated by what you're trying to do. . . . What's the force of the scene? What are you trying to put across?" The same principle, he tells Schiff, applies when the camera goes on the move. "The film itself is really what dictates your camera movement," Schepisi says. "I'm very strong in thinking that a film should have a style, design, and discipline that are all true to it. You have a personal grammar and certain things you want to have a bit of cinema fun with, but it's always got to be completely in the service of the story."

Between them, he and Baker have developed a distinctive approach to filming dialogue. In the Fincina Hopgood interview, he explains his modus operandi. "I shoot dialogue as action, or, probably a better description, I shoot it as emotion. In the same way that, in theatre, you draw attention to some things and not to other things, I'm doing that all the time. It's about connections and disconnections." Both Baker and Schepisi identify *Six Degrees of Separation* as marking the genesis of the "prowling" camera style that characterizes the way they go about filming two people in a room talking to each other. Their chief inspiration, the "panther"-like intruder into the central couple's upper middle–class world, played by Will Smith.

In the "On Making Movies" interview, he also concedes that their approach often doesn't sit easily with collaborators unused to their style. "I have arguments with editors," he says, "because I don't like cutting backwards and forwards. Who should I be on? Again, who's the force of the scene? Who's the conversation affecting the most? I'll stay on them until it's important that we see what the other person is doing. To add to that, the movement creates a little bit of unease or maybe brings in something in the background that tells you something else."

In the same interview, Schepisi reveals what has led Gillian Armstrong to observe that "actors, of course, adore him." "I've found the very best actors all want to be directed," he says. "But what they really want isn't always to be told what to do. What they really want is a sounding-board they can trust. In a way, they want someone to hold a mirror up so that—obviously they don't want to watch themselves—they know what they're doing and what direction they should be going."

In the appendix, composer Paul Grabowsky, one of only three Schepisi has worked with over the years—the others are Bruce Smeaton (eight films) and Jerry Goldsmith (five films)—makes it clear that the director's eclectic tastes in music brought them together, with a little nudging from the musician, and that Schepisi hates clichés. "Fred hates film music that insists on telling you what you already know," he explains. "What I call 'pumping the movie with steroids,' which most action adventure films do."

He also testifies that, even if Schepisi trusts his instincts to guide his filmmaking decisions, there's nothing haphazard in this. "Fred is someone I'd describe as a structured filmmaker. He demands and expects an orderly roll-out of carefully prepared decisions. He has an incredible eye for detail and an amazing memory too."

Combine that with his other qualities, including his resilience and native cunning, and you'll have some insight into how this filmmaker has managed to survive over the years. Asked by Rennie Ellis about his strengths, Schepisi himself refers to the bloody-mindedness that has served him so well, "the sheer determination and energy and ability to outlast everybody and see the job through."

Thanks are due to many people, beginning with Fred Schepisi, who patiently reflected on his career for me; his valued collaborators, Ian Baker and Paul Grabowsky, for their time and insight; and the writers whose work has been included in this volume, including filmmaker Gillian Armstrong in the foreword. My dear friend, Barry White, provided invaluable technical assistance and advice. Catherine Gillam, chief librarian at the Australian Film Institute Research Library at the Royal Melbourne Institute of Technology in Melbourne, and her assistant, Harley MacDonald, were of enormous assistance as I deployed their irreplaceable filing system to track down interviews and background materials. Siobhan Dee, collection officer at the Melbourne branch of the National Film and Sound Archive, was equally helpful in providing me with access to Schepisi's pre-feature work. Others contributed along the way too: Jamie Wood, Peter Travers, Geoff Gardner, Mike Reed, Schepisi's assistant Rochelle Green, and Nigel Dawson. Most of all, though, I'm forever grateful to my wonderful wife, Debi Enker, and our awesome daughter, Madeleine Ryan, for their encouragement, support, editorial advice, and wise counsel in general over the eighteen enjoyable months it took to compile this book.

TR

Notes

1. Ryan Gilbey, "Unmade Freds," *Sight & Sound*, January 2002, pp. 12–13
2. Fred Schepisi, *Libido*, DVD commentary.
3. Ibid.

Chronology

1939   Born Frederic Alan Schepisi at around 3 a.m. on December 26 at the Epworth Hospital in Melbourne, Victoria, to fruiterer Frederic Thomas Schepisi (of Italian/Irish extraction) and Loretto Ellen Hare (of Irish extraction).

1944   Survives TB scare.

1948   Attends the Assumption College boarding school in Kilmore in country Victoria.

1953   Moves to the Marist Brothers' Juniorate in Macedon, in country Victoria for training for the priesthood. Having abandoned his studies for the priesthood, he enrolls for his Leaving Certificate (Year 11) at Marcellin College in Camberwell in suburban Melbourne.

1955   Gets a job in the dispatch department at Carden Advertising in Melbourne.

1956   Television is launched in Australia. Schepisi begins to work on writing, production, and media for TV commercials. He also takes evening classes in advertising.

1957   Takes charge of directing and producing TV and radio ads for Carden where, a year later, for a brief period, he works alongside friend Phillip Adams.

1960   Marries Joan Mary Ford. They have four children: Deborah (now Ashley), Janine, Quentin, and Jason. Moves to the Paton Advertising Service in Melbourne as television production manager. Phillip Adams is creative director.

1963   Becomes Victorian manager of Cinesound Productions.

1966   Buys the company, changes its name to The Film House, forms a partnership with Alex Stitt and Bruce Weatherhead, and assumes the post of managing director. Making advertisements and documentaries, the company goes on to become what has been described as "the most significant Australian production house in the 1960s" (Barbara Paterson, *Renegades: Australia's First Film School from Swinburne to VCA*, 1996). Wins the AFI's Best Public Relations Film award for *People Make Papers*. Joins the course advisory committee at the Swinburne Film and Television School, and becomes known by the students as "the guru." Several graduates subsequently find employment at The Film House: cinematographers Ian Baker, Ellery Ryan, and Wolfgang Kress; editor Jill Bilcock; directors Graeme Jackson, John Ruane, Jamie Blanks, and Gillian Armstrong. Schepisi's role represents the first stage of his ongoing role as a mentor to aspiring filmmakers.

1970 Directs the short film, *Party*.

1971 Directs the short film, *Can't You Hear Me Callin', Caroline*.

1973 Self-funds and directs *The Priest*, shot in six days and made for $13,000, his twenty-seven-minute contribution to the compilation feature, *Libido*. It wins a Silver Award from the AFI (Australian Film Institute). Marries casting director Rhonda Elizabeth Finlayson. Two children: Alexandra and Zoë.

1976 Writes and directs his first feature, *The Devil's Playground*, with a budget of A$300,000, approximately a third coming from the Australian Film Development Corporation (AFDC), and the rest from family, friends, and his own pocket. Shot in and around Werribee Park Mansion in country Victoria, the film is screened at the Director's Fortnight in Cannes, is nominated for ten AFI awards and wins six, including those for best direction and best screenplay.

1977 Directs *The Chant of Jimmie Blacksmith* with a budget of around A$1.2 million. Shot in fourteen weeks, mostly in rural New South Wales, the film creates controversy in Australia but is nominated for twelve AFI awards, winning three. Released in the US two years later.

1979 Drawn to the US by film offers.

1981 Directs *Barbarosa*, his first feature for Lew Grade's Marble Arch in the US. The $10 million production is mostly shot in the remote Big Bend National Park in Texas. After market testing, the film is shorn of twenty minutes by Universal, which then delays distribution. Only as a result of an outcry from major critics is it eventually released.

1983 Directs *Iceman* on location in Manitoba and British Columbia, Canada. It too falls foul of Universal's testing system and is released with minimal marketing.

1984 Directs *Plenty*, shot in London, Brussels, Paris, and Tunisia on a budget of around $10 million. John Gielgud and Tracey Ullman are nominated for BAFTAs (British Academy of Film and Television Awards) for Best Supporting Actor. Marries New York artist Mary Rubin. They have one child, Nicholas.

1987 Directs *Roxanne*, shot in British Columbia, Canada, on an estimated budget of $12 million.

1988 Directs *A Cry in the Dark*, shot in Australia, mainly in the Northern

Territory and Sydney, for around $14 million. The film is released in Australia and New Zealand as *Evil Angels*. Meryl Streep wins the Best Actress award at Cannes and is nominated for an Oscar as Best Actress. The film is nominated for eight AFI awards, Schepisi again winning for direction and (with Robert Caswell) screenplay, producer Verity Lambert accepting the Best Film award.

1989   Directs *The Russia House*, shot for around $21 million in Moscow, St. Petersburg, Lisbon, England (Pinewood), and Vancouver.

1991   Directs *Mr. Baseball*, shot for around $25 million in Nagoya, Tokyo, and Los Angeles. A slightly different cut is released in Japan. Schepisi wins the Australian Film Institute's prestigious Raymond Longford Award for services to the Australian film industry.

1993   Directs *Six Degrees of Separation*, shot in New York for $16 million. Reprising her role in the original Broadway production of John Guare's play, Stockard Channing is Oscar-nominated for Best Actress.

1994   Directs *I.Q.*, shot in New Jersey, including at Princeton University, for an estimated $32 million.

1996   Directs and reshoots parts of *Fierce Creatures* after Robert Young leaves the project. Responsible for "the last twenty-five minutes, some of the stuff at the beginning" (Tom Ryan, "Fred Schepisi on Making Movies," 2015). Shot in England, at Marwell Zoological Park in Hampshire, Pinewood and Twickenham Studios for around $25 million. The reshoots are reported to have cost around $7 million.

1999   Closes down The Film House.

2001   Directs *Last Orders* on location in England for $9 million.

2002   Directs *It Runs in the Family* for around $20 million in New York and New Jersey. Receives an Honorary Doctorate in the Visual and Performing Arts from the Victoria College of the Arts at Melbourne University (VCA), formerly Swinburne Film and Television School.

2004   Awarded an Order of Australia (AO) on Australia Day. Directs *Empire Falls* in Maine, for Home Box Office television on a budget of around $22 million. It screens as a two-part mini-series. Schepisi: "I shot it as a film" (from correspondence with editor). It receives ten Primetime Emmy award nominations, including for Schepisi with Paul Newman winning for Outstanding Supporting Actor in a Miniseries or a TV Movie for his final role.

2005   Diagnosed with prostate cancer and has "a radical prostatectomy that saved my life" (from correspondence with editor).

2006   Buys vineyard at Red Hill on the Mornington Peninsula in Victoria.

2009   Chairman of the Jury at the Moscow Film Festival.

2010   Directs *Eye of the Storm*, shot in Melbourne, Sydney, and far North Queensland for around A$15 million. The film is nominated for ten AACTAs (Australian Academy of Cinema and Television Arts Awards, formerly known as AFI awards). With Schepisi among the nominees, it wins three, including for Judy Davis as Best Actress in a Leading Role. Schepisi's daughter, Alexandra, features in a supporting role.

2013   Directs *Words and Pictures*, shot in Vancouver, for around $15 million.

2016   He and wife Mary are officially appointed Ambassadors for the Australian Prostate Cancer Council. Currently preparing three films: *Andorra*, based on the 1997 novel by Peter Cameron, adapted by Schepisi and Jamie Bialkower, to be produced by Lizette Atkins and Bialkower, and set to star Clive Owen, Toni Collette, Gillian Anderson, and Joanna Lumley. *Burnt Piano*, based on the play by Justin Fleming, first performed at Sydney's Belvoir Street Theatre in 1999; and *Hitches*, based on an original screenplay by Schepisi about "two bright-eyed, bushy-tailed lads who have to hitchhike from Melbourne to Queensland, rather reluctantly, because they'd rather fly" (from correspondence with editor).

Filmography

During the 1960s and '70s, Schepisi wrote, produced, and directed hundreds of advertisements and numerous industrial documentaries for The Film House, assisted by several of those who became long-term or occasional collaborators, among them Ian Baker, Alex Stitt, Brian Kavanagh, and Bruce Smeaton.

Industrial documentaries (incomplete)

THE SHAPE OF QUALITY (1965)
Director: **Fred Schepisi**
Writer: **Fred Schepisi**
Photography: Howard Rubie
Editor: Brian Kavanagh
Music: Bruce Clarke and Frank Smith
Narration: John Royle
27 minutes
Cinesound Productions

A HUNDRED ODD YEARS FROM NOW (1968)
Director: **Fred Schepisi**
Writers: Weatherhead & Stitt
Photography: Lars Gundlach
Design: Weatherhead & Stitt
Editor: Michael O'Donnell
Music: Frank Smith
Cast: Ian Bremner (Yockoo), Lew Walker, Will Timmerman, Susy Kendall
17 minutes
The Film House

PEOPLE MAKE PAPERS (1965)
Director: **Fred Schepisi**
Writer: **Fred Schepisi**
Photography: Peter Purvis

Editor: Brian Kavanagh
26 minutes
Cinesound Productions

ONWARD SPEED (1971)
Producer: Tony Fisher
Director: **Fred Schepisi**
Writer: **Fred Schepisi**
Photography: Ian Baker
Editor: Gail Norton
Cast: Rhonda Finlayson, Jon Finlayson
14 minutes
The Film House

THE PLUS FACTOR (1970)
Director: **Fred Schepisi**
Writer: **Fred Schepisi**
Photography: Volk Mol
Design: Weatherhead & Stitt
Editor: Brian Kavanagh
Music: Bruce Clarke
12 minutes
Comalco/The Film House

TOMORROW'S CANBERRA (1972)
Producer: Don Murray
Director: **Fred Schepisi**
Writer: **Fred Schepisi**
Photography: Ian Baker
Editor: K. Michael Reed
Music: Bruce Smeaton
34 minutes
The Film House for the Australian Commonwealth Film Unit on behalf of the National Capital Development Commission

Shorts

PARTY (1970)
Director: **Fred Schepisi**
Screenplay: Russell Beedles

Production Facilities and Technical Crew: Staff and Students, Swinburne College of Technology Film and Television Department
Cast: Jon Finlayson (Norman), Di O'Connor (Vera), John Hanson (Frank), Marion Edward (landlady), Martin Phelan (Felix)
20 minutes
The Film House

CAN'T YOU HEAR ME CALLIN', CAROLINE (1971)
Director: **Fred Schepisi**
Screenplay: **Fred Schepisi**
Production Facilities and Technical Crew: Staff and Students, Swinburne College of Technology Film and Television Department
Entertainment Media

THE PRIEST (1973)
[Part 3 of LIBIDO, a four-part compilation feature, the other segments directed by John B. Murray, Tim Burstall, and David Baker]
Producers: Christopher Muir, John B. Murray
Director: **Fred Schepisi**
Screenplay: Thomas Keneally
Photography: Ian Baker
Editing: Bruce Kavanagh
Music: Bruce Smeaton
Cast: Arthur Dignam (Father Burn), Robyn Nevin (Sister Caroline), Vivean Gray (elderly nun), Vicki Brey, Valma Pratt, Penne Hackforth-Jones
27 minutes
Producers and Directors Guild of Australia

Features

THE DEVIL'S PLAYGROUND (1976)
Producer: **Fred Schepisi**
Director: **Fred Schepisi**
Screenplay: **Fred Schepisi**
Photography: Ian Baker
Editing: Brian Kavanagh
Production Design: Trevor Ling
Music: Bruce Smeaton
Cast: Simon Burke (Tom Allen), Nick Tate (Brother Victor), Arthur Dignam (Brother Francine), Charles McCallum (Brother Sebastian), John Frawley (Brother

Celian), Jonathan Hardy (Brother Arnold), Thomas Keneally (Father Marshall), Jon Diedrich (Fitz)
107 minutes
The Film House

THE CHANT OF JIMMIE BLACKSMITH (1978)
Producer: **Fred Schepisi**
Director: **Fred Schepisi**
Screenplay: **Fred Schepisi** (based on the novel by Thomas Keneally)
Photography: Ian Baker
Editing: Brian Kavanagh
Production Design: Wendy Dickson
Music: Bruce Smeaton
Cast: Tommy Lewis (Jimmie Blacksmith), Freddy Reynolds (Mort Blacksmith), Ray Barrett (Farrell), Jack Thompson (Reverend Neville), Angela Punch-McGregor (Gilda Marshall), Steve Dodd (Tabidgi), Peter Carroll (McCready), Robyn Nevin (Mrs. McCready)
108 minutes
The Film House

BARBAROSA (1982)
Producer: Paul N. Lazarus III
Director: **Fred Schepisi**
Screenplay: William D. Wittliff
Photography: Ian Baker
Editing: Don Zimmerman, David Ramirez
Special Design Consultant: Leon Ericksen
Music: Bruce Smeaton
Cast: Willie Nelson (Barbarosa), Gary Busey (Karl Westover), Isela Vega (Josephina), Gilbert Roland (Don Braulio), Danny De La Paz (Eduardo), Alma Martinez (Juanita)
90 minutes
Universal

ICEMAN (1984)
Producers: Patrick Palmer and Norman Jewison
Director: **Fred Schepisi**
Screenplay: Chip Proser and John Drimmer
Photography: Ian Baker
Editing: Billy Weber (and, uncredited, Don Zimmerman)

Makeup Creator: Michael Westmore
Music: Bruce Smeaton
Cast: Timothy Hutton (Dr. Stanley Shephard), Lindsay Crouse (Dr. Diane Brady), John Lone (Charlie), Josef Sommer (Whitman), David Strathairn (Dr. Singe), James Tolkan (Maynard), Philip Akin (Dr. Vermeil), Danny Glover (Loomis)
100 minutes
Universal

PLENTY (1985)
Producers: Edward R. Pressman and Joseph Papp
Director: **Fred Schepisi**
Screenplay: David Hare (based on his play)
Photography: Ian Baker
Editing: Peter Honess
Production Design: Richard Macdonald
Music: Bruce Smeaton
Cast: Meryl Streep (Susan Traherne), Charles Dance (Raymond Brock), Tracey Ullman (Alice Park), Sam Neill (Lazar), John Gielgud (Sir Leonard Darwin), Sting (Mick), Ian McKellen (Sir Andrew Charleson)
121 minutes
Pressman Productions, RKO Pictures

ROXANNE (1987)
Producers: Michael Rachmil & Daniel Melnick
Director: **Fred Schepisi**
Screenplay: Steve Martin (from the play *Cyrano de Bergerac* by Edmond Rostand)
Photography: Ian Baker
Editing: John Scott
Production Design: Jack DeGovia
Music: Bruce Smeaton
Cast: Steve Martin (C. D. Bales), Daryl Hannah (Roxanne Kowalski), Rick Rossovich (Chris McConnell), Shelley Duvall (Dixie), John Kapelos (Chuck), Fred Willard (Mayor Deebs), Michael J. Pollard (Andy)
103 minutes
Columbia

A CRY IN THE DARK/EVIL ANGELS (1988)
Producers: Menahem Golan, Yoram Globus and Verity Lambert
Director: **Fred Schepisi**
Screenplay: Robert Caswell and **Fred Schepisi** (based on the book by John Bryson)

Photography: Ian Baker
Editing: Jill Bilcock
Production Design: Wendy Dickson, George Liddle
Music: Bruce Smeaton
Cast: Meryl Streep (Lindy Chamberlain), Sam Neill (Michael Chamberlain), Bruce Myles (Ian Barker), Neil Fitzpatrick (John Phillips), Charles "Bud" Tingwell (Justice James Muirhead), Maurie Fields (Justice Dennis Barritt), Nick Tate (Graeme Charlwood), Lewis Fitz-Gerald (Stuart Tipple)
120 minutes
Warner Bros.

THE RUSSIA HOUSE (1990)
Producers: Paul Maslansky and **Fred Schepisi**
Director: **Fred Schepisi**
Screenplay: Tom Stoppard (based on the novel by John le Carré)
Photography: Ian Baker
Editing: Peter Honess (and, uncredited, Beth Jochem Besterveld)
Production Design: Richard Macdonald
Music: Jerry Goldsmith
Cast: Sean Connery (Barley), Michelle Pfeiffer (Katya), James Fox (Ned), Michael Kitchen (Clive), Roy Scheider (Russell), John Mahoney (Brady), J. T. Walsh (Quinn), Ken Russell (Walter), Klaus Maria Brandauer (Dante/Yakov)
123 minutes
Metro-Goldwyn-Mayer/Pathe Entertainment

MR. BASEBALL (1992)
Producers: **Fred Schepisi**, Doug Claybourne and Robert Newmyer
Director: **Fred Schepisi**
Screenplay: Gary Ross and Kevin Wade and Monte Merrick (story by Theo Pelletier & John Junkerman)
Photography: Ian Baker
Editing: Peter Honess
Production Design: Ted Haworth
Music: Jerry Goldsmith
Cast: Tom Selleck (Jack Elliot), Ken Takakura (Uchiyama), Aya Takanashi (Hiroko Uchiyama), Dennis Haysbert (Max "Hammer" Dubois), Toshi Shioya (Yoji Nishimura)
108 minutes
Universal

SIX DEGREES OF SEPARATION (1993)
Producers: **Fred Schepisi** and Arnon Milchan
Director: **Fred Schepisi**
Screenplay: John Guare (based on his play)
Photography: Ian Baker
Editing: Peter Honess
Production Design: Patrizia von Brandenstein
Music: Jerry Goldsmith
Cast: Stockard Channing (Ouisa), Will Smith (Paul), Donald Sutherland (Flan), Ian McKellen (Geoffrey), Mary Beth Hurt (Kitty), Bruce Davison (Larkin), Richard Masur (Dr. Fine), Heather Graham (Elizabeth), J. J. Abrams (Doug)
112 minutes
Metro-Goldwyn-Mayer

I.Q. (1994)
Producers: Carol Baum and **Fred Schepisi**
Director: **Fred Schepisi**
Screenplay: Andy Breckman and Michael Leeson
Photography: Ian Baker
Editing: Jill Bilcock
Production Design: Stuart Wurtzel
Music: Jerry Goldsmith
Cast: Tim Robbins (Ed Walters), Meg Ryan (Catherine Boyd), Walter Matthau (Albert Einstein), Lou Jacobi (Kurt Godel), Gene Saks (Boris Podolsky), Joseph Maher (Nathan Liebknecht), Stephen Fry (James Moreland), Tony Shalhoub (Bob Rosetti), Charles Durning (Louis Bamberger)
95 minutes
Paramount

FIERCE CREATURES (1997)
Producers: Michael Shamberg & John Cleese
Directors: Robert Young and **Fred Schepisi**
Screenplay: John Cleese & Iain Johnstone (and, uncredited, William Goldman) based on an idea by Terry Jones & Michael Palin
Photography: Adrian Biddle and Ian Baker
Editing: Robert Gibson
Production Design: Roger Murray-Leach
Music: Jerry Goldsmith
Cast: John Cleese (Rollo Lee), Jamie Lee Curtis (Willa Weston), Kevin Kline (Rod McCain/Vince McCain), Michael Palin (Adrian "Bugsy" Malone), Ronnie Corbett

(Reggie Sea Lions), Bille Brown (Neville Coltrane), Carey Lowell (Cub Felines), Robert Lindsay (Sydney Lotterby)
93 minutes
Universal

LAST ORDERS (2001)
Producers: Elisabeth Robinson, **Fred Schepisi**
Director: **Fred Schepisi**
Screenplay: **Fred Schepisi** (based on the novel by Graham Swift)
Photography: Brian Tufano
Editing: Kate Williams
Production Design: Tim Harvey
Music: Paul Grabowsky
Cast: Michael Caine (Jack), Tom Courtenay (Vic), David Hemmings (Lenny), Bob Hoskins (Ray), Helen Mirren (Amy), Ray Winstone (Vince)
109 minutes
Sony Pictures Classics

IT RUNS IN THE FAMILY (2003)
Producer: Michael Douglas
Director: **Fred Schepisi**
Screenplay: Jesse Wigutow
Photography: Ian Baker
Editing: Kate Williams
Production Design: Patrizia von Brandenstein
Music: Paul Grabowsky
Cast: Michael Douglas (Alex Gromberg), Kirk Douglas (Mitchell Gromberg), Rory Culkin (Eli Gromberg), Cameron Douglas (Asher Gromberg), Diana Douglas (Evelyn Gromberg), Michelle Monaghan (Peg Maloney)
109 minutes
Metro-Goldwyn-Mayer Studios Inc., Furthur Films

EMPIRE FALLS (TV movie, 2005)
Producer: William Teitler
Director: **Fred Schepisi**
Screenplay: Richard Russo (based on his novel)
Photography: Ian Baker
Editing: Kate Williams
Production Design: Stuart Wurtzel
Music: Paul Grabowsky

Cast: Ed Harris (Miles Roby), Philip Seymour Hoffman (Charlie Mayne), Helen Hunt (Janine Roby), Paul Newman (Max Roby), Robin Wright Penn (Grace Roby), Aidan Quinn (David Roby), Joanne Woodward (Francine Whiting), Dennis Farina (Walt Comeau), Danielle Panabaker (Tick Roby), Theresa Russell (Charlene)
188 minutes
HBO Films

THE EYE OF THE STORM (2011)
Producers: Gregory J. Read, Antony Waddington
Director: **Fred Schepisi**
Screenplay: Judy Morris (based on the novel by Patrick White)
Photography: Ian Baker
Editing: Kate Williams
Production Design: Melinda Doring
Music: Paul Grabowsky
Cast: Geoffrey Rush (Basil Hunter), Charlotte Rampling (Elizabeth Hunter), Judy Davis (Dorothy de Lascabanes), Alexandra Schepisi (Flora), John Gaden (Arnold Wyburd), Robyn Nevin (Lal)
114 minutes
Paper Bark Films Pty. Ltd.

WORDS AND PICTURES (2013)
Producers: Curtis Burch, **Fred Schepisi**
Director: **Fred Schepisi**
Screenplay: Gerald Di Pego
Photography: Ian Baker
Editing: Peter Honess
Production Design: Patrizia von Brandenstein
Music: Paul Grabowsky
Cast: Clive Owen (Jack Marcus), Juliette Binoche (Dina Delsanto), Bruce Davison (Walt), Navid Negahban (Rashid), Amy Brennerman (Eslpeth), Valerie Tian (Emily), Adam DiMarco (Swint)
111 minutes
Latitude Productions, Lascaux Films

Other Films as Producer

BOYS FROM THE BUSH (TV series)
—WEDDING PREZZIES (Season 2, Episode 2, 1992)

Producers: Verity Lambert, David Shanks
Executive Producers: **Fred Schepisi**, Peter Beilby, Robert Le Tet
Director: Rob Marchand
Photography: Martin McGrath
Editing: Peter Carrodus
Production Design: Paddy Reardon
Music: Brian Lang
Cast: Tim Healy (Reg Toomer), Chris Haywood (Dennis Tontine), Nadine Garner (Arlene Toomer), Mark Haddigan (Leslie Duckett)
50 minutes

THAT EYE, THE SKY (1994)
Producers: Peter Beilby, Grainne Marmion
Executive Producers: **Fred Schepisi**, Tim Bevan, Robert Le Tet
Director: John Ruane
Screenplay: John Ruane and Jim Barton (based on the novel by Tim Winton)
Photography: Ellery Ryan
Editing: Ken Sallows
Production Design: Chris Kennedy
Music: David Bridie, Helen Mountfort, John Phillips
Cast: Jamie Croft (Morton "Ort" Flack), Mark Fairall (Sam Flack), Lisa Harrow (Alice Flack), Amanda Douge (Tegwyn Flack), Peter Coyote (Henry Warburton)
105 minutes
Beyond Films Ltd./Working Title Films

LEVITY (2003)
Producer: Richard N. Gladstein
Executive Producers: James C.E. Burke, Morgan Freeman, **Fred Schepisi**, Doug Mankoff, Lori McCreary, Andrew Spaulding
Director: Ed Solomon
Writer: Ed Solomon
Photography: Roger Deakins
Editing: Pietro Scalia
Production Design: Francois Seguin
Music: Mark Oliver Everett
Cast: Billy Bob Thornton (Manuel Jordan), Morgan Freeman (Miles Evans), Holly Hunter (Adele Easley), Kirsten Dunst (Sofia Mellinger)
100 minutes
StudioCanal/Revelations Entertainment

SAY I DO (2006)
Producers: Joe Forte, Tricia Linklater, Ron Vignone
Executive Producer: **Fred Schepisi**
Director: Ron Vignone
Screenplay: Joe Forte & Ron Vignone
Photography: Christopher C. Pearson
Editing: Ron Vignone
Production Design: Felicity Nove
Music: Steve Bissinger and Jamie Blanks
Cast: David Bel Ayche (David), Samuel Bliss Cooper (Michael), Don O. Knowlton (The Best Man), Benjamin Koldyke (Ben), Rebecca Rosenak (Patricia), Pamela Moore Somers (Sydney)
90 minutes

Music Clips (incomplete)

BREATHE
Kaz James featuring Stu Stone
Director: **Fred Schepisi**

Appearances

PART ONE 806 (undated)
Producer: Chris Lofven
Director: Chris Lofven
Cast: **Fred Schepisi**, Captain Matchbox Whoopee Band, Spectrum, Daddy Cool, Hans Poulsen

THE NAKED BUNYIP (1970)
Producer: John B. Murray
Director: John B. Murray
Writers: John B. Murray, Phillip Adams & Ray Taylor
Photography: Bruce McNaughton
Editing: Brian Kavanagh
Cast: Graeme Blundell (Graeme), Barry Humphries (Edna Everage), The Very Reverend F.M. Chamberlin, **Fred Schepisi**, Rennie Ellis, Jacki Weaver
139 minutes
Southern Cross Films Pty. Ltd.

THE MIKE WALSH SHOW (Episode 8101 of TV talk show, 1978)
Host: Mike Walsh
Cast: **Fred Schepisi**, Rhonda Schepisi, Laurel Lee, Tommy Lewis
60 minutes

AUSTRALIAN MOVIES TO THE WORLD (1983)
Producer: Peter Beilby
Directors: Gordon Glenn, Scott Murray
Writers: Gordon Glenn, Scott Murray
Photography: David Haskins
Editing: John Dutton
Cast: John Stanton (narrator), Gillian Armstrong, Bruce Beresford, **Fred Schepisi**, Mel Gibson, Nicolas Roeg, Peter Weir, Jack Thompson
96 minutes
Film House TV Pty. Ltd.

RIGHT SAID FRED: FRED SCHEPISI FILM DIRECTOR (TV documentary, 1993)
Producer: Don Featherstone
Director: Don Featherstone
Writer and Research: Steve Warne
Photography: Steve Newman
Editing: Frans Vandenburg
Music: Peter Kaldor
Cast: **Fred Schepisi**, Stockard Channing, Meryl Streep, Donald Sutherland, Andrea Stretton (presenter)
54 minutes
SBS-TV and Don Featherstone Productions

TODAY (TV talk show, 1994)
Episode in which Fred Schepisi is interviewed about his career.

THE CELLULOID HEROES (TV mini-series, episode 4, 1995)
Producer: Anthony Buckley
Director: Robert Francis
Writer: Robert Francis
Cast: Bryan Brown, Graeme Blundell, Bruce Beresford, **Fred Schepisi**, Gillian Armstrong, Phillip Adams, Judy Davis, Mel Gibson, Paul Hogan, Graham Kennedy
55 minutes
Film Australia

I THINK I CANNES (1997)
Producers: Jeffrey Alan, Larry Cuneo
Director: Phyllis Stuart
Screenplay: John Brodie & Phyllis Stuart
Photography: Marie Pedersen
Cast: Phyllis Stuart, Atom Egoyan, Curtis Hanson, **Fred Schepisi**, Harvey Weinstein, Michael Moore, Woody Harrelson, Demi Moore, Arthur Hiller
97 minutes

BRAVO PROFILES: STOCKARD CHANNING (TV documentary, 2001)
Producer: Terri Randall
Director: Avner Tavori
Writer: J. M. Stifle
Editing: Jose R. Casado
Cast: Tony Roberts (narrator), Stockard Channing, John Guare, **Fred Schepisi**
44 minutes
Bravo Cable

THE FAT (episode in TV panel-show series, 2003)
Series Producer: Damian Davis
Director: Damian Davis
Writers: Damian Davis, Nick Price, Tony Squires
Panellists: Rebecca Wilson, Sam Kekovich, **Fred Schepisi**
60 minutes
Australian Broadcasting Corporation

NOT QUITE HOLLYWOOD: THE WILD, UNTOLD STORY OF OZPLOITATION! (2008)
Producers: Craig Griffin, Michael Lynch
Director: Mark Hartley
Screenplay: Mark Hartley
Photography: Germain McMicking and Karl von Moller
Editing: Jamie Blanks, Sara Edwards & Mark Hartley
Music: Stephen Cummings and Billy Miller
Cast: Russell Boyd, Richard Franklin, Alan Finney, **Fred Schepisi**, Antony I. Ginnane, Phillip Adams, Greg McLean, (Dr.) George Miller, Philippe Mora, Russell Mulcahy, Quentin Tarantino
103 minutes
City Films Worldwide

Fred Schepisi: Interviews

Fred Schepisi

Sue Mathews / 1984

First published in *35mm Dreams: Conversations with Five Directors* by Sue Mathews, Penguin, 1984. Excerpted by permission of the author.

Beginnings

Sue Mathews: How did you come to pursue a career as a film director?

Fred Schepisi: When I was fifteen, I decided I wanted to leave school—because I was impatient with it, not because I wasn't any good academically (as one writer reported, much to my annoyance). My parents didn't object because I was fairly headstrong, and they knew that if I didn't want to do it I wouldn't. I worked with my father for a while in the car yards, but I was always very good at English. My mother thought we should find something for me to do—she always thought I was going to be a journalist. So when it was suggested to me that advertising was somewhere I could get paid very well for being good at English, I thought, "Well, that sounds okay," being fifteen years old and not knowing what the hell it was.

I went to a vocational guidance test, and the guy said, "What are you interested in?" I said, "I think I'm interested in advertising." He said, "Well, let's find out," and held up three cards: I got the colors right, and he told me I was perfect for advertising. I got a job in an agency as a dispatch boy. I did that for a while until I convinced the company that they didn't need three dispatch boys and would be better off with a driver and a car. That fixed that. We all got absorbed into other places in the agency, and I went through press production, typesetting, and layout. I wanted to become an account executive because, in those days, account executives did everything. But, with me only sixteen, they could hardly make me an account executive.

Fortunately television arrived in Australia and I got sidetracked into the television department. Most of the production companies were pretty raw at that time, so we were all experimenting together, both in writing and directing, though guessing was more what it was. At the same time, I was getting very interested in "Continental films," as we used to call them. They were so different from American and English films, not to mention hornier, which, for a kid of fifteen or sixteen, was fairly important. They seemed just extraordinary; they were so rich and involving. Clouzot's *Wages of Fear* (1952), with Yves Montand, and Bergman's *One Summer of Happiness* (1951) were the first two I remember, then Visconti's *Rocco and His Brothers* (1960) and *The Fiends* (1955), another Clouzot thriller.

I went to see *One Summer of Happiness* because I thought I was going to see someone naked. It was the biggest disappointment of my life—I found out that the reason it was on the Catholic condemned list was because it made fun of priests. But what I saw was a fantastic film and that piqued my interest from then on. I joined various film societies, and I'd go to the Melbourne Film Festival. I went to see every different kind of picture I could.

SM: I imagine in that early period in TV advertising you were able to get quite extensive experience?

FS: I was very lucky from that point of view. I got to touch film, play with it, and get involved with the editing. We were always experimenting with techniques, trying to do something different. We would try to translate still-photography techniques, like bar relief, strange separation techniques, and high contrast things. And we'd try to come up with different ways to find a look without lighting.

What struck me in French and Italian movies was how beautifully different the lighting was. Then filmmakers like Kurosawa began to influence the work I was doing with their use of exteriors and the way they used chemistry. I actually think we were the first people to use fog in commercials as a glamorous thing, to use weather textures and make them beautiful or exciting, to give energy, which is what Kurosawa does so incredibly well. As well, I was working with a number of art directors who helped influence the way I work now: in different styles, in patterns, on the square, and so on.

SM: Are there any commercials of that period that you are particularly proud of?

FS: Lipton jigglers [*Jigglers Unlimited*, 1971] was probably the most well known, I think, and we did a great many of the Marlboro commercials, with horses running through silvery water. We were among the first people to use white limbo as a negative space, simply placing elements in it.

SM: When did you set up your own production company?

FS: When I was twenty-four, I took a job as manager of Cinesound in Victoria. We made a profit within the first year, and, by the end of the next year, we were making more money than the parent company in Sydney. That was when I found out about loss companies. But it turned out to be for my benefit because, with my partners, I was able to buy the place.

SM: Cinesound had been one of Australia's most productive '40s and '50s it became best known for its movie-theater newsreels. Were the newsreels still important in your time?

FS: We did newsreels, but when we bought the company I didn't take over the newsreels. I wasn't a very good newsreel person. I stopped my news crew going out when the Beatles came to Melbourne because I thought the mass hysteria was so ludicrous and dangerous that I didn't want to add to it. Another day, there was an aeroplane that had dropped an engine and was in big trouble. It was coming in to land and, of course, my news guys got all excited and were leaping into their car to go out. I thought it was incredibly ghoulish—it didn't seem to me to be reporting, just a desire to have a sensational piece of footage. So I took the keys and wouldn't let them go out. Newsreels were dying by then, anyway.

There was only one person in the editing department when I arrived, an assistant editor named Russell Boyd, who had been there for six months. Now, of course, he is one of Australia's foremost cameramen.

SM: Where did you find the money to buy out Cinesound?

FS: Three years before, when I was twenty-two, I had borrowed £80 from a very sceptical bank manager to go up to Sydney with another guy to see Sir Norman Rydge, the head of Greater Union [one of three major exhibition-distribution chains in Australia], which owned Cinesound. I had a one-and-a-half page report, and we made him an offer to let us take over the Melbourne end of Cinesound for no money and eventually pay it back. To my amazement he actually listened to us for about three quarters of an hour. Of course, we didn't convince him to hand over Cinesound, but subsequently I got the job of managing it. After two years, I went back to him and said, "You remember me? I've been running your company, and you can see what I've done. So let me put it to you this way: why don't we do it on the terms I suggested before?" He agreed and I bought Cinesound for almost no money down, with a promise to pay back specific large amounts over a couple of years. He seemed impressed that I'd tricked my way into the joint and made money, so he let me have it. That's how my company, The Film House, started. I thought I was going to make movies straightaway.

SM: Was that the motivating force from the age of sixteen?

FS: I liked advertising when I was sixteen, but I lost that urge very quickly. I just didn't like the business at all. The idea was to make money to make films, but then there's the reality of what films cost. Also, you get involved in a business, and suddenly you're involved in it fifteen hours a day. You're as busy as you can possibly be. You are expanding and getting equipment and maybe doing a lot of turnover, but you've got to keep churning the money back to improve the facilities. You find yourself on this amazing wheel where you seem to have a lot of money, but if you get off the wheel you lose it all. So I got caught up in business in a big way, in a nightmarish way. I didn't have holidays, I managed the place, I wrote most of the commercials, I wrote the documentaries, and I directed them.

The Revival Begins in Melbourne

SM: Was anybody making feature films at that time?
FS: There was the odd film here and there. Tim Burstall was doing a lot of the spade-work: he was the original battering ram. At that time he was doing *2000 Weeks* (1969), a feature which was a lot better than people gave it credit for, and not long after, I think, he made *Stork* (1971).

SM: Was there a circle of people interested in filmmaking in Melbourne at that time?
FS: Tim Burstall was part of a group that was based in the outer suburb of Eltham, at an art colony [Montsalvat] that had been established in the 1940s. They were into every form of the arts, and Tim led them into film. They really put everything into it, with no money, no help, no backing. They made a lot of pioneering inroads. Then there was the Carlton push [in inner-suburban Melbourne] which was a later development, a younger group that came out of universities and technical colleges. And then there was the professional ring, the would-be filmmakers working in related areas such as the ABC, who really weren't doing anything.

Burstall was a key person in the PDGA [the Producers and Directors Guild of Australia], and I got involved in it because I hoped I'd meet a lot of theater people. I wanted to learn about play structures and dealing with actors and performances and how theater was different from film. The PDGA turned into quite a catalyst: we all fired one another up and began trying to generate things for television, film, and stage. We recognized a need for unity and help. We would run competitions for scripts and produce them on stage, on film, and on television.

SM: You did all this in your spare time?
FS: Yes. At the same time, I was involved in the Experimental Film Fund as one of the assessors, sometimes referred to as "the assassins." We used to deliberate for hours over hundreds of scripts. We used to take every one at face value, trying to think from the writer's point of view, and trying not to do any smart dismissals. In most cases we were only talking about giving $300 grants, but that amount was so precious that we really had to take it seriously. The Experimental Film Fund did a remarkable job—it got *Stork* off the ground and gave people some basic opportunities to experiment or prove themselves.

SM: Was the activity in Melbourne very different from what was going on in Sydney at that time?

FS: The Experimental Film Fund was going in Sydney as well. The film course at Swinburne Technical College was already going in Melbourne, quite some time before the National Film and Television School started in Sydney. The attitude to making movies in Sydney was much more Hollywood. They wanted job demarcation, unionization, more glamor, and more money. In Melbourne, we used smaller crews, and there was more cross-pollination of jobs, with everybody working to one end. We were closer to the Czechoslovakian or Swedish approach. Even among the competitive commercial companies in Melbourne, we would all help one another. If someone had a problem, they would ring up, and, if we could solve it for the other person, even though we had just lost the job to them, we'd do it. I think that had a lot to do with us actually getting things off the ground.

SM: Your first involvement with a feature film was *The Priest*, the episode you directed of the four-part *Libido* in 1973. How did you come to be involved with the project?

FS: Through the PDGA, we had been encouraging people from other media to write for film, television, and stage. We asked people to submit scripts on the theme of the libido, and we produced the film ourselves. I knew Thomas Keneally, the novelist, was submitting a script. At that time, I was planning on writing *The Devil's Playground*, but I didn't know if I was capable of it, so I thought that maybe I should get to know Tom Keneally, just in case I got into trouble.

The other thing that attracted me to Keneally's story of the nun and the priest was that directing two people in one room for half an hour was probably the most difficult thing I could handle at that time. So I went right for it—I didn't give anybody else a chance at that one. And while we were discussing *The Priest*, Tom Keneally had *The Chant of Jimmie Blacksmith* in galley proofs, and it was then that I started my campaign to get that. It took me a few years to get it off him.

SM: It's interesting that your first two feature productions have to do with sexual repression and the Catholic Church.

FS: Well that's coincidental because of the rather arbitrary way I selected *The Priest*. On the other hand, I was passionate about *The Devil's Playground*. But I liked both subjects and I'm glad I did them. My ex-wife, Rhonda, did the casting for *Libido*, and we had two fine theater actors, Arthur Dignam and Robyn Nevin. They had never acted in a film before and so were very interested in the process. They were a great help to me and vice versa. I wanted to work everything up out of the camera, a bit too much I think, and I had worked out a very definite camera structure to enhance the drama. I thought the script was overwritten, and we took out a lot of words in rehearsal, a lot in shooting, a lot in editing . . . and we could probably have taken out more. It was a terrific experience: two actors and a crew who really cared, and Gillian Armstrong, who was a student in the film course at Swinburne, was doing the tea.

SM: How long after that did *The Devil's Playground* get under way?
FS: I had done the screenplay shortly after *Libido*, and it took me two and a half years to raise the money. In fact, most of it came from my own earnings. The Film Commission initially would not give me any money: I applied to them again and again and again. But even though they weren't enthusiastic, nobody in Australia had won as many awards as I had in both documentaries and commercials, so eventually I got about $100,000 worth of acknowledgement. I put $154,000 in, and I raised the rest in lots of $1,000 and made the film.

When I finished it, nobody liked it or wanted to distribute it, so I had to raise the money to distribute it myself. It meant that I came off that film exhilarated but had to go straight back to work doing commercials. I would work during the day and do a second lot of work at night. The film was being edited at the same time. It was not the happiest period of my life. It was very tough, but I insisted that it was a commercial picture and made sure that it was treated that way.

SM: You had been thinking since 1971 of doing that film. How long had the idea of doing an autobiographical film about that period of your adolescence been an ambition?
FS: I was reading a lot of books looking for a subject, and around 1971 it just crossed my mind that it might be an interesting world to explore in a film. I made notes for nine months: plots, thoughts, pieces of action, and possible endings and middles. I wrote lots of ideas in a book and then somebody stole it. It was horrendous for me as well as being vindictive.

SM: You think it was a deliberate sabotage?
FS: Yes, I fired somebody around the same time. So I couldn't face it for a long time. Sometime later, I was writing a documentary for Film Australia—I used to shoot commercials and run the business during the day, then write at night. One night, I finished more quickly than I expected and went to bed four hours early. Then *The Devil's Playground* started coming, so I got back up and started writing. It took me about two months. I used to work every morning until three or four and then get up and go to work. I'm not sure I could do that anymore.

SM: To what extent did you draw on your own experiences? How much of you is there in the character of the boy, Tom?

FS: It's semi-autobiographical. When I was thirteen, I decided I wanted to enter the monastery, and I think my parents made the wisest decision and let me do it. I left a year and a half later, by which time I'd got it out of my system. The Brothers are combinations of various people, the events are combinations of what happened to me and to other people, and some of them are made up. Once, when I was about nine, I was in the infirmary of my Catholic primary school, which happened to be right next to the Brothers' billiard room, so I could hear some of the conversations. And once I stayed back for a few days at the end of term; they were more relaxed under those circumstances, so I briefly got inside their world. The film was really made up of what I thought it would be like, and what I thought was going on, or, if you like, extensions of what I thought I might have become.

SM: You would see yourself presumably as closest to the Nick Tate character, who is the most approachable, and the most confused, of the Brothers.
FS: I hope so. I'm sure I wasn't that far away from the Arthur Dignam character either. No, I hope I'd never let that beast out.

SM: How do you feel about that period of your life? Do you feel any anger or resentment?
FS: No, I don't. It's just what I went through. I think a lot of it is very silly, and I'm definitely against it. But, no, I don't feel any bitterness about it. I don't think that those people were doing that to me deliberately or with malevolence: they thought they were doing the right thing.

SM: There's a point where the Nick Tate character is reflecting on how he feels about life in the seminary and he says, apparently without irony, "I love all this brotherhood. I feel I belong here." I was wondering how you intended that?
FS: I believe that. He didn't agree with it all, and quite clearly hadn't come to terms with a lot of it, but he liked the life. And that's a fact, they do. I wasn't trying to paint the Brothers as black. They are products of a system and were trying to do the best they could, believing they were doing the right thing while maybe doubting some things. They taught obedience which is one of the vows, so it's pretty tough.

SM: The Arthur Dignam character is very bitter and repressed, with his punishments of the boys and guilt-ridden visits to the public baths to watch women undressing. It's a very extreme characterization.
FS: That's what you think. I don't care what anybody says; I back-pedalled a long way on how extreme I made the characters, mostly because I didn't think people would accept it if I gave them any more eccentricities. I can tell you that the Arthur Dignam character is a mere shadow of a couple of the people I encountered. When

the film came out, people used to ring me up and write me letters and burn their T-shirts and send them to me. Almost any Catholic boy who has been to boarding school will say of that character, "That was Brother so-and-so." There was one in every school, and they'd say to me, "Oh, you were kind to him."

SM: How similar to Tom's was your experience of deciding to leave?
FS: I did run away once, but, really, it was quite different. I got to the point where I thought, "This life's not for me," because I liked girls a lot. Though, like Tom, I used to wet the bed a lot, and the part where he is given the Lourdes water to cure his bedwetting is true. I made a small deal with myself that, if the Lourdes water didn't work in one month, I was going to give it all up. It didn't work. So I told them I wanted to leave, and they actually pulled me out of class one day when I least expected it, saying, "Get your pen and leave," and drove me home. They were quite nice about it, though not being able to say goodbye was very strange. I never wet the bed again.

SM: That was your first feature. Were there many lessons that you learned or surprises about the way it turned out?
FS: Sure, but I can't tell you what they were. I think the saddest thing was that I didn't have the opportunity to immediately go on and apply the lessons that I had learned, the economies of doing things. I actually learned more out of seeing it recently than I did at the time.

SM: What sort of things?
FS: There are some things—like how cold the water in the showers is—that are repeated so often that I thought, "If you say that again, I'm going to tear the screen down." Probably because I did some of the cutting myself there are some set-ups missing, and some things seem to come in right out of the blue so that you think, "Where the hell did that come from? It has no relevance to anything." And the writing was a little overwrought in places, a little too clever. Amazingly though, an incredible energy and honesty comes through which overrides and excuses all of it. It doesn't excuse it for me, but it does for the audience. But it's very raw. I've come a long way since then.

SM: The director of photography, Ian Baker, came to The Film House from the Swinburne film course, and he's worked on all your features so far. How closely together did you work on deciding how something was going to look?
FS: I like to work up my action out of the camera, so we work very closely, very cooperatively, because each composition is affected by a range of things—for example, by the sound I'm using off screen, because that's giving information I don't

need to put on screen; or by the approach I'm using in design and cutting. Composition adds an emotional impact as well. We discuss the lighting, then Ian does it, but we do the composition together because it affects the cutting, not just a specific shot. As years have gone on, we speak less and less because we know what we're doing and why we are doing it.

SM: There are some terrific shots in *The Devil's Playground*, like the repeated one of Tom running down the stairs where you are looking almost through the floor.
FS: One of the reasons we picked that particular location was because the stairwell was open at one end. So we were able to do that. It's a crane shot and what makes it work is the lighting—that's why you need real cooperation with your director of photography.

SM: I like the opening too, where the camera slowly tracks along the river to where a group of boys are diving and playing.
FS: Yes, we were hanging off the front of a boat. That water is so shallow, you wouldn't believe it: when they dive-bombed, they hit the bottom. It was also freezing cold. We wrote the film to be shot in a number of seasons and planned to do certain things in autumn and into winter. But, in fact, the lake shot was screwed up: we had a camera shaft break on us without us knowing. And we lost the first—and hottest—day's shooting, so we had to come back and do it on a very cold day, much to everybody's delight.

SM: Another shot I liked very much comes towards the end, where Tom and the old Brother, Sebastian, are talking on a balcony. They are framed above the line of stone columns.
FS: That was originally going to be done in the sun—I thought I'd like to repeat the opening, where Tom first sees Sebastian sitting in the sun. We only had that particular actor for three weeks. We scheduled the scene five different times, and each time the weather just blotted us out. So, in the end, I had to come up with an entirely different concept, had to say, "Where can I shoot this thing where it's kind of outside and isolated and away from other people but protected from the rain?" Answer: the balcony. And it makes it doesn't it? Providing you know why you are making the film or what your discipline is, you can make those adjustments. It's like going down a river, where as long as you stay between the banks, you're okay.

SM: How was it working with the young boys? Were they professional actors?
FS: No, not really, though the lead actor, Simon Burke, has gone on to an acting career. We spent a lot of time in rehearsal and training, and everybody was given a very definite character and biography, a nickname and an attitude to other people.

If you get the right kids, you find they really like acting. If you can tap that and lose the embarrassment, you've got it made. And we really had terrific kids. Rhonda Schepisi put an extraordinary amount of work into selecting the cast.

SM: A lot of the subject matter deals with issues like masturbation that must be difficult for kids—for anyone—to deal with in public in that way?
FS: It was handled very carefully, and I tried to grade the shooting to lead up to that, and I kept talking about it, so by the time it arrived it was "Come on. We've got ten minutes. We've got to be out of here. We haven't got any time for this messing around. Get on with it." So there was no choice. I used every trick a director has for getting something out of somebody, from coercing, to taking breaks, to lecturing, to getting tough, to getting nice.

SM: The final shot is of Tom in the car. He realizes that he's got away—it's a lovely expression on his face—and then the focus shifts to the reflections of the trees and the sky on the car window going past. Had you decided from the start that you were going to end it like that?
FS: Oh yes. Heaven and earth, definitely. We shot that on the first day. I figured, no easy introductions, let's get the kid off the ground in a big way.

SM: You mentioned working with the writer Thomas Keneally as early as *Libido* in 1973, and you gave him a small part in *The Devil's Playground* as the priest who preaches on the horrors of hell and gives Tom Lourdes water for his bedwetting. He also appears briefly as a cook in *The Chant of Jimmie Blacksmith*. When did you manage to extract the rights to the book from him, and how closely did you work with him on the adaptation?
FS: It wasn't until after I'd done *Devil's Playground*. There were quite a few people in various places in the world trying to get the rights. Tom really wanted to sell it internationally—at that time, there was nothing much happening in the film industry in Australia. But I think he liked what I'd done with my films, and I was able to offer him cash, split across a couple of financial years. That's what finally swung the deal: he wasn't terribly wealthy at the time.

He'd written the novel during what he considered a black period of his life, and he didn't quite like some of the attitudes of the book. So, in fact, I wrote the screenplay on my own. I showed it to him when I finished, and I remember he kept rushing to the book to find out whether the good bits were his or mine. They were mostly his. I really did try to encourage him to get involved, but he didn't want to at that time. He was taken aback by the power of the thing, and I think he was very worried that it was going to unleash some kind of riot. The imagery was so violent and strong on film, and maybe it made him feel rather strange about what he had written.

SM: How did you go about the process of adaptation? How closely did you refer to the novel as you were writing the screenplay?

FS: I broke the book down on a series of little cards and stuck them on the wall. Then I wrote two movies in structure form, using the cards. I wrote the movie I made, and I wrote a movie that started with the school teacher being kidnapped, which comes at the end of the story chronologically. The running-time of the movie was the whole time they had him kidnapped. I did it that way because I was interested in doing it in flashbacks. The school teacher would be wrangling with the kidnappers, so you would be instantly involved in action and threat. Under that tension, the audience, like the school teacher, would be trying to learn who these threatening characters were. The teacher and the audience know they've been killing people, and you'd flash back to pieces of what they'd done. In a way, you'd prepare the audience for the horror so that, by the time you unleashed it, the audience would be both prepared for it and would understand why it happened. I'm not convinced that that might not have made the film a lot more commercial, but I liked the way we went anyway.

SM: Had the theme of the movie been important to you for a long time? What was it attracted you to the book in the first place?

FS: The story of a man at odds with the system who just wants to be himself and get on in the system. That's probably what attracts me to most material.

The story is about a young part-Aboriginal who has been brought up by a white missionary in the nineteenth century. He tries to find work and establish a life for himself in the first part of the film.

SM: Had the treatment of the Australian Aborigines been an issue of particular importance to you?

FS: Not particularly. It had always disgusted me, but I wasn't actually doing anything about it. The story caught me. It seemed to me to be a very entertaining way to explore the plight of the Aborigine, and it had such imagery in it. A number of elements attracted me to it.

It was never meant to be the definitive Aboriginal picture, as everybody seemed to expect, because that's just not possible. They are more complex than we are, and there are more diverse groups or tribes.

SM: How did you research it? I find it easier to imagine how you'd familiarize yourself with the classic stuff of anthropological research than with the shanty town scenes. Where did you develop your ideas of how they should look and what they should feel like?

FS: From seeing films from the past. From being in places like that, in the Northern Territory and around Alice Springs, and by doing research. You've got to give

Wendy Dixon and the art department an enormous amount of credit. They did a lot of research and a lot of incredibly clever work. The design on that picture is quite phenomenal, right down to the one thing that probably nobody knows—the book that the school teacher kept wanting to take with him. "My Palgrave," he kept saying, "I want to take my Palgrave." What the hell is that? Is it boots, or a scarf? It's a little book of poetry which Wendy had on a shelf, annotated in the character of that school teacher, so that when the actor walked on the set and was looking around, he discovered the Palgrave and it just heightened the performance. Wendy's design was beyond something that you see as an audience: it created an atmosphere and ambiance for the actors which I think is just incredible. In fact, everyone's contribution on that film was extraordinary. It always tends to come out as "the director did it all," which is nonsense. The sound is terrific, and a lot of credit must go to Roy Stevens, who was production manager, because he made me contain the picture. We had to cancel locations and come up with new locations, and he made us go that extra ten percent, take that extra time, but cut that corner whenever possible.

SM: Had you seen many of the other films that had been made in Australia about Aborigines?
FS: To tell you the truth, I thought most films made about Aborigines were wrong. They seemed superficial: they always had them with the spear and the leg up on the knee, standing on the horizon. I don't think Aborigines would be that silly. They were part of the earth; they were in harmony with it. They lived with it, so I tried to construct every shot so that you had to look for the Aboriginal in the frame before you found him, because he was so much a part of it. He was always shot down into the earth, against a hill, in amongst the trees, so that he never stuck out on the horizon. He was always part of it, in harmony with it, whereas the white person stuck up out of the earth. He was at odds with it, taking from it.

SM: You use a lot of close-ups of insects, textures of bits of wood and bark, and so on.
FS: It's a discipline of the film. The Aboriginals perceived the bush as alive with food, insects, nature to cohabit with, where we tend to see nothing. Sometimes those shots represented the passing of time. Sometimes they were a comment on the action. Sometimes they were just showing what was in the environment.

SM: You also emphasize the chooks that seem to be on all the white farms.
FS: Well, they were the animals that were being used then. And there was the suggestion of violence, with the farmers chopping their heads off and hanging them up. I was trying to say that the whites were used to killing, more than we are today. They were used to violence; it was part of the way they lived and ate.

SM: Where did you find the Aboriginal actors?
FS: We had searched through black theater in Sydney, where we did find a lot of our actors, and we searched all up the coast of NSW. We found Tommy Lewis, who plays Jimmie, in an airport. My wife and I had been grounded by fog. I noticed him and then Rhonda noticed him. We talked it over and she chased after him and chatted him up. We tested him over about four days. Tommy was a student at the time, and we went to a break-up party for his course where a couple of other blacks came along. One of them was Freddy Reynolds, and the minute he walked through the door, I said, "That's Mort." He was just right.

SM: What have Tommy Lewis and Freddy Reynolds done in the time since making the film?
FS: Freddy has not done very much, unfortunately. The last I heard, he was lecturing at schools. People didn't exactly rush them with roles, though I don't know why. It's difficult. It took a long time for people to understand how good Tommy was: they somehow thought it was me and Michael Caulfield, the acting tutor on the film, doing it. But you can't put a CinemaScope camera right in on the eyes of a person and have that subtlety of emotional change register unless it's coming from within the person, unless he is doing it. Now, of course, he is getting work in TV and films which is terrific.

SM: It must be a very difficult adjustment to make, for people who've never been performers.
FS: That's true for anybody who gets into that limelight. I was very careful, as I was with Simon in *The Devil's Playground*, to say, "This is an event. This is a holiday. It may never happen again. When it's over, remember the holiday: it was great, but don't chase it for the rest of your life." But when you've got somebody like Tommy, who is in every scene, and you don't want him to move, you deliver him things—a cigarette, a drink, you wipe his brow—and then it's not very long before he's demanding, "Cigarette!" The first time you hear that you've got to stop them, admonish them, send them off the set for arrogant behavior, get them back to earth again.

Then there's the publicity tour afterwards, and the girls. Those guys pull birds like you've never seen in your life, and it's a big high.

SM: It's a real responsibility, getting someone who's not an actor, who's not prepared for it, into that sort of experience.
FS: Yes, definitely. And the pressures aren't just from this side of the fence; they are also from their own people. Take someone like Freddy who's been really screwed by the system, a full-blood Aboriginal with no tribal heritage whatsoever, taken away

from his parents at a very early age and shoved in some white boarding-house somewhere. He's been at war with the whites since he was five, and then we take him and dote on him.

The strain on anybody fresh walking into a movie is extraordinary and the strains on somebody like that are beyond the pale, I'm afraid. With Tommy, while on the one hand he liked to be in the city, he couldn't be there very long because he really was a person who would go out hunting, and he liked that. I think he's found a reasonable balance in both worlds. Finding a balance between ordinary life and the life when you're in a movie is hard for all actors—both worlds don't keep going constantly. Even Jack Thompson is out of work for long periods of time. So we tried to keep setting precedents as the picture went on. But, at the same time, when you make a movie, you increase your family in a lot of cases. It's a very intimate and enjoyable experience, and you are never totally separate from then on.

SM: At the time it was the biggest budget film that had been made in Australia, wasn't it?

FS: "Death of the Australian film industry," they said, "the biggest, most disgusting budget ever." Why did I want to make a big budget film? I wanted to make *The Chant of Jimmie Blacksmith*, and I wanted to make it on the scale that it should have been made. There wasn't one penny spent needlessly. Today, executive producers are ripping off $200,000 and more for putting a package together. For writing, producing, and directing *The Chant of Jimmie Blacksmith*, I got $36,000, plus I paid cash for the rights. I didn't even get paid in the end, but that was what I was written down for. And I invested $250,000 in the film. Everybody got stuck with rotten money, and it was done in the most economical way possible. It just happened to cost that much.

SM: There was a big publicity build-up at the time it was released and while it was being made. Was that a conscious marketing decision?

FS: Yes, of course, but there was one major problem. We achieved something that nobody else had achieved in getting into the Cannes Film Festival's international competition. Given the politics of the Cannes festival and how prizes are awarded, to be the first of the new crop of Australian films ever to get into that festival was an end unto itself. It was the award. The problem was that suddenly everybody was predicting we were going to win awards. That's when I thought the publicity had gone crazy. I tried to stop it, but how do you stop it? When I came back, the customs officer said, "Gee, sorry about you failing overseas." We didn't fail; we got a five-minute standing ovation.

SM: How did that feel?
FS: Extraordinary. I always get embarrassed with that stuff, so I think the people who were with me, my father-in-law and brothers-in-law, got more of the feeling that I would have liked to have got out of it.

SM: Was the Cannes screening before or after the film's Australian release?
FS: Before. I'd walk down the street in Melbourne and someone would say, "Sorry about your film, buddy." And, then, everybody expected it to be definitive, they expected every dream they ever had of an Aboriginal picture to be in it, and they certainly didn't expect it to hit them across the head.

SM: How do you feel now about the graphic violence in the film?
FS: It was necessary; you can't not have it. The film is making a very definite antiviolent statement. It's not glamorous, it's not romantic, and it certainly didn't sell tickets, but it's necessary. The point is that violence happens when you least expect it, to the people that you least expect or want it to happen to, and it is committed by a person who you don't want to do it. It's sickening and vile, and all it does is beget violence.

SM: Did you expect the character of Jimmie Blacksmith to retain the audience's sympathy?
FS: I clearly expected to lose it the minute he killed. I expected to get it back through the affability of the brother, Mort. The intention was to use Mort to bring the audience back around to Jimmie again. I don't know whether I did that for you. Did I?

SM: Well, no, not really.
FS: It's fifty-fifty: with a lot of people I did and a lot of people I didn't. Some people are drawn right into the film from the beginning and have no trouble with what's happened to Jimmie or why. But the same element that sucks people in seems to push others right outside the film—there's no middle ground.

SM: Part of the reaction against the film may be a sense that you don't judge Jimmie, that you let him off too easily.
FS: He gets the shit beaten out of him. He's not let off by the people. I do not say that he is guilty; I say he was pushed to the edge, split between black society and white society. He is not a black, he is a half-caste, and he can't belong to either society. So, in the end, it is just inevitable that he strikes out. It isn't what he should have done, but what the hell else was he going to do?

SM: There are a lot of other things he could have done apart from picking up an ax and chopping people up.

FS: Maybe it was the white component that made him take up the ax, and not the black component, maybe it was forces beyond his control? He struck at women because of tribal things against women and because it was women whose love he most desired but couldn't get. It was an act of frustration, a moment of frenzy without really realizing what he was doing. But why try to pass judgment on it? It's a fact, like many criminal acts, and the film is an examination of what brought it about.

SM: What sort of models did you have of how to present the violence? Was Sam Peckinpah an influence at all?

FS: No, definitely not. There was very little blood in the film. In fact I tried to develop something that would attenuate the experience of death, the horror and the pain of it, by cutting unexpectedly to people's faces, maybe to a face you didn't expect, then on to the face you did expect, but with an unexpected reaction. There is very little actual violence, but somehow the experience is worse than if there was more.

SM: Did you re-edit the film for its overseas release?

FS: Yes, the version of *Jimmie Blacksmith* that was released overseas was much better. There is about twelve minutes missing, mostly after the killings. I decided that once those killings had happened, you really owed it to the audience to wrap it up and let them out of the theater to get a breath of air. What I was doing in the original version was going on and exploring what was happening to the country, people's reactions, and other reasons for it happening. I now realize—and this is something I learned even more on *Barbarosa*—that there's a certain point beyond which you mustn't introduce any new information that requires you to go off and think in a new direction. There's an emotional drive that you have to follow and allow to be concluded, and any new information must pertain only to that, otherwise you dissipate the energies of the film. It's not a novel; it's a film: it's a physical experience as much as anything else, and you've got to let that drive take you through.

Reflecting on Directing

SM: Do you think that Australian films have a recognizable look?

FS: To a certain extent, but I think that's because of the light of the country. The light varies in different countries. For instance, we don't have the strange clear light that the Swedes have, that very whitish pure light. The local light dictates a lot of what you do or what you pick up on if you're good at it, whether it is the haze, the colors on a specific day, or the folds in the hills.

SM: *The Devil's Playground* certainly captures the winter light around Melbourne very clearly.
FS: *The Devil's Playground* was pretty unique at the time because we used very little artificial lighting. We gave ourselves a lot of agony using very fast lenses, which give you very little depth of focus but mean you can light a match and have the light just explode on the actor's face. The sequence in the hotel is the best example of that. We wanted the film to look not lit, to look as natural as if you just walked into the room. Somebody said as an insult after they saw *Libido*, "They didn't even light the bloody thing." I turned around and said, "Thank you very much."

SM: Thoughtfully composed shots and images are a hallmark of your films. Do you feel that you learned lessons in advertising about ways of putting things on the screen that were carried over into film?
FS: Sure. In commercials I had a chance to experiment with groupings, with positionings, which I see now in good theater, ballet, and paintings. Groupings are a terrific, dynamic thing, and I was able to play with elements like that. Also to shoot through things: I like a very wide frame because then I can shutter it down to the format that I want or explode it out by using objects that relate to what's going on, but block the camera's view. Ian Baker and I like doing that without using optical effects. The experience with positioning of things, the use of negative space, the working against white helped me a lot. That and working with good designers. I don't like doing production shots: every shot has got to be advancing the story in some way or making a point, so that I am not just saying, "Here we are in this beautiful country." I'd rather be saying, "How small these people are in this country" or "How isolated that person is." I think that is important, and I like to set something up at one stage that will make a point later.

SM: How do you feel about the presentation of sexuality in Australian films? Would you agree that in general it's something we don't do very well?
FS: Gee, I hope I do it well. I think the sex in *Jimmie Blacksmith* is terrific. I think perhaps some of our early films were a little too exploitive and straining to be erotic. I think being erotic is actually a lot easier than that, because it's a textural thing you can do in a film. I don't think many of our subjects have really given us that opportunity—I think, fortunately, that most of us have avoided being exploitive and dropping it in just for the sake of titillation or commerciality. If it is part of the story and is essential to the story, it goes in, and if it isn't, it doesn't.

In George Miller's film *Mad Max 2* (1981, released in the US as *The Road Warrior*), the dog and the woman get killed. That doesn't happen in Hollywood because they are looking at it from a purely commercial standpoint. We don't care; we follow the dictates of the story, and I think that's a great plus. But it's true that we haven't really explored sexuality; maybe we are still a little embarrassed. When an Australian says, "I luv ya," it's not quite as romantic as "je t'adore." It reflects the way Australians deal with sex—there's a tendency to be a little blunt, I think.

SM: What are the qualities about Australian cinema that you like?
FS: It isn't always there, but it's the freshness of approach, the openness, and the unabashed honesty. It's Australian in what you are looking at, in the way it's photographed, in the way it's written, and the way it is structured, in the acting and the humor. The better films are the films that have an indigenous subject matter, that are by us and about us and with us. They may have a universal theme, but they are our point of view and they're different. The films I don't like and the films I believe have failed are the ones that have sopped to the international market, either with international stars or international themes or subjects—pseudo-American horror pictures or pseudo-American thrillers or whatever. It's nonsense; you are not going to do that better than the Yanks. I think that our films are refreshing; they are simple without being simplistic.

But I certainly don't think they are all so very wonderful. I think too few people working in film care enough about using the medium to its fullest—sound, picture, composition, cutting—all of which can be used differently, can avoid being formularized.

SM: Do you see yourself as an artist?
FS: Probably. I'd like to . . . Yes, I do, but not in a pompous way. I certainly don't see myself as just churning out stuff. I would like to make as many films as I can that deliver a new experience, though that's not always possible.

SM: How do you see the role of the director working in the team?
FS: A good director is open to surprises and enhancement from the actors and the crew, providing that happens along the lines of the discipline and design of the film. Those people are not just there to supply you with what you've already imagined. Hopefully the crew members are as talented in their area as you are in yours, and they will take you somewhere further. That's where the real role of the director comes in, because he is the focus of all the talents, the one who directs everything between the riverbanks.

The director is the one who is responsible for the vision, in that he makes sure everybody contributes to a specific end. But, of course, directors work in extraordinarily different ways. A lot of directors don't direct camera at all and know nothing about the camera or lighting or lenses. Then a lot of directors do camera only and never tell the actors what to do.

That's the biggest complaint I've heard in the US, that actors don't know what they're doing because they're not being directed or told. Then there is the system in America where the stars won't do what the directors tell them, and that's untenable as far as I'm concerned.

SM: It's often remarked that there's at least the appearance of a lot more democracy on Australian film sets than American ones.
FS: Nonsense, total nonsense. What that might come from is that Australians don't think they have bosses. Now that's okay, but some people do necessarily have positions of authority. And maybe the lines of demarcation are more clearly drawn in Hollywood. In America people call you "sir," but they call any head of department "sir," and they call their fathers "sir"—so I don't think it's "sir" in the way it's used in England. Nobody does that in Australia, and everybody eats together and does things together and is a closer kind of group. But that's phony in one respect—underneath it all, it really isn't any different. Directors might seem to be nice blokes in Australia, but they're not really. I know most of them, and they want what they want.

SM: Which directors do you particularly admire?
FS: A long list. Kurosawa and a lot of the other Japanese directors: Mizoguchi, Ozu, Oshima. I like the English directors from the kitchen-sink, new wave era—*Look Back in Anger* and so on. As much as the directors, there was a school of writing that came out at that time. I tend to name directors because that's what I knew about then, but a lot of the credit should go to the writers. I think writers are very badly forgotten—the basis of all films is the script; if the script isn't good you don't have a good film. I like the Czechs—Jiri Menzel is still there, making the most charming, whimsical films, and Milos Forman and Ivan Passer are in the US. I like Satyajit Ray from India, Luis Bunuel from Spain, now Mexico, and I liked the French and the Italians who came out at the same time. Of the American directors, there's John Huston; I like a lot of his films: *Fat City* (1972), *The Treasure of the Sierra Madre* (1948). I'm not a John Ford fan, though. I like Bob Fosse. I think Woody Allen is sensational. Billy Wilder I love, and William Wyler. Often it is the actors you remember from those films, like Hepburn and Tracy and Clark Gable and Claudette Colbert.

The Devil's Playground: An Interview with Fred Schepisi

Brian McFarlane / 2015

Previously unpublished. Printed by permission of the author.

Brian McFarlane: Was the semi-autobiographical element the main source for the film?
Fred Schepisi: Yes, absolutely. Probably a lot more than semi-autobiographical. One of the reasons I did it was that I thought that what I experienced was something a lot of people didn't. And one of my philosophies is that, within every walk of life, you always have the full range of personalities. Whether it's architects or plumbers or construction workers, you'll find the optimist, the pessimist, the bright one, the dull one, and, in the monastery, among all the Brothers, you'd find the same range of personalities. So that was the starting-point: the exploring of different attitudes and the different ways that people look at things in the same environment. Also, what those Brothers represent, what any one of those young boys was likely to become, depending on, in the first place, their basic personalities and the influences they're exposed to.

BMcF: Beyond that, I wonder if there was a bigger, more universal idea behind it: the idea of a conflict between natural development and the things that restrain it?
FS: I guess so. As I was saying, all of those Brothers had quite diverse personalities, perhaps representing what each of those boys might become if they stayed in the monastery, depending on who had the most influence on them and on what path they started to choose for themselves.

BMcF: The range of Brothers suggests you were trying for a balanced view of the Brotherhood: how important was this to you?
FS: Very important. A lot of people have a strange memory of the film: that it was dealing with the sorts of problems that have emerged in recent times. But it

wasn't about that. In fact, I never experienced that in boarding school or in the monastery, nor did I know anyone at the time who did. It wasn't about that. It was really about the monks and how they were trying to lead a life they were called to, as it were, but sometimes struggling with what that meant, with the exigencies of that life, particularly because of celibacy.

BMcF: It doesn't seem as if you were out to deliver a broadside against the Catholic Church, but would you agree that there is an element of critique in it?
FS: Yes, but it wasn't something I was forcing as a bias. It was just something that emerged from the facts I was looking at. It's really a matter of trying to reach an understanding of what people in that walk of life would go through, the things they'd enjoy and the things they'd miss.

BMcF: How difficult was it to set up the production at the time? There were several other films in a period setting about young people's growth. Was their popularity a helpful factor?
FS: No, not at all. I think that was just coincidental. It took five years to get it together, and there was considerable resistance to it. The money was mostly from my own savings and friends and relatives, some from the AFDC (Australian Film Development Corporation). It wasn't until someone said that I wasn't going to get any money from the government unless I was prepared to be tough and play politics that I got tough and played politics. At that time I'd won more awards than anybody in Australia and internationally for my commercials and for my documentaries, and I'd done a couple of short films and part of the portmanteau film *Libido*. I had to raise a bit of a hue and cry along the lines of "If I'm not worthy of a bit of support, then who the hell is?"

BMcF: As I understand it the budget was about $300,000, which doesn't sound like much now, but was a substantial figure then . . .
FS: Yes, that's right. Then I had to go on and distribute it myself and hire cinemas myself. Phillip Adams led me to the guys who ran the Bryson in Melbourne and a couple of theaters in Brisbane as well, so I started through them. I had to market it through them, and it cost me as much as I'd put into the film.

BMcF: How successful was your film in box-office terms? It did pretty well, didn't it?
FS: That's the perception!

BMcF: What is more than a perception is that it was a big critical success . . .
FS: Yes, and it seemed to touch a nerve that I didn't expect. That is, young boys

going through puberty got as much out of the film as anyone might have got from the religious aspect. It's really as much about growing up, going through those changes we all go through, and there was a real identification with it among younger people as well as with those who'd gone through Catholic education.

BMcF: Which critical responses did you feel came nearest to what you were aiming at?
FS: I do remember when I was taking it around to get it distributed that a lot of people liked it.

BMcF: Was it ever distributed in Britain? I couldn't find a review of it there.
FS: Don't remember. I do remember selling it to Columbia and walking round Soho with cans in my hand, and they might have done something with it. But I guess it would have been a very limited release.

BMcF: How did you settle on Simon Burke for Tom?
FS: We saw a whole lot of boys, and we tried casting it here in Melbourne. Then we went up to Brisbane, then to Sydney, where we went to the Nimrod Theatre where Robyn Nevin and Arthur Dignam were involved. We went to see them in a play. At interval, the people we were talking to said, "See that young boy over there by the concession stand. You should go and talk to him; he's a keen little theater boy." He was trying to be an actor and had a bit part in something. So we started talking to him and liked him a lot, and we got him to come along and see us the next day and subsequently have a test. There was another young boy up for the part, but Simon just seemed to have the naturalness and the qualities of innocence that that boy needed to have.

BMcF: How easy/difficult was the rest of the casting? Where did you recruit the kids from?
FS: Most of them came from Melbourne. We cast a very wide net. My wife at the time, Rhonda, was responsible for a lot of that. She was connected to a lot of revue theater. We just held a lot of auditions.

BMcF: How easy was it to direct a large bunch of kids like that?
FS: Actually they were pretty good. It was part of the selection process. Whenever I'm auditioning anybody, I try to test out their flexibility, their ability to have ideas in the first place, but then to listen to what is required of the character and then to be able to adjust as needed to what's required. They were all pretty good, nice raw material that was good to build on.

BMcF: You got together a very good adult cast. How easy/difficult was that?

FS: First was the old guy, played by Charles McCallum. I auditioned a lot who found the dialogue is really hard. Then he came in one day. He was the right age. The others were generally much younger trying to be that age, and the minute he started to talk he was just perfect. And he had a bit of the shakes.

BMcF: They're all physically as well as psychologically distinguished from each other . . .

FS: I had a belief that it's good to cast sculpturally, so that you're physically casting different shapes and sizes.

BMcF: Was it mostly shot at Werribee Park? Where is the guest house? Is it Ard Rudah in Macedon?

FS: Yes, it is. Werribee Park was a godsend. Trevor Ling, my production designer, and Rhonda both kept saying this was the place, whereas I'd been trying to get the juniorate at Macedon. We'd been looking everywhere. Trevor and Rhonda said I needed something much bigger than that so that you have room to work in. But by the way you shoot it, you make it look smaller than that. I resisted that for a while because I didn't quite understand what they meant; then I suddenly got it. So, for the refectory scene, we moved all the tables and chairs up one end when we were shooting one way and then had plenty of room for the crew, then moved everything up the other end when we were shooting the other way. It gives you room to work, and you create the actual size of the room.

BMcF: I greatly admire the look of the film and wonder how importantly you regard Ian Baker's collaboration.

FS: Oh, it was extremely important. He had a very difficult job, and he had to work very quickly. I wanted that natural light look, and he had a way of re-creating that. And he had to because, as he said, the sun moves in the sky and so do the shadows, so we'd better be controlling that. He was very much part of the process, and he did it beautifully. It's hard to know where I stop and he starts. Bruce Smeaton, the composer, thought it was good to open with a sort of an overture as part of educating the audience as to how it's going to view the film and to bring you down from being out on the street and into the cinema and another world.

BMcF: I've been watching the recent miniseries and wonder if you have seen it and whether you'd agree that it's the product of a very different time in relation to the church and society? If you were remaking your film today, would you adopt a different tone?

FS: No, I really liked what they did. They wanted me to be involved, but I just gave it my blessing. They were going to use some extracts from my film but then wisely decided just to let their work stand in its own right. I liked the way you couldn't be certain who was doing what to whom and who was the bad one.

BMcF: I've enjoyed the miniseries but wonder what you think of a comparison I'd make: that is, that it is much more strongly plotted. What I most admire about your film is that it seems more observational, that its concern is with character and ideas rather than a more conventional narrative.
FS: That's true. Someone said it was the first film he'd seen that seemed like a novel. I guess with me it was instinct and the reason I was doing it.

Playboy Interview: Fred Schepisi

Rennie Ellis / 1982

> Published in *Playboy* (Australia), July 1982. Reprinted by permission of the author's estate.
> © Rennie Ellis Photographic Archive.

When Fred Schepisi was in his early twenties and working for a Melbourne advertising agency, he set himself three goals. At twenty-five years of age, he said, he would be managing director of his own company; at thirty he would have directed his first feature film; and at the ripe young age of thirty-five he would win the open competition at the Cannes Film Festival.

As a friend recollects, "Fred was never one for tip-toeing through the tulips." Schepisi is brash, direct, and, at times, boastful in that semi-playful, semi-serious way that one can never quite dismiss as being merely facetious. Behind his boyish chuckle, wide-mouth grin, and the loud Aussie banter is an ambitious and committed writer and director who is determined to expand the frontiers of a film language he first learned making TV commercials in Melbourne.

He was running his own film production company by the time he was twenty-five, his first feature, *The Devil's Playground*, was completed five years beyond his self-appointed deadline, and he hasn't won Cannes yet. But, as everyone will tell you, he went damn close in 1978 when his second feature, *The Chant of Jimmie Blacksmith*, was the first Australian film accepted as an official entry in the open competition at the world's premier commercial film festival.

Influential overseas critics who previewed the film before Cannes were unusually generous in their praise, and Schepisi became the dark horse tipped to pull off the big one. He got a standing ovation the night it was shown, and the blond, boisterous boy from Melbourne was the toast of the town. But *Jimmie Blacksmith* didn't win the coveted Palme d'Or.

"Look," says Schepisi, "there were all sorts of expectations but politically it couldn't win. The prize was being accepted, getting in ... breaking down a barrier. 'That was enough kudos for the Australians that year,' was the judges' attitude."

Whatever the ramifications of Cannes politics, *The Chant of Jimmie Blacksmith* did signal to the rest of the world that Australian films had something to offer an international audience hungry for a good story told with unusual flair and flavor.

Schepisi, along with Peter Weir, Gill Armstrong, Phil Noyce, George Miller, and Bruce Beresford, formed the nucleus of Australia's new wave directors whose films were to have a considerable impact with critics and audiences alike. Australian films had arrived and a lot of the right people were talking about them in very favorable terms. Since its US release, *The Chant of Jimmie Blacksmith* has appeared on several prominent "top 10 of the year" lists. Reviews by critics of the stature and influence of Pauline Kael and John Simon have been excellent.

In Australia, *Jimmie Blacksmith*, set up by an exceptionally effective publicity campaign prior to its release, received mixed reviews. There was an air of disappointment about it and perhaps an element of resentment because of the nature of the subject. Australians are not yet free of their racial prejudices. Based on the novel by Thomas Keneally, which was itself based on the true story of Jimmie Governor, an Aborigine, the film examined black/white relationships in Australia's early colonial days when the detribalized black was an easy mark for the white supremacist boot.

When Schepisi made the mandatory trip to Hollywood, it was no cap-in-hand pilgrimage to the celluloid czars but as a highly respected writer/producer/director and at the invitation of 20th Century Fox. However, his decision to move to Los Angeles with his family and make films in America was derided by some misguided Australians as a sell-out. They behaved as if Schepisi had some filial duty to perform in the home country, especially once he was accepted internationally. The way he saw it was that Hollywood was an international center for making films and, at this particular stage in his career, that was where he wanted to be to expand and hone his talents. Currently, he is working in one capacity or another on seven different development projects.

Schepisi's entry into the cut-and-thrust world of the Hollywood money men has had all the implications of a double-edged sword. While he is continually frustrated by their lack of concern for a film's content and by the slick maneuvers one is obliged to make in order to stay in the game, he is also elated by the completion of his first American film and the knowledge he has gained in the process.

"I am a much better director through making *Barbarosa*," he volunteers.

With a $10 million dollar budget—far in excess of any Australian-produced film—he tackled the almost sacred American genre of the western with country superstar Willie Nelson and veteran movie actor Gilbert Roland. Like his two previous films, *Barbarosa* is concerned with a character at odds with his fellow man. The theme of the outsider coming to terms with his alienation seems to weave its way through Schepisi's work.

"*Barbarosa* is about a legendary character who takes a young boy under his wing and teaches him how people need people," says Schepisi. "It's also about a vendetta and how men can be united through hatred. Basically it's an adventure story of the Butch Cassidy and Sundance Kid type. It's supposed to be a very different kind of western, but it still delivers the basic elements of the genre."

The film opened in America while Schepisi was on a brief visit to Australia, where he still has a major interest in The Film House, the company he started back in 1966. Earlier this year *The Devil's Playground* received its first US release. This, his first feature, was based on his childhood recollections of life in a Roman Catholic junior seminary. It won several Australian film awards in 1976 and was chosen for Directors' Fortnight at Cannes. The April edition of *US Playboy* gave it an excellent review.

Barbarosa also won good reviews from influential critics like Pauline Kael, yet it was taken off by Universal after a very brief southern states run. Says Schepisi, "Universal treated it like an exploitation western, which it isn't. All I want to do now is get it back and show it properly."

Rennie Ellis: You first went to the US in 1978 just a few months after *The Chant of Jimmie Blacksmith* had been so well received at the Cannes Film Festival. Was that when you set up the deal to shoot *Barbarosa*?

Fred Schepisi: No, it just doesn't work as easily as that. I'd signed with an established agent named Sam Cohn—he's the one they all thank on the awards nights—and he arranged for 20th Century Fox to invite me over to talk about an idea I had for a script called *Bitter Sweet Love*. And, on the basis of that idea, we made an agreement for me to write, produce, and direct that script. I then came back to Australia to write it. But during that time, there were a series of management upheavals at Fox, and the people I'd done the deal with got shafted—escorted off the lot, in fact. It was all very dramatic. Luckily the new president, who I knew from London, wanted me to continue. He gave me two months to finish. But the day I arrived back in the States, hot script in hand ready to talk business, he resigned.

The whole experience was quite traumatic for both sides. But I got an office, did my rewriting, and collected my money. The new management and I agreed to shelve the project for a time. The script was set in the US, and, by then, I knew I needed to get inside the fabric of American society much more. I was beginning to realize that the Americans are as different from us as the French are.

RE: So why set an idea you developed in Australia in America—an America you hadn't yet come to grips with?

FS: Firstly, I wasn't aware at the time that America was so different. Secondly, it was an important project to me, and I wanted it to speak to a larger group of people and I wanted to do it on a large scale.

It's about a man who's been married twice and is having an affair. It examines relationships in three stages—one that's over, one that time has soured, and one that's blooming and new. And it juxtaposes them in a funny kind of way, using time jumps and strange overlaps. The thing I loved about it most was that it shows how the idiosyncrasies of a person are frequently the things that attract you, but they're also the first things that drive you nuts.

RE: How much did you get paid for taking the script to first rewrite stage?
FS: I got fifty grand. My writer's fee for the film was, I think, $150,000. And the way you get paid is that you get so much for doing a first draft and a set of revisions, then you get so much for the next draft, then you get a bonus of the remainder of the money if you get the sole screen credit, or a bit less if you share the credit.

But as I was also producing and directing there was the same amount of money available to me again, plus I had fifteen percent of the profits. But of course it never got to the pay or play stage.

RE: Pay or play? What exactly does that mean?
FS: They're the secret words. Once the studio makes a commitment to the picture you are "pay or play." This means, even if the film in fact never gets made, the studio still has to pay you the full fee they agreed upon for you to write or direct or whatever.

RE: A writer's fee of $150,000. A director's fee of $150,000 to $200,000. This sounds like big money by Australian standards.
FS: Not necessarily for directors. I imagine Peter Weir, for instance, got a similar amount of money for *Gallipoli* (1981) to what I did for *Barbarosa*. In America, the director's contract states that the minimum money you can receive is $50,000 plus five percent of the net. Of course, to define the net would take twelve pages. If you become a big star like the guy who made *Alien* . . . his next fee was a million dollars.

Look, $150,000 may sound like a lot of money but consider that you're tied up on a project for between one and two years, you lose up to a third with fees to lawyers, agents, business managers, a percentage goes on your industry cards, you lose half of the remainder in tax, and then you've got to remember you've set up house with your family in a country where it's very expensive to live. My rent for a pretty ordinary house on the wrong side of Beverly Hills is $2,100 a month. The idea is to be involved in several development projects to help out. And then again, it's not so much the fee that's the important thing. It's the percentage you negotiate in the profit returns because, if a picture really takes off, that's when you can make big money.

RE: I've heard it said that "the deal" is the new art form in Hollywood which suggests that a film's content and form are secondary considerations. Where does this leave you in terms of personal integrity and commitment to the script?

FS: Well, that's more or less true. And it leaves you frustrated and disappointed. Without a word of a lie, I've had 120 scripts offered to me since I've been there. Now, a good deal of those have come to me on rotation—they go to everybody. What they look for is a "name" person who's popular with studios or financial groups of a specific type who might help finance the movie. It simply means they've come to you so you can be part of a package that may attract money. I have been offered, on a much more serious basis, about fifteen very definite projects. And I have turned them down because I did not like the content. Some of them would have made me a lot of money.

I have been working on seven projects. You have to have irons in several fires over there. In Australia, you say, "I want to make that film," and then all your energies go into raising the money and producing that film. In America you need a number of projects. It's extremely hard to make individual pictures in the mainstream because the nature of the business is "show me the poster," "where's the hook?" and "what's the package?" And there, as you said, is where the art form is—the package.

The heads of studios are now ex-agents and ex-lawyers, and they changed the whole business in the sixties. What they want to see is this scriptwriter, that director, and these two actors. And, on these people, he can pick up the phone and pre-sell territories around the world and lay-off money here and set up a specific television sale there. So the whole thing is done by numbers. They want to know if a certain script is on line at the correct time, the demographics of it, et cetera. It's like advertising—our audience is twenty-five-year-old white females or something or other, and it would seem that the making of the picture is the least important part of the process. I find that completely frustrating because I don't find any forward vision. I don't find any exciting entrepreneurial attitudes to new and innovative material. However, you have to admit that some extraordinary films get made despite that system.

RE: So in order to make it over there as a writer or a director you have to be one helluva wheeler-dealer, as well as an artist, or you get taken to the cleaners?

FS: Yeah, and you need to be thick-skinned. And you must have very good agents and lawyers.

RE: So, with one project shelved, how did you get to do *Barbarosa*?

FS: While I was writing *Bitter Sweet Love* and the management shuffles kept happening, my agent put me in touch with other studios, and, in fact, I was brought back to America by two companies—Universal Studios and Lorimar Productions. Lorimar fronted for my visa and agreed to pay me an amount of money to supervise the rewrite of a picture called *Partners*, which I was subsequently going to direct. Universal was paying my expenses on a verbal agreement to work on a script with Bill Wittliff called *Raggedy Man*. I took that project because I met the writer. I found there was more in the writer's head than he had put in the script, and I knew how to get it out. I liked the project also because Sally Field was to star in it. And that meant I could deal with one American star and work that system out.

In actual fact, Sally Field messed around. We had to find another star, and that star turned out to be Sissy Spacek. We were involved in very delicate negotiations with her—she likes to read draft after draft of the script before she makes up her mind. At the same time, my agent recommended me to Paul Lazarus, the producer of *Barbarosa*. Lazarus was shown *Jimmie Blacksmith*; he went crazy and wanted to make me an offer—pay or play with a guarantee of the film being produced within a specific period of time. Now the important thing to do is to make films, not money. You can go pay or play, and you can get paid even if the picture doesn't come off. But you're out of circulation for a year or so, and you're not making films. So the guarantee of making the movie is the important part of the process.

So we warned Universal of the situation and gave them the opportunity to sew me up, and they started to say, "Well, negotiations with Sissy Spacek are very delicate. We can't be putting pressure on at this time." I said, "It's very simple. If you think I'm to be the director, just sign this piece of paper, and we'll all believe it." You know, there's a strange thing over there—everyone keeps their options open.

So my agent and my lawyer, who are two of the best in the country, said, "You must take *Barbarosa*. It's guaranteed." I say yes, but I've put four months into *Raggedy Man*. I'm emotionally committed to it. I've broken its back.... I understand it. I know what to do with it. I don't want to leave it. And they said, "You have to trust us because *Raggedy Man* may never happen, and you can't take that chance when there's a guaranteed film." For once in my life, I listened to the pragmatic view and I signed. This was Friday. On Monday I was told Sissy Spacek's husband, Jack Fisk, was signed to direct his first picture "pay or play" on *Raggedy Man*, and she too was signed pay or play. Had I not signed for *Barbarosa*, I would have been out in the cold. That's how I got to direct *Barbarosa*. It's a long-winded answer, but I think it's important that people understand that, in Hollywood, it is that complicated.

RE: What was it that made you want to go to Hollywood in the first place? Was part of it the disenchantment you must have felt because of the poor reception *Jimmie Blacksmith* received from Australian critics, while overseas they raved about it? Were you pissed off with hometown reactions?

FS: Actually about seventy percent of the critics in Australia liked it. The bad reaction came from columnists rather than film critics, probably the result of over-publicity. But, to answer your question, no, it wasn't the reaction to *Jimmie Blacksmith* that made me go to America.

RE: Did it contribute to it?

FS: No, not at all. Although I should say that I was a little disappointed at one or two fellow filmmakers trying to destroy the success of the picture for their own gains. That's when I got cross.

RE: How could it be to their gain?

FS: I've no idea. There was one man writing under a pseudonym . . . and writing not exactly truthful things about a number of filmmakers: disparaging articles about Peter Weir, Bruce Beresford, and me. By putting us down, he'd been putting himself up. He was entitled to his opinion, but readers ought to know whose opinion it was and where his interests lay. There was another producer in Melbourne who did an interview saying that what happened with *Jimmie Blacksmith* in Cannes was a lie, that people didn't stand up and clap at the end. That it was all publicity hype. What upset me especially was the inability of these people to understand that every Australian film that was successful made it easier for the rest of us. The more we were successful, the greater the aura created around Australian films, the easier it would be for everybody. But I'm digressing . . .

The reason I went to America had nothing to do with all this. I wanted to go to America firstly because I wanted to get paid good money. Everybody forgets that I put in major amounts of money in all my films—that is, my company's money. For instance, for *Jimmie Blacksmith*, it was more than a quarter of a million dollars. You can't keep doing that.

I wanted to work on a whole series of pictures in a row. I wanted to be able to apply immediately what I'd learnt in one picture to the next. I wanted to work just as a director on great scripts. I wanted to work just as a writer and have somebody else direct or just work as a producer. I wanted to hone each skill separately to make sure that I was using them properly in relation to my own work. I had a lot of subjects that were not specifically Australian, and I thought it would be better to make these films in a place like America. I wanted to see what the Americans had to offer in skills in all the various departments right through to marketing. I wanted to make a name for myself, to make it easier to market Australian films for myself and . . . well, for a million reasons, not the least being that if you sing opera you want to sing in La Scala, and you want to sing at the Met. You play tennis, then it's Wimbledon. Athletics, it's the Olympics. You want to pitch yourself against the best in the world for two reasons—to see if you can tune yourself to a finer and better degree and to test your theories and beliefs and give yourself confidence in them.

RE: Some people may disagree with you that the best in the world are to be found in Hollywood.
FS: And they would be right. There are other places where top people are working. I don't look at Hollywood as America, but as an international center for making films. There are Germans and French and Yugoslavs and Poles and Poms—all kinds of people who are often mistakenly thought of as Americans. Hollywood is a pressure cooker. And the films that come out of the place are international as opposed to indigenous type films, which is what we should be making in Australia. Films about Australia, our people, attitudes, history, lifestyles, and so on that are important here but that will also reach out and touch other people. This is especially so when funding is coming from government bodies.

RE: Are you committed to Hollywood, or do you hope to return to Australia eventually and make films here?
FS: A few weeks ago, I nearly came back. The frustration in Hollywood mounts up, and sometimes it starts to get the better of you. I was watching *A Town Like Alice* (1981) on the box, and I just got very homesick. I loved that series. I thought it was just spectacular. So, every Sunday, I used to pack my bags before I sat down to watch it. Look, there are several projects that I want to do in Australia, not the least of which is the Norman Lindsay story. But I felt that before tackling a project like that I needed more experience.

RE: And has the American experience made a perceptible difference to your filmmaking yet?
FS: Yes, yes. I am a much improved filmmaker since doing *Barbarosa*. I learned so much. I've just written a screenplay adaptation of a novel, a beautiful romance, and it's the best thing I've ever done. This also fitted one of my criteria for going to America—of trying to find refined story content and structure and all those things to appeal to large groups of people and to get all the message and feelings and things I have to say in it, so it kind of bubbles up through it. In this way, I have a top layer that attracts large audiences but, beyond that, there are layers of meaning and feeling for people to discover depending on their intellect and sensibilities. I felt the Americans had something to offer in that way. I didn't want

to go over there and copy them but to try to combine my attributes with some of their methods and technique—something that would allow me to express myself in an original way but to large groups of people.

RE: Does *Barbarosa* work in this way?
FS: *Barbarosa* is an interesting picture in which there are some levels of stuff going on, but it is primarily an entertainment picture. I would say that, having made it, I'm twice the filmmaker I was. I learned so much about story, drive, forward motion, energy centers, people having goals. For instance, there's a point where you can no longer introduce new intellectual information into a film, where the physical and emotional attention of the audience is peaking. You must be very aware of these things. You have to know how to satisfy your audience in these areas. There are certain things that have to be brought to climaxes from both a physical and intellectual point of view. There is a point where one takes over from the other, and to deny it is to deny your audience a proper appreciation of the film.

RE: I'm not sure I understand exactly what you mean here.
FS: Somebody said a great line to me the other day—originally it was applied to novels but it's the same for films—"don't lose them." Because the minute you lose them, you lose this wonderfully complicated thing that you've weaved and all of its intricacies. You lose an audience for a few minutes, and you've killed off whole thought patterns and experiences that the film was creating. I've learned an extraordinary amount in this area.

RE: Did you find your own personal film guru, some master who instructed you?
FS: No, mostly out of myself. Out of being there and being put under certain pressures, which I responded to in my own way, which is not necessarily the Hollywood way. They have certain rules and regulations and beliefs when it comes to picture making: the way scripts are written, the way actors are handled, the way crews work. Pictures always take on their own life. No matter what you've written, what you've designed, what your direction is, a picture becomes like a living organism, like a river, and once you're on it you have to go with it. It's no good trying to go to the bank and drill a hole because that's where you want the river to go. You've got to follow its course for the best ride, if you like, and you've got to adapt to it without losing sight of where you're going.

In *Barbarosa*, this was especially obvious to me. There are some haunting, involving, mythical things in the picture that in another film would really hold your interest. In this picture, there are times when the relationship between the two men has such energy and is so attractive that you just have to stay with it and subjugate certain other textural elements of the picture in order to keep that sudden energy alive. When it's hot, you know you've got to go with it. It's an amazing experience. You've got to try to make the film come out the way you want it, but, at the same time, you want to pick up on this energy, this thing that just evolved.

RE: Is there a hard and fast dividing line between art and entertainment?
FS: No, I don't think so at all. I don't see why there should be a difference.

RE: You said *Barbarosa* is basically an entertainment film as if you were excusing something about it.
FS: No, I'm not excusing anything about it. I guess I was differentiating between *Barbarosa* and *The Chant of Jimmie Blacksmith*. While *Jimmie Blacksmith* is a good story, it is also packed with messages and pleas and exposes. It's a very serious statement about what we did to our blacks. *Barbarosa*, on the other hand, is much lighter; it's not meant to carry a heavy message.

RE: When does a film stop being just entertainment for the masses and become art? When the critics say so?
FS: I think it becomes art if it delivers an experience that uses the full spectrum of the medium. And in an inventive and innovative manner that excites you in a way you haven't experienced before. Or, if it's a genre film, like a western, it becomes art when it's so incredibly polished that it achieves the above. A film is not art just because it is arty or precious or deep or intelligent or... There is another thing and that is when the filmmaker has made it with passion. When there is something to the person being expressed, a substance beyond the surface gloss.

RE: Is it easier to get money for films in the US than it is here in Australia?
FS: It's easier to get money for some kinds of films. I would hate to go to America unless I was highly regarded and went in on some sort of star basis. I would not like to be running around town looking for work.

I think the circumstances regarding film finance in Australia have changed radically since I left in '79. I'm sure the tax incentive situation has made it much easier to fund a project here now.

RE: Do you feel let down in any way by your American experience?
FS: I think my biggest disappointment, apart from the frustrations already mentioned, is that I expected to find an expertise in showmanship, in producing knowledge, and in those entrepreneurial marketing skills I thought the Americans invented. I was looking forward to having a really great producer who understood film and has a real commercial sense. And I expected to find writers of great skill. All of this is your illusion of the film industry over there, isn't it?

RE: Sure. I always thought the Yanks past masters of all that.

FS: Forget it! There are pockets of it, but that's all. I expected more brain power, more knowledge being used in the selection of production material. What I did find that was great was on the crew level. The crew I worked with were very generous and giving people who had experienced everything.

RE: Yet, despite your praise of US crews, you used Ian Baker from Australia as your director of photography on *Barbarosa*. I believe you were obliged by the unions to employ an American cameraman even though you never used him.

FS: Yes, we had to do that. I used Ian because he shot both my films in Australia, and we had built up a very special communication. There were basic communication problems with the Americans because of the idiosyncrasies of Australian and American English and because my style of expression and my approach to filmmaking was, to them, unconventional, and it took time for them to get used to me. But "Bakes" and I have an understanding: we communicate in shorthand, and, when you're trying to advance your art in an environment you're not familiar with, you need that kind of security. Apart from that, I know of no other cameraman who is better.

RE: How did your approach to filmmaking differ from what the Americans were used to?

FS: The conventional way of making pictures is that you shoot a master shot, then you do the medium shots for that scene, then you work the close-ups. In other words, you establish the scene in the master shot, you sell the proposition of the scene, the essence of it, in the medium shots, then you get into the details with the close-ups. Well, I think that's nonsense. The way I work is that I take the whole film as a canvas, and I have different rhythms and textures in each scene. The story content dictates the style.

RE: When you direct, how much of it is intuitive and how much is worked out beforehand and carefully structured?

FS: It's all very carefully structured, but, when you're actually shooting, it has to change so much because of all the variables, like the weather, technical and mechanical problems, the dictates and pressures of time, and the actors and their moods. So you have to improvise and make decisions on the spot. But you must also have a solid base and a direction so you don't lose sight of where you are going.

RE: Did you find that working with American actors was any different from working with Australian talent?

FS: As a rule, American actors require much more of a director's time—much, much more than we are used to giving in Australia. American actors are used to it and expect it. It's slower because they tend to want to take the whole discussion process beyond the rehearsals and on to the floor while you're actually shooting. They like strong direction and reassurance. In America, if a guy is a star then he's used to being treated in a certain way. I think Australian crews don't always understand that. When an American star works in Australia they expect him to be one of the boys, eat and drink with the crew and so on. And if he wants his own motor home on location and wants to prepare alone and in silence, they think he's a snob or something. But he's not there for fun and games; he's there to perform. I've talked with Kirk Douglas since he came back from Australia after filming *The Man from Snowy River*, and he had those kinds of problems. They created some unfortunate friction.

RE: In *Barbarosa*, Willie Nelson plays the lead. Is he an actor or a singer who acts?
FS: He's an actor in my film.

RE: You also had the famous old-time star Gilbert Roland working with you. What was he like?
FS: He was so great—tremendous ability, a man whose career spans the time from the silent era right up to now. He's been up in the superstar category and down again. He has such a professional approach to the business. He was always on the set on time, prepared, ready, and he probably has more knowledge about the whole process of filmmaking than me. Yet he was totally responsive to me as a director. He'd done it all before. He knew exactly when to turn his head, hit a certain line, and he knew instantly if I was capable as a director of protecting him—whether he could put himself in my hands. It was the kind of professionalism that I wanted to experience in Hollywood.

And, you know, he had the same costume fitting as he did forty years ago.

RE: Because of Australian Actors Equity regulations, it's very difficult for overseas actors to work in Australia. Do you think this kind of protection is a good policy, or does it get in the way of expanding the international appeal of our films?
FS: I understand the reason for those attitudes. I also take the point of those producers who believe an actor with some kind of international star rating is a plus when it comes to getting the money together for a film, although I doubt if their presence really helps sell a film. There are few bankable people in the world today, and they change weekly. I can't see that paying someone a million bucks to appear in your film is going to result in a million bucks more in sales.

But to get back to the question. There's a fine line between what is good cross-pollination between cultures and what kind of cross-pollination helps uplift our experience. I think each project should be considered on its merits. Australians should be looked after, but there are also economic considerations and the benefits of good and appropriate casting. It's the excesses of the way they interpret these regulations that drive me mad and can be bad for the industry. When they try to say Robert Stigwood is not Australian. Or look at Tim Burstall's trouble with *Kangaroo*, when they ruled that Olivia Newton-John was not Australian. You know what I call that? They're looking for extra ways to levy money out of pictures.

Look, I believe in protection, and I believe that if you're going to have government money in a film then it ought to go to Australians. And certainly I don't like the idea of Americans coming out here to play Australian parts. But let's be sensible and realistic in the interpretation of the rule.

RE: How do you find living in Los Angeles? Is there a great difference in the lifestyle?
FS: I do tend to think of LA as Sodom when people are paying $14 million for a house! There are seven or eight pages in the Sunday paper devoted to advertising properties worth one million dollars and over. It is the most expensive place to live in that I've ever experienced. I live in an old country-style house up the back of Beverly Hills, and I'm alarmed at the rent I pay. It costs me $2,100 a month, and that is a bargain by their standards. Yet, I'm still astounded that I have to pay that much. We've got a pool, but it's certainly not the kind of house you'd expect to get for that sort of money if you use Australian criteria.

I just think that LA is so weird. It's got no center, no focus. At first you're totally alienated. It's not so bad for the man of the family because he's out working and meeting people. But, if you're at home, you hardly ever see anyone because people drive everywhere whenever they go out. There's few places to meet people. It's difficult for a woman and kids to get settled, make friends, and make a life. It takes a long time to settle down and adjust. My little kids are five and three, and they've already got American accents. They figured they couldn't communicate, so they'd better learn how.

RE: Is Hollywood still Tinsel Town?
FS: No, that went in the sixties when the studio system broke down ... Maybe in some areas still where they hang on to the idea of the past—movie stars and contract players and all that sort of stuff. Hollywood can be a lonely kind of place. It's a company town so you tend, unfortunately, to be only involved with people in the industry. I'm used to being involved with people on a much broader scale. So I

have fewer friends there and few outside interests. You find you're always talking about box office and deals. There isn't the communication between writers and directors that I would have liked to be involved in. Whereas I love New York—in New York, it's much more exciting. There you talk about the theater and the arts and the content of something rather than the deal. I wouldn't mind doing a play in New York or a musical on Broadway as an in-between thing.

RE: Will you be doing any television work?
FS: I've been offered a prestigious series about Robert Kennedy. But I don't want to do television at this point. The reasons are that you have to compromise too much and you have to censor too much. You can't express yourself fully, but you still have to put in the same kind of energy.

RE: What projects are you working on at the moment?
FS: At the moment, I've got an office and a secretary provided by Warner Bros., and I'm working on my script out of there. They have first right of refusal on my ideas and the work I produce. MGM is trying to negotiate a similar but more enriching deal, and we're close to coming to terms on a Judith Ross screenplay—a very witty, sophisticated comedy about infidelity. And there's another development project about a Japanese World War II soldier who turns up in the Borneo jungle and returns to Japan and has to cope with all the changes that have taken place in Japanese society. I want Tom Keneally to write it. I want to get into multi-screen stuff. It's a wondrous thing. And there's another script written by James Goldman, an Academy Award-winning writer, about diplomacy under pressure.

RE: Do you have a special ambition for the future? A goal you set yourself?
FS: By 1990, I hope to come up with an entirely different form of film expression. By then, I will have served my apprenticeship and be confident enough to try something very special. My belief is that everyone is trying to make bigger and bigger films so they become an event and get people away from the box. And with cable TV coming on big and all the diversity that will offer, it's going to be harder and harder to attract film audiences. But if you can offer them a new experience, not just an event, but something much more involving and complex and enriching, but, at the same time, as simple as films are now . . . well that's where I'm heading, that's what everything I'm doing now is building up to. I'm going to give you something that is stylistically stunning on the simplest of levels but with more there if you want it. I want to deliver something that is stimulating and exhilarating with great emotional impact—a totally new experience.

RE: When you make a film, how conscious are you of your audience? For instance, a painter may just paint for himself and be aware only of his own personal vision.
FS: Unfortunately, you can't do that with $10 or $20 million. But I do believe that a film has to be a personal expression. There's a great line from Nabokov about the role of the novelist, and I think the same applies to the filmmaker. He said you have to be a story-teller, a teacher, and an enchanter. And that's how I see it. Film is about the precision of science and the beauty of poetry.

Fred Schepisi: The Australian Director Talks about His New Controversial Film, *Barbarosa*

Michael Sragow / 1982

Published in *Rolling Stone*, April 29, 1982. Reprinted by permission of *Rolling Stone*. Copyright © Rolling Stone LLC 1982. All Rights Reserved.

Forty-two-year-old writer-director Fred Schepisi is definitely the most controversial and arguably the most talented of all Australian filmmakers. With only three feature films to his name, he's won an international reputation as a sensual visual poet and an intrepid explorer of volatile subject matter. He's viewed as an individualistic outsider—with good reason. He not only wrote and directed his first feature, *The Devil's Playground* (1976), but promoted it and distributed it down-under virtually all by himself.

This tragicomic study of life in a Marist seminary swept the Australian Film Awards and finally opened in New York in 1981 to rave reviews. Schepisi's next film, the incendiary *The Chant of Jimmie Blacksmith* (1978), from the novel by Thomas Keneally, outraged home audiences with its frank depiction of racial violence in nineteenth-century Australia but was also hailed by American critics as a masterwork.

Schepisi's first American movie, a visually arresting, spirited western, *Barbarosa*, has yet to open outside the South and Southwest. Its distributor, Universal Pictures, chose to market it regionally as a conventional shoot-'em-up instead of premiering it in the major northern cities to take advantage of Schepisi's large critical following. Though the film stars both Willie Nelson and Gary Busey at their best, Universal is now debating whether to open it elsewhere or cut its losses. When I met Schepisi a few weeks after the movie's regional opening, he spoke quite frankly about its failure to find an audience.

Michael Sragow: Why is *Barbarosa* in trouble?
Fred Schepisi: I think the problem is that Universal didn't like the film. Studios

are able to convey their feelings to everyone who sees a film. They had an exhibitors' screening in New York and managed to make it quite clear that they were not keen on the film and that it was not high on their list of priorities. Both trade reviews led off by saying the film would be difficult to market. That's no coincidence.

I was in advertising myself, so I'm not just speaking as a director. I think the people who didn't like the film wanted to be proved right. They want to think they're good marketers. But a good marketer is a person who's able to take a difficult film, figure out what its audience is and how to reach that audience and then market it. These days, everyone is after the big one. No one's content with a modest success.

MS: What attracted you to *Barbarosa* in the first place?
FS: It has this roguish, picaresque quality, and it allows me to examine hatred as a catalyst for uniting people. The Mexicans unite against Barbarosa the way the American people united against the Ayatollah Khomeini.

MS: All your films are about what unites and separates different cultures.
FS: Arthur Dignam, an actor who was in *The Devil's Playground*, told me I always deal with individuals outside of a system who are struggling to become part of a system and yet remain individuals. I guess that's right. On the one hand, I'm conservative—I'm suspicious of extremist factions in society. On the other hand, I'm anti-authoritarian and against institutions.

MS: *The Devil's Playground*, which is, in some ways, critical of the Catholic church, contains a real respect for ritual.
FS: Rules and regulations are usually set up for good reasons. When I was running my own business (a film production company specializing in commercials), a couple of university people studied it as an example of open management. As long as people did their jobs, that was it. We all shared in the goodies. Well, I cannot tell you. One man came in drunk. I lost some people. One man came in crying, saying, "I'm becoming a bum. You've got to tell me what to do." I had to become a benevolent dictator. But you have to create a balance. You can't let regulations become rigid.

MS: Why do you think *Jimmie Blacksmith* upset Australians?
FS: Australians are basically racist, and they are able to avoid facing it because most Australians live in cities. The black populations that remain, that weren't killed off, are either confined to a specific suburb or live in country towns or right outside of country towns. So most Australians can live a whole lifetime and never come into contact with blacks on any day-to-day basis. They can have

very liberal attitudes without ever having to put them to the test. This film put them to the test.

MS: There are some visual similarities between *Barbarosa* and *Jimmie Blacksmith* . . .

FS: The running scenes are somewhat similar. But in *Blacksmith*, all the shots of the Aborigines were directed to look as if they grew out of the landscape. The whites in the movies were shot as if they were alien to the landscape: up and out, so that they were fighting against it, and there was violence in everything they did. *Barbarosa* is shot differently, except for the Mexican banditos all tucked down in the canyons. There are two things I tried to do visually: to show you the beauty of the countryside as it looked to Barbarosa—he does stay there because he likes the joint—and to convey the reality beneath the surface, that it's harsh and rocky and thorny, that it hurts.

MS: What bothers you the most about American moviemaking?
FS: You spend more time making deals than you do making the films. You don't get to make many of the films you work on, and if you do, there are so many compromises along the way that the film you make is very different from the film you agreed to make. Fighting with the powers that be can be depleting for an artist.

MS: But if what you say about hate is true, then artists could band together against the businessmen.
FS: Well, I hope it's not true. I hope there are greater motivating forces than hate. The Ayatollah united this country, but so did the US Olympic hockey team. When they won the gold medal, I'd never seen such a national explosion of joy!

Fred Schepisi's *Iceman* Cometh: Altered States in the Great White North

James Verniere / 1983

First published in *Film Comment*, September/October 1983. Reprinted by permission of the author.

When *The Chant of Jimmie Blacksmith* was released in 1980 in the US, Fred Schepisi (rhymes with Pepsi) was hailed as the great Australian director. Since his emigration to the US four years ago, Schepisi has completed only one film, the pseudo-mythic western, *Barbarosa*, which also received good reviews but was given only a minor release by Universal. However, the studio obviously has faith in Schepisi: he is now at work on Universal's *Iceman* in Vancouver, British Columbia.

On the face of it, this hardly seems like a Fred Schepisi project. Produced by Norman Jewison and Patrick Palmer, *Iceman* is the study of a prehistoric human (John Lone) revived by a team of cryobiologists (headed by Lindsay Crouse) after forty thousand years frozen in Arctic ice. Timothy Hutton plays hotshot anthropologist Stanley Shephard, whose efforts to communicate with our thawed-out forefather is a struggle to bridge the gap between modern and primitive man. The project seems more a combination of *The Wild Child* and *Quest for Fire*—a kind of *Altered States* in the Great White North—than anything in *Blacksmith*'s ken.

"The only science fiction in this film is the first heartbeat," says scriptwriter John Drimmer, sitting in a trailer in a bus depot in Vancouver, where some *Iceman* interiors have been built. Drimmer is echoing the sentiments of the director and the producers. Apparently, the word is out to soft-pedal the science-fiction elements of *Iceman* and to emphasize its "human drama." Clearly, though, it will be more than a caveman-on-the-loose film. Though the genre is a science-fiction and action film cross, *Iceman*'s creators are seeking to convey its serious philosophical underpinnings: a pop variation on Hobbes and Rousseau. "It will be much more than a grunting Alley Oop," adds Drimmer.

Outside the trailer, an assistant director blasts a pocket horn at regular intervals to warn that the cameras are rolling in the vivarium, a $500,000 reproduction of the Iceman's natural environment where the scientists have placed him to observe his behavior. The vivarium is an enormous hollow full of cliffs and caves, built out of chicken wire, burlap, and ABS foam on a skeleton of steel scaffolding. In the center, on a wooden ramp, a Louma crane is perched. Above is a great, plexiglass dome.

Inside, Schepisi is directing Hutton and Lone (a Chinese American who won an Obie Award for his galvanic performance in *The Dance and the Railroad*, which he also staged and scored) in their first meeting. Lone makes a formidable protohuman. Squat but muscular, he sports the ridged brow and bulbous cranium of our evolutionary forebears. Unlike the Neanderthals of *Quest for Fire*, Lone's primitive is more human, despite his oversized teeth and nails and the ceremonial scars that crisscross his chest.

Only two weeks of shooting remain, and the mood of the cast and crew vacillates between giddiness and exhaustion. A local doctor has been by to give shots of B-12. The locations have been murderous: in Churchill, Manitoba, where the temperature dips to fifty below zero; on ice fields near Summit Lake and Bitter Creek; and on the Salmon, Chickamin, and Bear glaciers.

The frustration level is high as Schepisi directs the first, violent encounter. He commands retake after maddening retake, but the result is a testament to his demanding style: this evening's dailies will bristle with tension. None of the principal actors sees the dailies, but Schepisi looks and limps around (he broke his foot Indian wrestling on location). Cinematographer Ian Baker grunts his approval from the back of the room. John Drimmer is clearly impressed, contrary to the myth of the disgruntled screenwriter. Everyone is drinking beer and munching pretzels.

Logistically, *Iceman* is Schepisi's most arduous film, requiring five helicopters to ferry filmmakers to the ice-bound locations. "Which means," he explains, "that you have to try to maximize the number of shots in one drop, which sometimes isn't possible. We got down to very few shots a day at one point." *Iceman* is over schedule. "We evacuated three times to avoid getting caught in a white-out," the director says.

The ice-bound locations also forced Schepisi to alter his shooting style. "Ian and I like to work with very long lenses, which packs things up and forces the perspective, like painting. And a very long lens on faces can blow the background away so it becomes a patina. It gives you a dimensional effect of the person being pushed off the screen. But when you're working on ice you sometimes can't get the effect of why you're there unless you're on a wide lens. At the same time, you can't get the scale without a long lens. It was really a quandary. We couldn't apply a single rule."

Schepisi's involvement in *Iceman* has always been perplexing—even he admits that at first the film was not his cup of tea. "Before I was offered *Iceman* I was involved in a debacle over a film called *The Consultant*, which was to star Jacqueline Bisset and Roy Scheider. It was supposed to be a 'go' picture, but as it turned out they didn't have the money, and it seemed I had to be approved by Jackie Bisset. After a number of meetings, she said she didn't feel she could work with me. That kind of thing happens all the bloody time."

Schepisi bridles at the suggestion that he might be making more films if he had stayed in Australia. Despite being bogged down by *Raggedy Man* (which he was scheduled to direct before Sissy Spacek's husband, Jack Fisk, took over) for nine months, and losing several more on *The Consultant*, Schepisi argues he has kept pace with Weir and Beresford. "Australia is just as tough in a different kind of way. I was accused of destroying the Australian film industry, because it cost $1.2 million to make *Jimmie Blacksmith*. Now executive producers take a $250,000 fee for doing fuck all. I didn't have the problems I'm having here because I did everything in Australia, and I'm going to try to get back to that here. I don't want to get all excited and put considerable work and emotional energy into a project like *The Consultant* and have it drop because of somebody's neurosis."

So, finally, what convinced Schepisi to stake his career on the *Iceman* script? "I saw a lot of prospects in it. I thought it could be a thought-provoking but also commercially successful picture, full of pace and energy. I thought this film could have—as Nabokov said—'the precision of poetry and the intuition of science.' But I have to be careful: I don't want it to be too poetic. What I'm searching for is the perfect balance: a good picture that people will bloody go and see."

Fred Schepisi: Taking Hollywood by Drizzle

David Edelstein / 1984

First published in *Village Voice*, May 1, 1984. Reprinted here by permission of the author.

In his 1978 masterpiece, *The Chant of Jimmie Blacksmith*, Australian director Fred Schepisi (pronounced Skep-see) first achieved the epic form that has (unwittingly, it turns out) become his signature. The film concerns a half-white, half-aboriginal laborer, who, pushed to the limit by Aussie discrimination, goes on a killing spree, and its mythic story is rooted in a welter of physical detail. Schepisi's work teems with quick shots of wildlife and vegetation as the characters scramble over the terrain; he takes almost no detail for granted, building his universe from the ground up. And while the subject of his films is generally a radical individual at odds with society, Schepisi's movies encompass virtually all points of view—the oppressor, the oppressed, and everything in between.

Schepisi was in town last week promoting *Iceman*, a big-budget sci-fi film about a forty-thousand-year-old man found frozen alive and the conflicts in an Arctic station between the young scientist (Tim Hutton) who wants to befriend him and the researchers who want to keep cutting him up to find out why he lived so long. The movie has been hailed in most quarters as a breathtaking technical achievement (with bravura grunting and bellowing by stage actor John Lone as the Iceman), weighed down by a dumb script, and it's doing only so-so at the box office. (His first American film, the prickly western, *Barbarosa*, had poor distribution and failed commercially.)

Several days before I spoke to him, Schepisi was married in Palm Beach, Florida, the home of his new wife's parents, and the "honeymoon" was interrupted by troops of reporters and photographers and by a thief who'd gotten into his suite at the Sherry-Netherland and made off with a string of his wife's pearls. He was also negotiating the financing and casting of *Plenty*, the film of David Hare's popular play set to star Meryl Streep. (Only a force like Streep could get *Plenty* off the ground; the project couldn't be financed with the original star, Kate Nelligan.)

Schepisi, forty-five, is a large, beefy man who exudes an ingratiating aura of masculine chumminess; in his faded jeans and red turtleneck, he looks out of place at the plush Sherry, yet seems delighted to be there—like a big, serene tomcat. Along with Australian colleagues Bruce Beresford, George Miller, and Peter Weir, Schepisi is working like mad to be accepted by Hollywood. But in the last several years, he has had a staggering number of projects cancelled or turned down. He's used to hustling his wares—it took him nine years of "working like a slave" making television commercials to finance his first feature, the quirky, sardonic *The Devil's Playground*. But in this country, he says, the problems run deeper than money.

"My own projects have been called 'soft,'" he explains. "Here they try to kick movies into acceptable packages. It's an interesting philosophy. But you can't make an *Entre Nous* here. I suppose *The Big Chill* in its own peculiar way is as nonnarrative as *Entre Nous*, but there's no comparison between them." I ask what it's like going from head honcho of his own production company to dealing with business executives who wear a lot of jewelry. "Yeah, well, there do seem to be a lot of corporate executives. I didn't find any of the entrepreneurial attitudes I expected to come across or any of the showmanship or guts. What I found were a lot of corporate executives who were not empowered to say yes. So their role in life is to come out winning if a film's bad or good, so somehow they can go, 'Yeah I told you so,' or else take the credit. Which is unfair to them, quite frankly." I ask if he enjoyed the Oscars. "God, didn't they all puff themselves up?" he says. "That's pretty amazing for a place that ignores the most talented people in the business."

Schepisi attributes his style to a few impressionistic documentaries he did in the '70s and to his experience in commercials. He never uses master shots—those single all-purpose takes that bind close-ups together—but tends to skip around a scene, photographing it from many different angles and assembling the pieces later (which makes a lot of studio people nervous). He and his steady cinematographer, Ian Baker, often simply discover things in the landscape and turn the camera on them, but the process, he explains, is calculated. "Through building detail, you can add other facets of a situation or a world to enrich the story. In *The Chant of Jimmie Blacksmith*, the use of animals and insects was to tell you that what looks to you like a barren landscape is full of life. Life that you can be supported by and life that may also be threatening to you. And the Aboriginals were shown completely in the landscape, in harmony. They were never above the horizon line. Whereas the whites were put above the horizon line. So visually I'm making statements that I then don't have to make in language in the film.

"In *Barbarosa*, there's a photographic style that absolutely everything is shot on very, very long lenses—it completely throws crews off, I wanna tell you. Because the landscape to me was the faces of those two guys. So a wide shot was done on a thousand millimeter lens, which means the camera was three miles away on a hill. But it pulled everything up and kind of put the landscape in and around the characters instead of pushing them out from it. In *Iceman*, there are three styles of photography that cumulatively create an ambience that I think will make a statement. The environment is shot awesome, majestic, powerful, simple. Something to be overwhelmed by both spiritually and, if you're not careful, physically. In the vivarium [an enormous, tank with rocks, trees, and animals, in which the Iceman is placed], it's very simple; it's allowed flow and play. In the scientific facility, the shots are full of cages, and it's to show how those people are trapped. They're shot through the equipment instead of the equipment being in their control. A little more deluged than they should be. And shooting through glass all the time so that you constantly have reflections over the people: anxieties, pressures, all the layers we impose on ourselves. How ridiculous in this beautiful simple place to have all this silly shit around."

I ask if Schepisi is a pantheist, and he replies that he doesn't think so but doesn't know what it means. I tell him it means God is in all the workings of the universe—nature and so on. "I certainly don't believe in God," he says. "I mean, if he exists he's a sick fella." Most of the interesting thinkers in Australia went to Catholic school, he points out, and none of them believe in God. Schepisi (who dropped out of the seminary at age sixteen—a decision chronicled in *The Devil's Playground*)—doesn't believe in the noble savage, either. "I believe in the directness of communication, and in the innocence and simplicity of living."

Life has been anything but simple and innocent in Tinsel Town. "I was gonna do a musical for David Merrick. I've written two comedies: one's a battle-of-the-sexes comedy, one's a family-relationships comedy. I've written a romantic film set in the late '30s, which is based on a novel. I wanted to do *Romantic Comedy*, actually, and I would have done it a lot better. But Bernard [Slade, the playwright] didn't think I was funny enough. The producer and the two stars wanted me to do it, but the studio didn't see any comedy in my work. Yet if you see *Devil's Playground*, fifty percent of the time you're laughing. People are always asking about my involvement with myth. But there are other pictures I expected to have slotted in that haven't come into being."

He describes with great relish the two musicals that never quite happened. For *Partners*, he created a series of lively production numbers—among them an "echo dance" on the marble steps of the Stock Exchange—but quit in disgust when the studio tried to halve his budget and cut the big dances. *Roadshow* would have featured Liza Minnelli and Tommy Tune, with music by Cy Coleman, but was shelved when producer David Merrick fell ill. "Musicals I love," he says, "because they're romance, they're fantasy, they're sheer joy. But also they allow you to show off some of the pyrotechnics that you have to subjugate in some other films." He'd even like to do an MTV video.

At one point, I accompany Schepisi to the offices of the BBC to meet with *Plenty* writer David Hare. Hare has a tape of a British television show featuring an actor who might be suited for the male lead in the film. The tall, mild playwright is nervous. A brilliant British comic has somehow taken it into his head that he's being considered for the lead and has left a buoyant message on Hare's London answering machine. Hare and Schepisi exchange helpless looks. "It's your problem," says the playwright. "You get out of it." Schepisi shrugs meekly and orders me not to mention the actor's name. They discuss finances, the appointment of designers, the stiff laws of the British film unions. The clip, meanwhile, is deadly, the actor as stiff and inexpressive as most aristocratic British protagonists; but the problem is principally the script and direction. "He has an interesting face," says Schepisi of the actor's hawkish mug. "You could do things with it." He decides to meet with the man in a couple of weeks. I ask, as we leave, whether he plans to make more movies in Australia. "Yeah, after *Plenty*, I'm set to," he says. "Unless something goes wrong with *Plenty*." I ask if he anticipates that. "Well, I've become so cynical."

Schepisi is predictably bitter about the failure of *Barbarosa*. "It was for Universal—not the regime that's there now. They wouldn't listen to the fact that *Barbarosa* was a special picture that needed exposure to critics in New York. They didn't believe that anyone in New York would like it, so we set about proving it to them. When we proved it to them, they ignored the information. Now that's when I got mad, because they were intractable. They said to me, 'No one will see this, this has Mexicans in it.' They said people hate Mexicans and don't wanna see them."

He's puzzled by the critical reception to the script of *Iceman*, though he concedes it has structural problems. "In the end, I wanted to make the statements through the photography. I wanted this to be the latest impression of the Neanderthal and to show some kind of ties between him and us—the spirituality, the beginning of human qualities, the directness of communication. It's a thought-provoker. Could the writing have been perhaps cleverer? I actually don't know. Maybe we distilled it too much—took out the more sophisticated arguments and left too simple ones. But I kind of like having a surface layer that's accessible on a relatively easy level for a lot of people and then put layers underneath it, or, as a French guy once said, let the other stuff bubble up through it. Have the other stuff there for people if they want to discover it. That's tricky. I think I'll be learning to do that properly for the rest of my life."

Man of Plenty

Brent Lewis / 1985

From *Films and Filming*, December 1985.

Despite being born in theater, *Plenty* seemed confined and shrunken there. To express its panoramic qualities properly it needed cinema.

Fortunately it's been shepherded from stage to screen by Fred Schepisi, a film-maker with affinity for the epic form. This Australian-born son of a greengrocer has an uncanny knack of deciphering that enduring English anachronism, the class society, and its manners and behavior are searchingly scrutinized in *Plenty*.

Burly, blond, with a down-to-earth manner and guarded cheerfulness, Schepisi relishes his work despite being an unremitting perfectionist. I'd watched him filming in the streets of Pimlico and the haughty elegance of the National Liberal Club (which also lent its splendors to *Ragtime*) and spoke to him at Twickenham Studios where he was bringing his conception to final clarity, piecing together thousands of feet of film. Through the juxtaposition of images and the alignment of the myriad of elements necessary to film, he's hoping to share his vision with the cinemagoer. That's not assured. Despite fine reviews, Schepisi's last two films—*Barbarosa* and *Iceman*—were seen by few. He's optimistic about *Plenty*, but admits that, despite a potent cast headed by Meryl Streep, it's not likely to appeal to those who want Spielbergian adventure in every film.

Thanks to two impressive films—*The Devil's Playground* and *The Chant of Jimmie Blacksmith*—Schepisi became one of the great hopes of the emerging Australian film industry of the late '70s. Naturally the Americans wanted him and won him over with offers too tantalizing to refuse. Since then, he's suffered the difficulties that plague too many working in an erratic industry. "I wanted to apply lessons from the last picture to the next, refining skills," he says, remembering thwarted hopes. "It didn't work out that way. I did a lot of scripts and was close to doing a lot of pictures that never happened. I learned a lot about the American film industry, but it was the sort of knowledge I could have done without. I learned how to make deals, but I wanted to make films. Films often seem to be the last thing a director ever makes there."

Now, with *Plenty* finished, he can assess that arid time without rancor. *Plenty* is his lifeline—a prestigious picture—the type Hollywood loves to be associated with. Its success while not guaranteed, will ensure that, for the first time in years, Schepisi's once more in charge of his career.

The project came about by chance after Schepisi had seen the play in New York and was convinced of its filmic qualities. He met its writer David Hare: "We hit it off. He liked my openness and decided I was right for the project." The only problem was to raise the $10 million necessary to make it. "People weren't convinced of its filmic qualities. I, however, saw it as a film with epic qualities. It really is a broad canvas of English society and attitudes."

Casual, amiable Schepisi comes from a background which, in its own way, is just as repressive as that explored in *Plenty*. Sent to a Marist Brothers' boarding school, he would explore the peculiar experience of his Catholic childhood in *The Devil's Playground*, his first feature, which he made ten years ago. "There's a real heart and passion there which override even the flawed craftsmanship that I've learned since. It was my apprenticeship to feature filmmaking."

It was not, however, Schepisi's initial contact with the world of film. For that we have to go back to 1963 when he, then twenty-three and an eight-year veteran in the advertising industry, became manager of the Melbourne section of Cinesound which made newsreels and commercials. Economically the Melbourne branch was a dodo, but Schepisi made it profitable within seven months of taking over. He bought the company in 1966, giving it a new title—The Film House—which he still owns with a partner. While the company continued producing newsreels he had little interest in them, preferring to shoot documentaries, one of which—*People Make Papers*—won an Australian Film Institute Award.

Through making documentaries and commercials, he was becoming a versatile filmmaker with a single-minded objective: "I wanted to make feature films, and, no matter how long it took, I never swayed from that." The fact that Australia had no feature film industry was something of an impediment, but the establishment of the Australian Film Development Corporation in 1970 presaged the return of indigenous filmmaking several years later.

Schepisi's first chance came with one episode in the four part feature, *Libido*, in 1972. Scripted by Thomas Keneally, a writer much admired by Schepisi, *The Priest* was shot by Ian Baker, Schepisi's close collaborator and cameraman ever since.

It took three more years for Schepisi to make *The Devil's Playground* and then only when he put up half of the film's A$304,000 budget. The film is obviously a report from experience, but was it also an exorcism? "As it turns out, no, although in a personal quandary ten years after those events, I arrived at the same point I was ten years before. I thought it was a great place to set a story, to take people into a world they've thought about yet never seen." Although he emerged from school an atheist, Schepisi doesn't regard *The Devil's Playground* as antireligious. He was more interested to explore the paradox of a society ruled by superstition and censorship "and how that created a surging passion for the things it tried to protect us against." So speaks the happy reprobate.

The Devil's Playground won the best film prize at the 1976 Australian Film Awards, which meant that the A$1.2 million to make *The Chant of Jimmie Blacksmith*, the most expensive Australian film up to then, was quickly raised. He still recalls with amused annoyance the criticisms for extravagance he received then. "I never understood what that charge was about. A film costs what it costs; no one was being indulgent. Everyone was down to a share, and I invested one fifth of the budget. One Australian journalist wrote that 'Fred Schepisi's *Chant of Jimmie Blacksmith* maimed the fledgling Australian industry.' That's gobbledygook! The twerp!"

In fact, Schepisi feels the real reason for the outrage was the film's depiction of the roots of Australian racism. "I think Australians didn't want to face up to the fact that Australian history is quite racist." Is the bigotry still there? "Oh yeah! Just ask an Aboriginal and you'll learn about indignities."

Despite their reputation, neither of Schepisi's Australian films made much money, which led me to ask whether he felt such uncommercialism was seen as a sign of his integrity. "That's really one compliment I could do without. You make the films you want to make, and you hope there is an audience for them, although a filmmaker's interests and those of the audience can be quite far apart. I suppose what satisfies me most about those two films is that an audience today can watch them and be absorbed."

His move to America was not out of any dissatisfaction with Australia. "I just had the strong belief that I could make films even better if I went out into the world. I'm not going to say I was enamoured of my time in LA. I couldn't see why I had to keep nine or ten projects going at once, but that's the way they do it." Schepisi drifted on through a miasma of unrealized projects with the awful thought that *The Chant of Jimmie Blacksmith* might well be his last, until he found an unlikely savior in Willie Nelson.

The country music star, who'd made an impressive debut in *Honeysuckle Rose*, happened to see *The Chant of Jimmie Blacksmith*. Admiring the stupendous use of landscape in that film, he was convinced Schepisi was the man to direct a western he dreamed of making called *Barbarosa*.

Eventually the film was made and received nice reviews, but suffered the bad promotion that's affected all of Schepisi's films. "I just wish they'd listen to me," he says plaintively. The idea of a mythical outlaw who lives beyond death is central to the theme of *Barbarosa*, as it is with a West so intersected with fable that history and legend merge. "The trick in *Barbarosa*," says Schepisi, "was to make you believe the myth despite what you see. I'm very proud of *Barbarosa*. A lot of people gave a great deal to it. It deserved to do better."

Which brings us to *Iceman*, whose virtues remain unknown to audiences in England, where it failed to get a release. Seen in widescreen, *Iceman* is a majestic revelation, justifying Schepisi's enthusiasm for "some of the most superb images seen on ice." Unfortunately it's also belabored with an inadequate script. That said, it's a far more distinctive and challenging film than most that make it on to the circuits. "I would never make formula, identikit films," Schepisi reflects, "You waste your life that way. To do a film I have to be captivated by some aspect of it, even if I can't properly articulate my fascination. I like things that become and seem other than what they first seem to be. I once saw a painting of a horse and a figure which seemed to merge. If I can achieve that in my films, then that's quite enough."

Man of Plenty

David Stratton / 1986

First published in *Cinema Papers*, March 1986. Reprinted by permission of the author.

Fred Schepisi has been away from Australia for six years. The last time I interviewed him was in mid-1979. Still depressed at the commercial failure of *The Chant of Jimmie Blacksmith* the previous year, he had signed with 20th Century Fox to direct, in America, his own original screenplay, *Bitter Sweet Love*.

Soon after our meeting, he sold his Melbourne house and left for Los Angeles with his family. I met up with him a few times during the intervening years. I had dinner at his home one evening, soon after *Bitter Sweet Love* (about a twice-married man having an affair with a young woman) had finally fallen through, mainly because of the alarming changes of direction at the top of the studio. We had dinner at a Beverly Hills restaurant soon after *Iceman* opened. And there'd been the odd meeting in between. But now, with his most successful film, *Plenty*, receiving good notices in Britain and the US and about to open in Australia, Schepisi was back at the Melbourne office of The Film House, working on a TV commercial for an insurance company.

He's made three features in those six years, and more than twice that many projects have fallen through for a variety of reasons. There was *Partners*, a tap-dancing movie for Lorimar, and *The Mandolin Man*, scripted by Herman Raucher (*Summer of '42*), to have been set in Sydney and to have starred Olivia Newton-John. There was *Double Standards*, also known as *The Other Man*, a screenplay by Judith Ross which, Schepisi says, "would have had an impact on this age like *The Moon Is Blue* had in the fifties." Even with three big names committed to the project (Gene Hackman, Roy Scheider, and Ann-Margret), the film, a sophisticated sex comedy, was rejected by the majors as "too old" and still didn't get off the ground when recast with William Hurt and Karen Allen. "I had them," Schepisi says, barely concealing his frustration, "but they still wouldn't make the bloody thing. I stood there with Freddie Fields, then head of MGM, underlining the funny bits in the script with a yellow pencil to show him it was a comedy! I'm serious! He couldn't see how funny it might have been."

There was also *Meet Me at the Melba*, an original screenplay by Schepisi set in Atlanta in the 1930s, about a repressed man and a free-spirited woman. "'Too soft,' said the people at Warners. I don't think they even read the bloody thing," says Schepisi. *Misconceptions* was another original screenplay, a comedy about journalists, a kind of modern Tracy-Hepburn subject. There was a comedy about Robin Hood, to be made for Mel Brooks's company. There was a subject about the media people who get politicians elected, which was to have starred Jacqueline Bisset and Roy Scheider, but this one was vetoed by Bisset (who had director approval and claimed there were no vibes between her and Schepisi).

The only one of these films that eventually did get made, but not by Schepisi, was *Raggedy Man*. Written by William D. Wittliff, this was a story set in 1940 about a young wife who leaves her husband when she sees him cheating on her with another woman and tries living alone in a small Texas town. Wittliff had seen *The Chant of Jimmie Blacksmith* and, soon after *Bitter Sweet Love* fell through, approached Schepisi to work with him on the project. Sally Field had been cast in the lead, but she had director approval, too, and it took an agonizingly long time for her to approve Schepisi. Eventually, she bowed out, and Sissy Spacek entered the picture, also with director approval. By this time, Schepisi had worked for months with Wittliff, reshaping the screenplay. In the end, however, the studio, Universal, bowed to Spacek's wishes: her husband, Jack Fisk, an art director with no previous directorial experience, took over the film. Schepisi's revisions were rejected.

Ironically, though, it was this major disappointment which eventually led to Schepisi's first American film, *Barbarosa* (1982), also scripted by Wittliff (who coproduced). This western saga, about the friendship of a Texas farmboy and a famous outlaw, had been offered to various studios, including Universal. It eventually ended up at ITC, Lew Grade's American production company, with distribution through Associated Film Distributors, a company set up to handle ITC and EMI releases in the US. The leads were already cast. "They interviewed me; I interviewed them," says Schepisi. He'd seen Gary Busey in *The Buddy Holly Story* (1978) and was very excited about him. "I'd heard he was difficult, but I didn't know he'd be quite as difficult as he turned out to be." But there was instant rapport with Willie Nelson.

Schepisi worked (uncredited) on the script and shot the film "with a great crew" on locations in Texas. That "great crew" included Australian Ian Baker, who'd shot both Schepisi's earlier features. Union problems were avoided because of the Texas location, and Schepisi was relieved to be working with his old friend and collaborator. Baker would later shoot both *Iceman* and *Plenty* and, says

Schepisi, is unequalled for balancing the quality of his work with the demands of the budget.

Sneak previews of *Barbarosa* revealed a few problems, exacerbated by the fact that the distributor, AFD ("Another Friggin' Disaster," says Schepisi) was collapsing at the time. Eventually, distribution of the film passed to Universal (where it had already been rejected at script stage), and, despite positive reviews, it was virtually dumped. One of the elements in the film that Schepisi looks back on with most pride was his own casting of veteran actor Gilbert Roland as Don Braulio. "He was fantastic: seventy-two years old and a consummate professional."

Despite the commercial failure of *Barbarosa*, Schepisi was offered other scripts. "In Hollywood, if you make an interesting film, whether it works or not, they appreciate what you've done. If you set out to make a commercial film and it fails, then they jump all over you." One of the scripts was *Iceman*, written by Chip Proser and John Drimmer, and picked up by producer-director Norman Jewison, a Canadian with many commercial successes behind him, from *In the Heat of the Night* (1967) to *Fiddler on the Roof* (1971).

The intriguing story deals with the discovery of a prehistoric man frozen in the Arctic ice, then thawed out into the twentieth century, and one of Schepisi's first problems was to discover what kind of film Jewison (who'd originally planned to direct it himself) wanted to produce. Overall, there was agreement between the two men, though they did clash over the final cut. Chief problem, though, was to cast an actor for the central role. A French-Tunisian boxer was considered, then a karate champ, then a French-Canadian from way up north in the Arctic. Finally, Schepisi settled on John Lone, whose training and experience had been remarkably varied (the Peking opera, method acting in New York). He was too slight for the part, but, after special training, he added weight and muscle, and his extraordinary grace and agility made him a memorable figure.

Critics were generally kind to *Iceman* (though some compared it unfavorably to Ken Russell's *Altered States*), but its release, in mid-1984 through Universal, was not very successful, and it has, so far, not played in Britain. Almost immediately, however, Schepisi was offered the opportunity to direct his next film, an adaptation of the very successful David Hare play, *Plenty*. The circumstances are unusually interesting. Hare himself had directed the original London and Broadway productions, which starred Kate Nelligan, and was actively preparing to direct his own first feature, *Wetherby*. But neither he nor his producer, Edward R. Pressman, wanted a British director to make the film. "They wanted someone not restricted by the very inhibitions the story was examining," says Schepisi. The first idea was to have an American, then Hare suggested an Australian ("'They're sort of like Americans'"), and several were considered. A screening for Hare of *The Devil's Playground* led to a meeting, and Schepisi, who had seen the Broadway production of the play and much admired it, got the job. The final choice, he says, was between him and George Roy Hill.

Kate Nelligan was seriously considered for the leading role of Susan Traherne, through whose eyes we see a Britain declining from the end of World War II to beyond the Suez Crisis. The trouble, says Schepisi, was the budget: Hare and Pressman wanted to open out the play, to give it greater scope and scale. "There was great scale which was only hinted at on stage, but it pervades the atmosphere. What is being said is greatly affected by where it's being said. The 'where' is sometimes a comment, sometimes a counterpoint, but always an essential character in its own right. If we did it with Kate, we'd have been limited to a $6 to 7 million budget, if the budget could have been raised. Even with Meryl Streep, it was still terribly difficult to get the money. Also, Kate's particular approach to the character could have been tempered and changed, but Meryl brings different qualities to the part. She's clearly the premier actress of her generation on film, while Kate is becoming the premier actress of her generation on stage."

As usual, Schepisi collaborated (without credit) on Hare's screenplay. "I shocked David by insisting he put more and more dialogue back into the film. He kept saying, 'Are you mad? Every director in the world wants to take the dialogue out!' But I said, 'Believe me, it'll work this way because, short of rewriting it totally to express it all visually, we should concentrate on the language.' It's a beautiful language piece. But it doesn't seem talky if you give it the kind of scale we did."

Nor was he worried, finally, at the casting of an American actress in such a very English role. It certainly helped that Streep had earlier been accepted in an English role in *The French Lieutenant's Woman*. During the scripting, Tracey Ullman's role of Alice was enlarged ("she was smaller and spottier in the play"), as was that of the husband, played by Charles Dance.

Ullman is known in America as a pop star, in Britain as a regular on TV variety shows; Sting, who plays Mick, is also still better known as a singer than an actor. Put them together with the eight-one-year-old John Gielgud, and you have some interesting interactions. "Gielgud was quite extraordinary," says Schepisi. "He gets angry with himself when he gets tired and can't remember lines, but he didn't hold us up."

Schepisi was amused when one US critic wrote that, although the film was "exactly the same as the play" and "nothing major had been changed," yet "somehow it all seems new." In fact, about a third of the material in the film *is* new, and the play has also been restructured. "The whole play was out of chronology," says Schepisi. "It was a set of ideas in random time placements, so you accepted the time-jumps backwards and forwards. In the film, we always went forward, though sometimes with long time-jumps, until the very end, when we go back to near the beginning again."

The fact that Hare had completed shooting *Wetherby* before *Plenty* started "gave him a better understanding of what I needed," says Schepisi. "It made him much more helpful as a writer. He never interfered with the direction; we had an extraordinary collaboration—very happy indeed. We had excellent communication, and we talked out our differences. Sometimes he changed my ideas; sometimes I changed his."

Schepisi has always been a bit cynical about critics, and *Plenty* hasn't changed that. Molly Haskell, in her review, listed all the things she liked about the film, and then said the only thing she really disliked was the blunt, overly physical direction. "But almost everything she listed as liking came about because of my input," says Schepisi. He's also amused when a reviewer, like Pam Cook in the *Monthly Film Bulletin*, reviews the film without even mentioning the director. "It's a compliment in a way."

And next? He plans to film a "wonderful" Steve Tesich script for Fox about rich but emotionally underprivileged kids in Boston and would also like to make another film in Australia. He might produce in Australia too, but his plans aren't fully formed as yet.

His six years away have certainly changed his life. He has a new, American wife, and a young family. He has survived and even prospered in a very tough world. He's as cynical as ever, but maybe a shade less naive. I wrote once that his films were about people trapped in a situation from which it's hard to escape. That was true of his Australian films and turns out to have been true of his three American films too: Barbarosa, trapped in a pointless family feud; the Iceman, trapped in a strange and hostile world; Susan Traherne, trapped in a stifling postwar Britain that offers little of the "plenty" she craves. But one feels that Fred Schepisi himself has broken free of his traps and seems to be looking to the future with cheerful confidence.

Dialogue on Film: Fred Schepisi

American Film / 1987

AFI's Harold Lloyd Master Seminar with Fred Schepisi ©1987, used courtesy of the American Film Institute. First published in *American Film*, July/August 1987. Reprinted by permission of the American Film Institute.

When *The Chant of Jimmie Blacksmith* was released in the United States in 1980, the name of Fred Schepisi joined those of Peter Weir and Bruce Beresford as leaders of the "Australian New Wave." Schepisi's wrenching film—it depicts in graphic detail a series of killings carried out by an Aborigine pushed over the edge by racial pressures—had been a critical success in Australia but did not fare too well at the box office there. It did, however, bring Schepisi to the United States to make his next film, *Barbarosa*. American audiences were also introduced to his first feature, *The Devil's Playground* (1976). Schepisi, who entered a Roman Catholic boarding school at the age of eight and went on to a seminary, admits that *Playground*—the story of a teenager's troubled time in a Catholic seminary—has autobiographical overtones.

Born in 1939 in Melbourne, Schepisi entered a career in advertising after dropping out of school at age fifteen. With the arrival of television, he moved into the media side of the business and soon formed his own production company. The Film House, the studio he purchased at age twenty-five, was a major source of inspiration for the new generation of Australian filmmakers. Schepisi, working on commercials and documentaries, established the reputation for innovative and experimental camera techniques that he incorporated into his later work in features.

His films made in the United States—*Barbarosa* (1982), *Iceman* (1984), and *Plenty* (1985)—all concentrate on main characters with a degree of isolation from the rest of the world: *Barbarosa* focuses on two characters trying to maintain the mythical freedom of the Old West; *Iceman* has a prehistoric man revived after more than forty thousand years frozen in the Arctic ice; Meryl Streep's character in *Plenty* sees her vision and ideals clash with and lose to the passage of time.

But with his latest release, *Roxanne*—a modern version of *Cyrano de Bergerac*—it looks as though Schepisi may have taken a more light-hearted approach to the outsider. Here, in contrast to the original, the main character ends up alive—*and gets the girl*. Now bicontinental in life and work, Schepisi may be succeeding in his own advice to filmmakers: "Get out there. Walk the tightrope. Experiment. Have fun."

American Film: You've made some films in the United States. Has that been easier than in Australia?
Fred Schepisi: Up until the late '60s, it was almost impossible to get an Australian film into an Australian cinema—mostly because the cinemas were owned by the Americans and the English! It's different now. I'd say it's much easier than being an independent or starting filmmaker in the United States.

It's easier to get a chance here if you come with a reputation, as I did.

AF: So how did you get *The Devil's Playground*, your first feature film, made in Australia?
FS: It took five years. I got half the money from the government and the other half of the money was mine and my friends'. When I finished the film, I immediately had to go back to making commercials—which was the worst thing I ever did in my life—just to get the money to keep paying for the film. And then nobody wanted to distribute it. Nobody believed in it at all. So I had to distribute it myself. Fortunately, it turned out to be a success. Everybody thinks it was a bigger success than it actually was, which is OK with me because that helped me finance the next picture quicker.

AF: It still took a few years to make *Jimmie Blacksmith*, didn't it?
FS: It wasn't that bad because I'd already been working on it while I was trying to get *Devil's Playground* going, and once that was commercially successful, I got the money for *Jimmie Blacksmith* very quickly.

AF: One of the elements in both *Jimmie Blacksmith* and your next picture in the United States, *Barbarosa*, is the land and man's feeling for it. How did you plan to make that apparent visually in each film?
FS: There were entirely different requirements for each film. The idea in *Jimmie Blacksmith* was that the Aboriginals are part of the land, and they see things in it that we just do not perceive at all. That was the reason that we had a lot of close-ups of animal and plant life that were a real sustenance to them in what seemed to us to be a barren landscape.

It is quite different in *Barbarosa*. There the barren landscape is the underbelly of the myth. There is another landscape also—the two people's faces. So what I tried to do was make that the important thing and get in on their faces all the time, and then every so often position them in their harsh environment.

AF: And the setting for *Plenty*?
FS: I was particularly interested in getting an institutional feeling throughout the film. So we used a lot of corridors and very enclosed spaces and alleyways and things like that to constantly crush in on the images. It was a little perverse in a way because I used anamorphic lenses. But it needed scope so you could see what was crushing in.

The production design was almost another character in that *where* something was being said was as important as *what* was being said. We also wanted to quickly establish the period: Instead of just doing random background action, there are a whole series of themes, such as the way people used bikes and prams, for instance. During and at the end of the war, they were used for carting personal belongings, sometimes coal supplies, all of those kind of things; and then in the background, you see them develop with the increasing affluence.

AF: Did you see *Plenty* on stage?
FS: Yes. I liked it and I was disturbed by it. I also thought it had some faults. It's an intelligent work on the writer's part, and the hardest thing was to do justice to that fantastic writing. So it took a while before I was convinced I could pull it off.

AF: Did you rewrite the original much?
FS: When I get involved with a writer like David Hare, my role is to interpret and make the best film that can be made of the work. I'm not there to change his work into mine. It becomes a collaborative effort. I hope to bring out all of the original richness and at the same time make it stand on its own as a film. Obviously, you've got to find your own point of view in it and express that. But it is still the writer's work. Because there's quite a jump from the stage play to the film, structurally, you have a lot to do. In rehearsals, with the actors and actresses, we really plumb the play, looking for things we might have lost.

AF: Can you talk about the casting?
FS: Joe Papp was one of the producers of the play, and he made what I thought was a pretty good statement: "There are good actors, and there's good casting." We needed to get an unexpected mix that would be attractive to a wide spectrum of people, so the draw wasn't just the subject alone. Also, I wanted people who had already achieved a certain amount of notoriety so that they wouldn't be fazed acting opposite Meryl Streep. We weren't just casting well-known faces; we were casting special actors. It's a good clue when casting to find out if you are all on the same wavelength. Because if you're not, forget it. It's just a pain in the neck.

I like to talk to actors well in advance of the shooting; we have individual discussions and then group discussions about their characters' places in the film, the needs of the other characters, the aims, style, and techniques of the film, before they get too set with their own biographies or visions.

Then, as the various other elements get involved, like costume design, I think you should still be there with them. Because everything the actors touch or put on or do is going to become part of their character, and you should be there to make sure it doesn't head off in directions that will cause you problems later. I like to rehearse things just up to the point where you suddenly discover the emotion in it. You get a little feeling at the back of the neck and you think, "Oh, it's there." And then you leave it alone.

AF: What about working with your cinematographers?

FS: All my pictures have been shot by Ian Baker, one of the best cameramen in the world. We communicate incredibly well. Because we've been exploring many times before, we can start a higher base level each time.

On nearly everything we've done, we set up a philosophy for the shooting. For instance, on *Iceman* it was: How do we film within the research establishment? It's very claustrophobic, very rat-mazed, the people are always seen through equipment of some kind. They're overwhelmed by their own technology; they're never seen out in the clear. It's about the complexity of modern society and how we layer stuff on to ourselves and cause our own anxieties.

In *Plenty* there's a repetition of images so that you're constantly introducing new places in exactly the same way. The idea is that, particularly for somebody who's been through a heightened experience, things keep repeating themselves. It's sort of like a déjà vu that throws them back to the glorious time they can't ever get over. Do you know what I'm saying?

I also think that sound is fifty percent of a picture, so, on *Plenty*, the same kind of things are happening in sound. We exaggerate the parachutes at the beginning of the picture and then constantly use that sound—the flapping of tablecloths and things—to suddenly pull you back to that first occasion. It's more subconscious than conscious.

I think of music in the same way—I've always worked with the same composer, Bruce Smeaton. I don't like it to signpost. I don't like it to overstate what you're doing. Mostly, I like it to add another layer. I think, if I'm correct, in *The Devil's Playground* there's actually only twelve minutes of music, but it feels like there's a lot more.

Now, in *Barbarosa* there is a lot of music. We used it entirely differently there because we found that people didn't quite know how to take the picture. We'd do something funny, they would laugh, and as soon as they were laughing, we'd stab them. They got a little uncertain, a little thrown off, and didn't know when it was okay to let loose. So we had to use music in a few cases to give them the clue that this bit was okay to laugh at.

AF: Your newest picture is *Roxanne*. It would seem to be a big change for you in that it's a comedy, a Steve Martin comedy. There is a lot of humor, certainly, in your other films, but is there a difference between directing comedy and directing humor?
FS: Yes. There sure is. I've been trying to do a comedy for a long time. Nobody would let me do it: "This guy's not funny. No way." And I keep saying that, well, you know, there's a lot of comedy in *The Devil's Playground*. There are certain comedy moments in *Plenty*, although it's of quite a different kind. And there's a lot in *Barbarosa*.

I got a chance—thanks to the efforts of one of my agents, who convinced Dan Melnick, one of the producers, that I'm really a funny guy. I met with him and was rather frank about the particular script we were talking about and comedy in general, and it seemed to coincide with his ideas. Then I met with Steve Martin, and we got on like a house on fire. So I got the chance to do *Roxanne*. It's a contemporary comedy loosely based on *Cyrano de Bergerac*. And it's fantastic.

The most incredible part about comedy is sitting in a theater with an audience that likes it. Of course, if they don't like it, I'm sure it would be horrible, but sitting in a theater and hearing people start laughing and laughing right at the beginning of your film—you suddenly realize: This is great! I really like this because it's instant gratification. With drama, you sit there and all you hear is silence and shuffling, seat kicking, or people running out, as they did in *Jimmie Blacksmith*, depending on which murder was onscreen.

AF: Can you talk a little more about your relationship with Steve Martin? Are there any pitfalls in working with an actor who is also a writer?
FS: There could be. I'm sure there could be. But Steve Martin is terrific. And you'll see a quite different Steve Martin in this picture, quite different, with a real acting range that will surprise you. He's very professional; he works incredibly hard and is constantly attacking the script. He's constantly searching to improve. And even when you're there on the day and you've got everything set, he's still searching, improvising.

There's a wonderful thing that happens with Steve—the camera turns and an extra button seems to be pushed somewhere and other stuff comes out. And you'd better be ready. It's a fantastic way of working because then you get involved and bounce suggestions off one another. You can see it also with Melnick, who has worked with a lot of comedies—particularly in the early days in television. There's a real thing in comedy of being collaborative. Steve liked to work with us there, so he could start writing and then try out ideas and get suggestions from us and turn it all back into his own script again.

AF: Is he serious or funny when he's writing?
FS: He's quite serious. But if he comes across a good joke, he laughs a lot.

AF: Was he the only one attached to the project when you were brought in? Were you involved in casting Daryl Hannah?
FS: Yes.

AF: Shelley Duvall?
FS: Yes.

AF: How did you tear Shelley away from her television commitments?
FS: Steve kind of convinced her that she should be in it. I think she wanted to work with me as well a little bit. It took a lot because she's really busy. But we said, "Oh, it won't take long. It'll just be a few days." We lied.

AF: So with all the work on the script, how long was it in the end?
FS: I remember us being up to twenty-one drafts. I think we may have been up to twenty-seven when we started shooting, and we wrote all the way through. Now, many of those drafts were just a few pages changed here or there. We did a lot of changing during rehearsals as well. You're still doing it in editing. Because no matter how much you know and no matter how much you plan it, when you get it all together, it has a different and sometimes unexpected impact, which means you have to keep searching. You should never settle for what you think is just "good." You should drive the editors and writers and everybody nuts until it's great. And if you don't go for great, you won't even end up with good. You've got to go beyond your wildest dreams because just the exigencies of filmmaking are going to smash you into ordinary.

The Making of *Evil Angels*: Director Fred Schepisi Talks about Private Moments, Public Realities and Dingoes

Philippa Hawker / 1988

Published in *Cinema Papers*, November 1988. Reprinted by permission of the author.

Fred Schepisi emphasizes that *Evil Angels* is not a "movie." He does a lot with those two syllables: he frames the word in contemptuous inverted commas, then expels it from his mouth with disdain. Despite the film's budget and its scale and its subject matter and its cast, all of which guaranteed it headlines, speculation, gossip, and media attention on an unprecedented scale, one of the things he was aiming for, he says, was the feel of a home movie. And there are no inverted commas around that last word.

He wants it to seem like a home movie, he says, "not in the sense of cheap or corny or amateur-looking, but for people to have the feeling that 'this is actually happening.' I wanted it to be something you experienced. I wanted the feeling that you were involved in the event."

Evil Angels takes its name and its origins from John Bryson's book, which established, with an air of passionate detachment and a fund of exhaustive detail, a convincing case for a miscarriage of justice in the (now quashed) conviction of Lindy Chamberlain for the murder of her baby, Azaria. Bryson showed how the presentation of evidence in court, the interpretation of those proceedings in the media, and an extraordinary surge of collective national superstition and rumor led to a widespread perception of her guilt.

Putting all that on the screen was going to be a different story. Shuttling between Australia and the United States, Schepisi had a passing acquaintance with the case. "But I was astounded by the passion and vehemence with which people held their opinions. Even very intelligent people would have a rational argument, examine the facts, and, despite everything, would end up saying, 'She did it.'"

Schepisi was approached; he read the book and spoke to producer Verity Lambert several times about directing it but always said no. "I thought it might be impossible to do the subject justice in a film," he says. "I might in the end be as guilty as the media have to be, in their brevity, of the very things I would be examining. I thought that to do the subject justice it would probably need six hours of television.

"I also thought, it's one thing to discuss a subject like this; it's another thing to present it as a film. What new light am I going to shed on this situation? Trial by media, trial by gossip, miscarriage of justice, we've seen and read many stories like that—does the world really want another one? How could I do it differently? Not just for the sake of it, but why would you want to go and see it?

"Verity said, 'Oh, you just don't know how to do it. That's the problem: you haven't found a way.' And that was true," Schepisi says with a smile.

"Bryson's book shows you how a lot of things were colored by the media. But it doesn't tell you, and it doesn't purport to tell you, anything about the Chamberlains. As it was expressed to me by my composer, Bruce Smeaton, there's a black hole in this book. That is in no way to denigrate it, but I believed that the Chamberlains had to be in the film.

"The film is the book *and* the private lives of the Chamberlains, so it becomes a film of personal drama. You get involved in their story, in what it must have been like for them; it's saying, 'This could be you.' Here are two people who were, if you like, somehow caught on a railway track, and a train bore down on them. When the smoke and the dust cleared and the noise died down, you realized that the train had fallen apart, but the people were still standing. That's how I saw the story."

With that in mind, and with Meryl Streep interested, Schepisi took another look at the project and, he says, found another way of doing it. "What it is, basically, is the public perception and the private reality. The whole film is about that, and the whole structure is about that. You get deeply involved with their private lives and deeply involved with what is happening in the public arena at the same time and with what the public perception is."

The only way to examine the private lives of the Chamberlains was to go directly to them. "[Screenwriter] Robert Caswell spent a lot of time researching and a lot of time with them personally. Subsequently I met them, Meryl met them and Sam [Neill] met them and we talked, having done a lot of study and research. We asked questions, and then we asked tougher questions. Then I wrote something for myself, a kind of psychological profile, which they read, although they weren't meant to. It was only a guide for me, a way of sorting something out, but I think it helped them to tell us more."

What they were looking for from the Chamberlains was an account of "those things in private moments that are always surprising, sometimes in their ordinariness, but which always have that little twist . . . We didn't badger them, and we didn't spend too much time with them because we had to keep doing it on the basis of the facts."

This does not mean the *Dragnet* simplicity of a single authorized version. "Their facts, the media's facts, the police facts—we've tried to present it all and let it speak for itself." The approach is exemplified, he says, by the handling of a speech Michael Chamberlain made on the night Azaria disappeared. "It was a difficult speech, it was religious, and some people found it very cold. Michael had one version of it, Lindy another, the people who were there had another still. Sam and I were trying to sort this out, and he came on and did something I thought was too emotional. Then I realized that every perspective was correct, once you combined them. If someone had lost their baby, and you didn't realize he was a minister of religion and a grief counselor accustomed to urging people to pray, his speech might seem to you to be an odd one. It was an important thing to establish: that reality was a combination of many points of view. We had to be very careful not to go for a specific point of view; this film is *not* Lindy's point of view."

Similarly, facts can be set in a new context. Lindy Chamberlain's inquest wear, a different outfit every day, sent many media commentators into a kind of "Fashion on the Field" frenzy. It was taken as an indication of her self-centeredness and callousness. "All those dresses were borrowed. Use the public perception, use the private reality—that's what it's all about.

"We did a lot of additional research, going through the transcripts, et cetera. We had a team of researchers, and Robert Caswell, who wrote the first draft, spent a lot of time with many different people. I spent time with Barker [the prosecution lawyer] and Kirkham and Phillips [the defense lawyers], so, between all of us, we managed to talk to a lot of people and get their side of the story."

Inevitably, re-creating events for the film led them all to reassess things they had taken for granted or not thought to question in accounts of what happened on the night of Azaria's disappearance. Shooting scenes with a dingo, for example, training it with a doll, Schepisi describes how it would "stand there with its neck held up, doing everything it was not supposed to do, carrying what we thought was 10.2 pounds, but which was actually 10.2 kilograms . . . And during the scene where Meryl's rushing in and out of the tent, tearing the place apart, and the camera's rushing in and out, and it's complete pandemonium, the young actor who was playing Reagan [the Chamberlain's four-year-old son] fell asleep for about three-quarters of an hour. Just as Reagan was supposed to have. It was one of those things that sounded unlikely, but it happened."

For those who see the film, the greatest revelation will be the strength of the Chamberlains' faith, Schepisi believes. "That was the unshakeable thing, their Seventh-Day Adventism, the thing they were most criticized for, and it will be the thing that will be most reconsidered," he says. He was concerned, he adds, to find the best way to portray their religious conviction. "If we did it wrongly, it could turn people's stomachs; it could come out cutesie-pie and Disney.

"But people will be astounded by Sam Neill, playing someone who tried to be strong and had a lot of faith and had great emotional difficulty handling the situation—it's a completely different role for him. And Meryl has truly caught what made people react in the way they did to Lindy, yet she shows you what a bad judgment that was and manages to make you understand the real person."

Schepisi says, more than once, that the film is telling people, "it could happen to you." Of the Chamberlains, he says that there were things that people "would consider off-center, like their religion—a respectable, ordinary, decent, middle-class religion, in fact.

"But nobody ever reacts to tragic circumstances and public pressure in the way they would like to think that they would. We judge people on a thirty-second telecast, when they're nervous or being deluged with questions, or what we're looking at is being manipulated or taken out of context. Yet we come to firm conclusions. "That sort of thing is so easy to do. The Americans were doing a trailer, and they were using something in a dramatic way. I said, 'I'm sorry. I'm just not going to let you do that. You cannot take that out of context because that is one of the things we are criticizing—the use of dramatic license to pump up a story. That's where the problem started.'"

At the same time, Schepisi says, lengthy explication didn't work. "If people explained things to one another or questioned things, you'd put that in. But what I found was that the more we tried to put those kinds of things in, the more we rejected them. It looked like we were making excuses. "You're rooted in reality: every time you try to take flight, your feet are stuck in the mud. You can't take license because you're dealing with people's lives. It can be difficult to make that live as a film."

The other difficulties included the need to rebuild everything, as the camping areas and motels near Ayers Rock have disappeared, and the courtrooms were in use. Much of the night shooting took place in a huge shed. Schepisi is full of praise for production designers George Liddle and Wendy Dixon and director of photography Ian Baker for the look of the film, moving between studio and arduous Northern Territory locations, where shooting took place in dust storms and 42 degree heat.

Northern Territory reaction to the filmmaking was, Schepisi says, "wonderfully ambivalent." "There was a resentment and suspicion about the subject matter," he says, "but, on the other hand, it was a 'movie'—Meryl Streep was in it. You could see people in this terrible quandary. In the end, people were very cooperative, but we felt the most aggravation in Alice Springs."

At this stage, *Evil Angels* is two hours long. "We arrived at what we thought was it, and then, with previews in America and other reactions, we realized that it would only delight some people. We wanted it to reach more than that. It forced us to relook at it, to free ourselves from the quantity of facts. I want people to get sucked into a story and then get carried away. That's all I want people to do. I want them to get involved and go on that journey. . . . Our best achievement is that it is deceptively simple, and I'm fighting to keep it like that all the way."

The Man Meryl Streep Trusts

Rennie Ellis / 1989

First published in *The Bulletin* (Australia), October 24, 1989. Reprinted by permission of the author's estate. © Rennie Ellis Photographic Archive.

With the personal approval of Soviet leader Mikhail Gorbachev, film director Fred Schepisi has just begun shooting, in the Soviet Union, a Tom Stoppard script of John le Carré's new spy thriller, *The Russia House*. Schepisi, his crew, which includes Australian cinematographer Ian Baker, and stars Sean Connery and Michelle Pfeiffer will spend many weeks on location in the Soviet Union before moving on to Portugal and London.

Schepisi and his New York agent, Sam Cohn, had been working on the film concept with Stoppard and le Carré well before the book was published this June, when it immediately jumped into best seller lists around the world.

Now almost fifty, Schepisi is a director who, with Peter Weir and Bruce Beresford in particular, continues to keep alive the notion of Australia as a source of good and popular filmmakers.

Rennie Ellis: What attracted you to the book as material for a film?
Fred Schepisi: My agent! (much laughter) John le Carré used the spy thriller as a way of exploring himself and, in a very cryptic way, of examining the Russian glasnost experiment. It is much more than just another spy story.

RE: How hard is it to translate the novel into a film?
FS: Very. Le Carré doesn't believe that he's yet had a great film made from any of his books, although he liked the television series made from *Tinker, Tailor, Soldier, Spy*. His works are very subtle, quite wordy, and there's lot of layers, all of which would seem to indicate that they are much better suited to the longer format of a television series than to the normally concentrated dramatics of cinema. So it's quite a challenge to try to extract the essence of the book and present it in a very exciting way without losing the complexity and the subtlety.

RE: What did you learn in your visits to Russia prior to moving the crew in and starting shooting?
FS: I realized that I would have to treat it as if we were filming in the center of Australia. It's necessary to take everything with us in terms of people and equipment. Our own trucks, our own catering, food, our own toilet paper . . . It would be chaos if we didn't. The problem is that the Russians work in a very different way and at a totally different pace from what we are used to.

For instance, their pay isn't all in terms of a direct cash salary, and their attitude is completely different from ours. We will be imposing a system on them, both economically and in shooting demands, that isn't really fair on them. They tend to do things by the book, and the system isn't very flexible.

They work a very short day in comparison to the number of hours of shooting we'd be aiming at. There is a great shortage of vehicles and petrol; in fact, there is a great shortage of food.

RE: It seems you're doing it the hard way. Why not shoot in Finland and pretend it's Russia like others have?
FS: What attracted me about the book was that it took a real good look at the people of Russia under glasnost. It was a rare opportunity to look at this country, which is going through a very significant upheaval. A country everyone is fascinated with and really knows very little about. It would be foolish to do it anywhere else. I want Russian people and Russian situations, and, besides, it's just not possible to re-create places like Leningrad.

RE: What's your strongest, most lasting impression of the country and what you encountered there?
FS: It's a very chaotic, disorganized place that is undergoing massive change that people are really having difficulty in coming to grips with. On the one hand, they seem to be enjoying it; on the other, they're very, very unsettled by it at a rather bad economic time, which makes it quite difficult for them.

The Russians passionately love their country, and they have a very wonderful way of looking at life. I found them a very warm, friendly, giving people. It was quite amazing. And they like a drink.

RE: How do you personally judge the success of a film you direct? How much does it relate to box office takings and how much to critical acclaim?
FS: Box office is in the lap of the gods. It is subject to too many whims to really indicate a film's success. The right release, distribution pattern, and advertising support can be critical. But you don't make them not to be seen, so box office is important. Critical success is nice, but it's not the be-all and end-all. Sometimes

things are very controversial. Fortunately, I generally do well critically. But how can you be excited by that when you don't necessarily like a lot of the critics?

The real success of it is whether you achieved what you set out to achieve. I believe if you get to seventy-five to eighty percent of your hopes, then you've done a wonderful job. Halfway through doing a film, you've already learned so much that you want to be on to the next film because you can't apply it to the one you're doing, or you'd mess up its style or internal logic.

RE: Does critical success or box office success determine the sorts of opportunities that open up to you as a director? Things like good scripts, big stars, and investment capital?

FS: Because I seem to have always made what in Hollywood terms are called "interesting" films, that is, not necessarily in the mainstream, I'm judged accordingly. If I set out to make a very commercial film and it failed at the box office, then I would definitely be making backward steps. When *Roxanne* came out and was a very big financial success, especially when it opened, it was amazing. You'd think you'd done something extraordinary. Suddenly you get all these incredible phone calls about the film's success, not about its quality. And people would say to me, "Why aren't you excited and enthusiastic?" And my answer was, "Well, it's the same film whether it made money or didn't take money."

As a matter of interest, to release anything in the US now it takes a minimum of $6 million and generally between $8 and $11 million, sometimes more, because of this nationwide mass release system they tend to use, which frankly I find questionable.

RE: Was *Evil Angels* a box office success in Australia and the US?
FS: A success in Australia. A break-even in America. In terms of release pattern and Academy Award timing and things like that, I think we got jockeyed because we were a pick-up picture rather than one done by Warners from the beginning. It had a small controlled release without a good follow-up.

RE: *Evil Angels* was nominated for four Golden Globes: Best Picture, Director, Actress, and Screenplay . . .
FS: . . . and it should have been Best Actor too! But we made a clean sweep. We got nothing. When I went in to the awards night, the head of the Golden Globes gave me a wink-wink, nudge-nudge and said it was great I was there and that she'd see me backstage later. To me this seemed like a pretty fair indication we were going to do well. And then we didn't get anything, and I thought, "Well, what was all that about?" The Meryl thing was even more bizarre. There were five actresses nominated in her category, and they had a three-way tie. I loved Meryl's comment:

"Thank God it wasn't a four-way tie." She was nominated for the Oscar and missed out on that too, but she won the New York Film Critics' award and the People's Choice and a couple of other things for that role.

RE: You've directed her in two films, *Plenty* and *Evil Angels*. She says you were very tough, and that was one of the reasons she liked working with you. What did she mean by tough?
FS: (Laughter) I like working hard and long hours. I work 'em pretty hard. Meryl and I have quite a relationship, a real collaboration, which isn't just to do with the acting or the part. It's to do with the whole film. We help one another a lot. I offer her a good eye and good ear, someone she can absolutely trust and someone who won't wilt under pressure by allowing a less than top performance to go through.

RE: She also said she could never see herself becoming a director because it was too demanding and it took over your life.
FS: I'm told that tests have shown that the two highest stress-producing occupations in the world are those of a fighter pilot and a film director. I'm sure it's true. You're out there with enormous responsibility. You're a bit like a general with an army. You're in control of a whole team who get their momentum and energy from you as the director. And there's an enormous money responsibility in that every decision you make can be terribly expensive. Then there's the absolute flip side where you're meant to be the sensitive artist who is balancing out a lot of emotional needs and trying to create a good story on film that will be very involving for an audience.

RE: What are your strengths as a director?
FS: In the long run it's fitness. The sheer determination and energy and ability to outlast everybody and see the job through. That's the ultimate thing because if you can't do that then you can't do the things you're supposed to be there for. Which you're good at, such as holding the vision and being sensitive.

RE: They say in Hollywood that the deal, rather than the film, is the art form and that agents rather than studios are the new powerbrokers.
FS: Very much so. The more powerful and the better of them are really acting like the old-time producers. They're putting the whole act together—writer, producer, director, stars.

RE: All the negotiating and the wheeling and dealing you have to go through to get a project locked in must be exhausting and often frustrating, especially when, as a director, I imagine, you would much rather use your energy and creative juice actually directing?

FS: That's right, but there are realities out there. You're asking someone to spend the volumes of money it takes to fund a film. For instance, the le Carré picture may cost over $20 million, so they've got to have people they believe are saleable commodities. As a director you'd better get involved in it so that you can turn what seems to be a logistical and statistical thing into a creative thing. You get involved to make sure you get the writer who is going to write the film you want. Or, if it's an actor, you don't just accept the name and make the part fit that. You try to find from the names available the best person for the part. Or you might try to convince people that, if the actor you want for the part is not a name actor, you use two or three name actors in the other parts.

RE: It seems any director working in Hollywood needs several projects in the pipeline at any one time: there's no guarantee any one of them will actually come to fruition.

FS: One of the things you have to face is that star availability and commodity thing, and it's not just in Hollywood. You have to juggle so many things. At the moment, among other things, I'm developing a Neil Simon project. Now here's something I like, but I feel it needs some work in a couple of areas. Here's something Robin Williams, as the potential star, likes and feels the same about. I would like to see Kevin Kline play his brother in the picture. A Robin Williams/Kevin Kline film would be just fantastic. So now the work's being done by Neil, who agrees with us. So let's say everyone likes it and wants to do it. So when are we all available to get together and do it? How many projects are they committed to? We might have to wait a year and a half, and in a year and a half who knows who wants to do what. So you need to be working on several projects at a time, or you could find yourself out on a limb.

RE: How much power does a big star have within a production? I've seen examples where the star has been able to wield a very big stick.

FS: Sometimes they come with the power because they actually carry the title of producer. But if they're the hook, the commodity that's being sold, then the people selling them are not very keen to upset them. They know they have the power at a certain point because the picture may have been sold on the basis of them being in it. The power increases when you're three weeks into the picture and you've spent an enormous amount of money. You can afford to lose the star at that point, and there are stars whose power games will increase from then on because they know they've got you. The producers will get rid of the director before the star because they are not going to spend $3 million reshooting.

You learn to keep away from certain actors, but you'll always have certain things with anybody who is a big star because they're going to want to be good and they get nervous about whether they're delivering what their promise is, what has made them a star. They want to preserve that, and you can't blame them. They probably get in the hands of some rather stupid people at times.

RE: We are hearing about how much stars get paid. How much does a director with a good reputation get paid for a film?
FS: Oh we're very poorly paid. Most good directors get a percentage, but you know . . . there's a percentage of net, percentage of adjusted gross, percentage of adjusted gross after break-even. And what it all means is that you never see anything. You know, there are some great stories . . . I think Sigourney Weaver was on quite a high percentage of net on *Ghostbusters*, which took about $500 million around the world, and they're still not in profit. You work it out. There are plenty of stories like that. The trick is to get as much up front as you can. And what you get depends on your standing. Some guys progress very well. Then they make a couple of bombs, and they go backwards in a big hurry.

You can do well out of it. It's really quite bizarre. The guy who did *Ghostbusters* was then paid $3 million to direct that turkey, *Legal Eagles*, that had Robert Redford, Darryl Hannah, and Debra Winger in it. Terrible. You think, goodness gracious me, what was he paid for because he certainly didn't direct as I understand the term. So it's commodity stuff. You've got to have produced a blockbuster to get anything like those kinds of terms because then they think you have the magic, that you can catch lightning in a bottle. So they'll pay you for it. If you're not making major commercial successes, then you're not making that kind of dough.

RE: What sort of money do writers get?
FS: Writers tend to not be as well paid as directors. The top twenty can probably get about $1 million a film. And that would be pushing.

RE: In Australia, now that the 10BA tax incentive scheme* is all but finished, is our filmmaking going to be able to attract enough local venture capital to fuel the industry?
FS: No. At Entertainment Media in Melbourne, where I'm involved with Robert Le Tet and Peter Beilby, we have a number of projects under way, and we're out looking for money. The people who would have invested under 10BA are now all gone into forestation, or whatever is the latest tax incentive scheme. They've been

---

* Introduced in Australia in 1981, the 10BA tax incentive scheme was designed to encourage film investment by allowing a 150 percent tax concession on their investment. [ed.]

spoiled in the past. Now you ask them to invest in a film, and they say, "We're used to getting this kind of deduction; what do we get now?" No, it's not easy to raise money in Australia. In fact it's almost impossible because even the entrepreneurs or angels that you found before have gone. Some of them are disenchanted. The 10BA did us a lot of harm, yet I'm rather sad it still doesn't exist in a modified form that is more reward-oriented. A tax incentive scheme that benefits investors in films that get released and actually make some money or have a chance of making money ought to be looked at.

RE: Filmmaking is a high-risk business. What percentage of films actually return profits to their investors?
FS: Yes, very high risk. We had a better success rate here for a while for getting money back on films than anywhere in the world. Maybe four in ten would get their money back and make a modest profit. A couple more will go close, and the rest are disasters.

RE: Do you get nervous before you embark on a new shoot? Do you ever think, "Am I up to it? Can I pull it off?"
FS: You're always champing at the bit. It's the waiting around. Once you're into it, there's too much going on to feel nervous. If you ever sat down and thought logically about most films, you wouldn't do them. You'd just know they're impossible and not even try.

Fred Schepisi

Peter Malone / 1998

Published in *Myth and Meaning: Australian Film Directors in Their Own Words* by Peter Malone, Currency, Australia, 2001. Excerpted by permission of the author.

Peter Malone: Before films, advertising?
Fred Schepisi: Yes, I started in advertising, and, in those days, there were a lot of writers at the advertising agency where I worked. It was quite a little hotbed, actually. Geoff Underhill, who used to write plays and worked for *In Melbourne Tonight* was there, along with Phillip Adams and Geoff Taylor. It was a little haven for people who wanted to be writers, playwrights, or whatever and couldn't make a living out of it in Australia in those days.

PM: How did *Libido* and your contribution to it, *The Priest*, come about?
FS: Well, I got into the business because I wanted to make films. I thought, that's easy, you just go into business and you make films. But it wasn't like it is nowadays; you didn't get paid upfront or anything like that. You had to outlay everything.

I wrote *The Devil's Playground* over five years before I did it. I was meeting a lot of actors, doing a lot of commercials and a lot of documentaries. So I joined the Producers and Directors Guild to try to meet people working in theater and television, to see other disciplines, as it were, because I wanted to go along and watch them direct plays and see what they did in that side of television.

Everyone in that group was not in there to be part of a guild; they were in there just to meet one another and help one another. So we started to devise projects. One year, we ran a scriptwriting competition. That's how I came across Thomas Keneally's script for *The Priest*, which tapped into the crises in the Catholic Church at the time. In a sense, it was prophetic of what has happened in the last twenty-five years to do with the priesthood, faith, and celibacy. It's always the writer that makes the material, and that came deeply from Tom's experiences, although it wasn't autobiographical. His wife was a nun, and Tom went right through almost to the end of the seminary course. So I do think the script came from deeply personal observations, and they happened to dovetail with my experiences and the questions that one comes up with.

A lot of people at the time reacted to Arthur Dignam's desperate portrayal by identifying that with Keneally but failed to remember that he wrote Robyn Nevin's lines as the nun as well, that he actually was presenting both sides of this relationship. The background was very real, afternoon tea with the nuns, the kind of conversation about the bishop and whether he would approve . . . it was so authentically Catholic that it revealed something of the church life of the past.

I think we both had a fair bit of knowledge in that area. Some of that is cinematic too, just the way you present that stuff, the veneer of politeness. It was good. If anything in that film, I got a little too gimmicky visually at one point, sort of whirling the camera around. I wouldn't do that now. Even though that might be what was going on in the character's head, I don't think I needed to reinforce it quite so much. I would do a variation on it. The energy was already there. We did that damned thing in six days.

PM: With *The Priest* and *The Devil's Playground*, you actually enabled Australian filmmakers and television-makers to explore church issues that otherwise they might not have. The TV series, *Brides of Christ* (1991), might not have happened had there not been *The Devil's Playground*.
FS: Right. I met Ron Blair who wrote the play, *The Christian Brothers* [in 1975]. He said he heard I was doing *Devil's Playground*, so he wrote like hell to get his play finished. I think it's rather significant, by the way—I don't think this is true now, but it was true then—that many of the people doing things, writing books, plays, getting into film, were ex-Catholics or traumatized Catholics. It was all strictly railing against that Irish Catholic severity and obsessiveness that I think most of us saw was counterproductive to what religion really should be doing. And I don't think it's any accident.

As my old colleague Phillip Adams and various people have written, not a lot of great cinema or anything, was coming out of Australia. It was a fairly complacent society, and there was not a lot to rail against, other than, say, mental torpidity or spiritual barrenness. Great work, unfortunately, seems to come out of oppression or deprivation. So I think at that time that area, oddly enough, was religion.

PM: Were there any cinema precedents for *The Devil's Playground*, or was it just so much part of your life?
FS: No, it was part of my life. I don't have cinema precedents; I just don't. I'm not stupid enough to believe that I haven't absorbed them, but I don't follow one style of filmmaker. The material dictates its needs. The thing I would say about *The Devil's Playground* is that I watered it down because, in fact, it took me five

years to get the money together. Over half the money was mine, and I had to put in that much money again to get it released. I had to hire the cinemas myself. Nobody liked the film until I got it out there, which I find rather remarkable. But, in remembering that I wrote it five years before, I knew if I went as far as I should go, everyone would go, "Oh, come on, that's not on, that's not possible." Nobody would believe it. So I deliberately pulled back in all sorts of things.

PM: Did you draw back in the presentation of the Brothers, the range of characters?
FS: In a way, they're all real men and combinations of two or three. What I did was this: every one of those Brothers represents the possibility of what he might become, depending on which side of his personality gets most influenced. Whether his sexuality gets so repressed that he goes down the Francine road or whether he's able to overcome that and be more joyful like, say, Brother Arnold [Jonathan Hardy], who's quite content in the spiritual life, or whether he's the middle guy who's more realistic, split the difference. But they're based on real people.

You can come across a great teacher here or there. I certainly did. There were a couple, in fact, and one very much in particular, Brother Osmond, who was very, very inspiring in every way, teaching music and Latin and geography and English. He made them great subjects for everybody. That can help. There really were some good people around, some very good people around, good Brothers too, and they were there with the sick buggers. The rest of it was just like misguided religious zeal.

PM: Now over forty years later and with the uncovering of repression as well as the exposure of abuse, we probably should look at it again in that light. However, even in ordinary Catholic schools, students were far more prudish in the early '50s, much less explicit in language than the characters in the film. Was the film a '70s perspective dramatizing of the '50s?
FS: No, I held back; believe me. I went to one of the Brothers at Assumption College, and I said, "You know, I have to tell you about all this bizarre behavior because I know you'd understand." He was pretty shocked, and quite a number of people got called out, sent away. I had decided to leave at that point. Pretty soon afterwards, the juniorate was closed down, and the students were put into an ordinary college. I don't think they really did know the extent of what was going on. I was doing it from a real belief that it doesn't need to be this weird. It was something like the Middle Ages. You know how the success rate of the juniorate turned out? At one point, only fifty percent of them kept going.

PM: In the late '70s, *The Chant of Jimmie Blacksmith* sparked reflections in Australia on Aboriginal issues. However, Ken Hall was quoted as saying that Australians won't look at films about Aborigines.

FS: He's right. I understand with *Dead Heart* (1996) that there was the same reaction. They won't. They won't because, you see, most Australians are nowhere near Aborigines, nowhere near in contact with them. It's not an issue in their daily life. They can have theories about them, but they don't have to test those theories. In certain areas of Western Australia, there's a lot more Aborigines in country areas. But in most of the cities you're not in contact with Aborigines at all, and the film bites you right where you think you're safe.

I remember a psychiatrist friend of mine with liberal attitudes and a seemingly intellectual character went to the premiere. When I got home, I found swear words across my front door, and it turned out to be the psychiatrist. I said, "Why did you do that?" He said, "Because you made me realize I was racist."

I think that's what *Jimmie Blacksmith* does for a lot of people; it makes them feel about themselves in a way they don't expect. It's a very violent film—on purpose. It was meant to be antiviolence, but all those things bring home a reality.

PM: In terms of church and religion, the film opens with Methodism, with Reverend Neville and his wife, and Jimmie eating with them. Then he goes to the initiation, another world. This gives you a hook on to the Australian audience with their churchgoing, confronting them with those issues. And, at the end, Mr. Neville visits Jimmie in prison and finds his religious world-view inadequate.

FS: Yes. Well, it's the cause of what happens, isn't it? I mean Christianity might not be the cause, but the churches' belief that their version of events is right and that they're going to go and save the heathen and take them out of that world is. Then, of course, the Aborigines are spiritually and culturally displaced. The world that they were being pulled into, at least at that time, and it's probably still fairly true now, does not accept them. They're not part of that world, and the world they've been pulled from rejects them. At the same time, the person is also internally conflicted, disliked by both societies. So that's the central conflict of the whole thing, those two issues.

There were a few priests who used to visit me because they had worked in Aboriginal missions. They were put in awful situations. They were out there seeing the Aborigine living in the life that is so particular to them, but trying to take them out of this world into another world, and then asking, "Why are we really doing this?" And then only being able to do this with the boys because they found girls unsettling. The priests were a bit sexually interested in a way they didn't expect to be, so they had to keep the girls away from them. They didn't deal with them, or treated them badly, emotionally badly.

One of the things I always thought was strange was that there was a lot of pressure on the missionary role of a person in religious life. It was always held up as one of the great things, you know, to go off to Africa or to New Guinea, somewhere like that, when right around the corner was a problem larger and more important than travelling to distant places. I was always unsettled by that lack of attention to the needs of the neighborhood, if you like.

One particular priest was spectacular about it. He would set up coffee shops and all kinds of things for people to come in and talk. His branch of the church hated it and stopped funding him. But I thought the number of people's lives that this guy touched effectively was fantastic because he was really working within his own community to help cure and solve problems. But they used to keep pulling him out of there and sending him off.

This is still the problem now for the churches, whether there is any need for the clergy to go to foreign countries as missionaries rather than collaborating with local churches to build them up with the people. This is far more realistic than the old-time missionary effort. It's a different world and so it should be a different church. We've been imposing our belief system on them or making them replace their system.

PM: Many Australians found *Evil Angels* very embarrassing. It challenged the way that a lot of people had reacted during the '80s to Lindy Chamberlain, especially. That whole question of rumor, all those scenes of tennis parties and dinner gossip, the cousin who knew this, the acquaintance who said that. You also challenged the role of the media . . .

FS: The really interesting thing about that film was the night when I'd just finished it and I showed it to Michael and Lindy Chamberlain. They were absolutely floored. They were in tears for ages afterwards because they had no idea of the scale of the thing, of what was against them. They had no idea. Just by proclaiming their innocence and insisting on proving it, they realized how much they inadvertently contributed to their own difficulty as well. It was something they put behind them very quickly, but they were devastated. I think nobody understood.

The difficulty of making a film like that is that there are no villains. It was the accumulation of so many things that just went to work against a person, at least five or six major things that contributed to the misunderstanding of those people. And, conventionally, in a film you wouldn't do that; you would reduce it. You would reduce the characters; you would reduce the dramatic through-line, et cetera. So, to me, the pleasure and the difficulty in doing that film was not falling into that trap. It's something that, quite honestly, I don't think you could do in Hollywood. I know because I tried to do it. I know you can't. I just fell on that sword again in withdrawing from *The Shipping News*. People think there's only one way of doing things.

Everything about that film was presented so that it was just the facts: not colored. We didn't emotionally color the music or any other aspect. We presented the facts, and the facts spoke for themselves. And when you're dealing with something, particularly since it was an ongoing case at the time, you can't take artistic flight. It's very difficult because you keep tripping over the truth.

What we did find, the thing that did take flight, is best illustrated by one incident. There was always a lot of talk about how strange Michael Chamberlain was, standing there delivering this message to the crowd that he was praying for them. It was religious, but it was kind of quasi-religious, very strange, God's will and all that stuff. Sam Neill and I were struggling with it. He could have just stood there and delivered his speech the way a preacher would, and it would have worked. But you're always looking for that deeper thing that gives it another edge, even if it's just to you.

The reports from that night were completely different. There were really three clear impressions given by his speech. And Sam found the way of delivering it which we were hunting for. He would say, "Let me try this or try that," and I would say, "We'll try this or try that." But, all of a sudden, he just hit a tone, a stance, a strangeness, and the hair went up the back of my neck and we knew. You could suddenly see: if you find the right way of being that person, you can then understand how many misconceptions could come out of it. So, in other words, you could always find the truth of the character.

And that became our guide. Every actor in the film was told, "We don't want you to present the pathologist as a bad person; we don't want you to present the prosecuting attorney as a bad person. We don't want that; that's wrong." We got them to go and talk to and spend time with those people, find out their point of view, find out why they were like that, take up their zeal, their enthusiasm, their belief and sell it. Say, "This is what I was like; this is what I actually believe; this is who I am." Far more interesting. And then let the truth lie where it lies.

Yet the staggering thing is that after seeing the film, people came up and said, "So what's the real story?" It used to make me so mad that I wanted to hit them. Now I just say, "Go away."

Seeing *Evil Angels* was the first time that some people understood something of the inner personality of Lindy Chamberlain. It was a strength of Meryl Streep's performance. Australians were all caught up in the exotic aspects of the case. Would it have made such an impact if the Chamberlains were not Adventist, if it had not taken place with dingoes at Uluru? That's why it stayed in the Australian psyche.

There's such a misapprehension about Seventh-Day Adventists and their cultish behavior and rituals. We think they're cultish. People think they're like Jehovah's Witnesses or Scientologists. They get all that off-to-the-side religion misunderstanding. And how are Seventh-Day Adventists different? Well, their main difference is that Saturday is the holy day, not Sunday. Is that worth fighting about? Because when it's Saturday here, it's Sunday over there, or vice versa. So, number one is that it's a basically decent religion.

PM: The opening scene with the trucker commenting on and swearing about the Adventists is an immediate challenge.

FS: My editor wanted me to take that scene out. The editor and the producer both tried to make me take that scene out again and again and again, and I said, "When you interrupt the film, it's always going to jar, because you're setting up a different grammar and it's always going to jar. I don't care. I'm going to jar you. I'm going to really jar you, and then everything after that will be easy." I think it's all right. It does confront you.

But the thing I hope comes out of it is that Lindy Chamberlain's faith is very real. She still truly believes that God will help her. Michael went around doing death counseling, but his belief was more a hope than a belief. So, even though he went around doing the right thing, he wasn't as convinced or as deeply convinced as she was that it was alright. He was very easily shaken.

Fred Schepisi: "Pushing the Boundaries"

Scott Murray / 1990

First published in *Cinema Papers,* August 1990. Reprinted by permission of the author.

In the 1970s, Fred Schepisi made two of Australia's finest films, *The Devil's Playground* and *The Chant of Jimmie Blacksmith*. Then, to the surprise and disappointment of many, he moved to the US, where after a period of aborted projects, he made the critically-acclaimed western, *Barbarosa*.

Today, Schepisi is one of an elite group of "A" directors. The commercial success of his 1987 American film, *Roxanne*, has given him the freedom to make films of his eclectic choosing. These include *Evil Angels* and the soon-to-be-released *The Russia House*, adapted by Tom Stoppard from the John le Carré novel.

Schepisi's work varies from astringent social criticism to refreshingly warm comedy, from a keen understanding of genre to a delight in the nuances of English mannerist drama. As such, his films are less easy to critically pigeonhole than those of most Australian directors. Each Schepisi film is an entity unto itself, with the director seeking and adopting a style peculiar to the material.

Scott Murray: How do you look back today on your first filmmaking experiences?
Fred Schepisi: They are good films, obviously. I wrote the first as an original and adapted the other, so I was right inside both of them. That was a good way to start working.

Financially, there was not a lot of room. *The Devil's Playground* cost $300,000, and we shot it in six-and-a-half weeks, paying everyone. *The Chant of Jimmie Blacksmith* cost $1.2 million, the most expensive Australian film at the time. That took fourteen weeks to shoot as it involved a lot of travelling—10,000 kilometres, if I recall.

I remember people angrily raving on about the indecency of spending $1.2 million on an Australian film. It was as if we were throwing money away in the Hollywood manner. That was absolute nonsense: in fact, we had to keep cutting corners all the way through the production. It kind of made me laugh . . . bitterly.

Still, *Jimmie Blacksmith* was a great learning experience, and, while we thought we knew a lot of things, we hadn't really appreciated the scale of what we were attempting. We knew a lot of technique from the commercials and documentaries we'd been doing, but applying it in emotional terms to the drama content of the picture is what you have to learn.

One thing that still wrankles me about those early days was the problems I had with some of the crew on *The Devil's Playground*. It was all to do with an attitude common at that time. A lot of them had started in the business at The Film House and then gone on to Crawford's and the other television production houses. They saw everything in an "eight minutes a day" mode: assistant directors would insist on setting up the shots and so on. They were "industry people," as opposed to people concerned with the art and craft of filmmaking. They thought they'd had a lot of experience but really hadn't. They made us feel unprofessional and quite shabby.

In fact, it was the support of my cinematographer, Ian Baker, that helped get me through it. He told me, "Don't let them upset you. They don't know what they're talking about. But, as they go through this experience, they will learn. Just care about the work and go on the way you're going because you do know what you're doing." Considering they also were getting up Ian's nose, I thought that was pretty good.

I guess the lesson that came out of that was not to listen to those kinds of criticisms. You should concentrate on what you are doing and organize all of the mechanics, like the scheduling, to give yourself the best chance of achieving things creatively.

All in all, doing *The Devil's Playground* was an incredibly rewarding experience. We had the advantage of all living on the location [Werribee Park]. And, because we had no dough, all the interstate cast used to live at our house on weekends. Rhonda [Schepisi], who did all the scheduling with me and the casting and had helped get the thing rolling, was also the second assistant director. But, of course, she was then my wife and, when everyone used to come back, she would cook meals. It wasn't exactly her day off! I think our tempers were a little frayed. (Laughs)

But because all the crew and cast stayed on location, we were like a big family. We'd all have dinner together, and I could do a lot of my directing at night, when people were relaxed. They would ask me questions that didn't seem to be about what they had to do tomorrow, and I could reply in a more acceptable framework. I think that really helped us to establish the camaraderie that you can see in the film.

I remember we got that location after having toured all of New South Wales and Victoria. Rhonda and [art director] Trevor Ling actually talked me into that place. I thought it was too big for the film I had in mind, but they kept saying to me, "You must make it smaller. Just imagine half the room is missing, and you will work more comfortably." It took them a while to sell me the concept! (Laughs) But they did, and I am really glad.

Then I went to the Victorian government—this was before Film Victoria had started—and saw one of the ministers. He rose to the bait, thought the film was a fantastic idea, and allowed us to use Werribee Park for $3,000, which he then invested in the film. As this happened only a week before we had to start shooting, I left that place walking three feet off the ground . . . and in tears.

There are two final things I'd like to say about working in Australia. On *Jimmie Blacksmith*, all the problems we'd found on *Devil's Playground* had been sorted out and things were far more professional. But it was a far, far bigger film than anyone had any idea of, particularly me. [Associate producer] Roy Stevens was really something in the way he helped me through that.

It was on *Jimmie Blacksmith* that I first came across the burgeoning unionism in the Australian film industry. I couldn't always afford to deal with it and had to keep coming up with deals. It didn't affect the film, but I let it bother me personally.

I was also angry at the rumors that were spread about the film. Everybody seemed to want it to fail. That is a disturbing trait in the Australian character: preferring people to fail rather than succeed. The only reason I mention this is because the otherwise good experience was tinged a little with bitterness.

When I came back ten years later to do *Evil Angels*, I thought I knew the industry and people in it. But I realized very quickly that, in those years, everything had changed radically and that I should treat coming back the same as if I were going to Canada or England or France. I had to select a crew here the same way I would in any of those places. There is a system for doing that, and I used it here.

To my surprise, I ended up with many of the people I had worked with on *Jimmie Blacksmith*. I got great pleasure out of that because I found that there was a genuine desire to achieve good work, a real adaptability. That was very thrilling for me. The *Evil Angels* crew was better than any crew I have ever worked with. I did not expect that, at all. In ten-hour days, we did exactly the same number of slates as we'd done in twelve-hour days on *Roxanne*. And we worked pretty swiftly on *Roxanne*.

Barbarosa

SM: After having made two of the finest Australian films of the 1970s, you moved overseas. Why the change?

FS: Both those films cost me a lot of money. About $300,000 of *The Chant of Jimmie Blacksmith* was Film House money, and half the budget on *The Devil's Playground* came from me. We also distributed that film ourselves, which cost as much money again. That is a lot of dough, and I had to work two shifts of commercials just to keep the money coming in, just to keep Film House on its feet. I found that a very difficult process and I wanted to make sure I didn't get lost making films again.

So, the first reason for going overseas was to get properly paid. The second was that I wanted to test myself in the international marketplace, to challenge what I had learned. I also had this funny idea that if I managed to do a couple of successful films in America and could build up a marketable name, that would make it easier for me to market any films I made back here. It was a real learning process.

On *Barbarosa*, I had a maniac of an actor named Gary Busey. He is a great actor but an absolute nightmare to deal with. The art form in that picture was getting Gary out of his motor home and on to location so that he could act.

I also had four producers! One was this guy who had been the head of Marble Arch, which was ITC in America, and had then been bumped sideways. As well, there was Willie Nelson, Gary Busey, and Bill Wittliff. What this really meant was that I ended up doing the work. Certainly, when there was any trouble I did the work. How I knew there was trouble was when I saw my producers driving away from the set, heading for Los Angeles on urgent business. (Laughs)

Ian [Baker] was just fantastic. We changed the way we worked three times within the first two weeks just to cope with the scheduling problems, Gary Busey, Willie Nelson's availability—all that sort of stuff.

The biggest shock for anybody going to America is the size of everything and the adjustment that takes. For example, an enormous amount of time is demanded of you by the actors, who resent your even looking through the camera. We also found ourselves with this huge circus of cars and machinery and drivers. We soon worked out that there is no way you can get this huge circus moving swiftly. So we set up these little runner units, and, while all the big stuff was back at base, we sent out the small units. That way we managed to get back to working the way we wanted. You can't defeat the machinery, but you must not let it defeat you.

SM: Where was *Barbarosa* shot? The locations are most striking.
FS: I had Preston Ames, a great, old-time production designer, come in at one stage. He told me to go to Big Ben National Park, but the producer said, "Over my dead body. It's too remote." Then I got Leon Ericksen in, who had done *McCabe and Mrs Miller* (1971). Leon is very eccentric and unusual, and I had a job convincing the producer he was the right person. Leon and I then went down to Big Ben National Park and Del Rio and found what we wanted. It was completely wilderness, but, because it was a tourist spot, there were tarred roads all through it. You could drive your trucks right to where you wanted, step off the road, and shoot. All the other locations that the producer had wanted, which were really ugly, you

felt you'd seen a hundred times before. They were also hard to get to, whereas this was so accessible.

The other great thing was you could do wide shots at both ends of the day because of the way that the mountains were formed. As you moved in to do closer work, there was always a direction you could point where you would get great light and good texture on the backgrounds. These are things American producers don't understand. Whereas we love to talk about light, over there there's absolutely no point talking to anybody about it. They don't understand light: they just want you to "shoot the story." (Laughs)

Anyway, to convince the producer of the sensibleness of this location, we all jumped in a jet and flew down. When we landed, he got out and he fell to his knees. I thought, "Oh, great, he loves it!" Then I heard, "How can you do this to me?" (Laughs)

But we did end up shooting there, in a very remote town with no television. I have to tell you, the impact of having no television on a group of people raised on twenty-six channels is really something to see. They are not like Australian crews who will make their own fun at night. These Americans had to make quite some adjustments. It was fun.

SM: In many ways, doing a Western as your first American film was a risky undertaking. Westerns haven't done well at the box office in years, and there is the difficulty of bringing freshness to a genre that many feel is played out.

FS: I agree. But the reason they chose me, which always makes me laugh, is that they thought *Jimmie Blacksmith* was a great Western. In fact, they even teach that in some of their film schools! A child of some of my friends was going to film school there, and her major thesis was on *Jimmie Blacksmith*. It was her teacher's specialty. So she asked me whether she could talk to me about it. I said, "Sure," and she brought over all her questions. I think I made her fail because I said, "Well, that's not right, and this is absolute rubbish." It was all to do with Westerns—very silly stuff.

Anyway, that is why I was chosen. In general, Americans want your originality, but not for original films. They want it applied to their kind of films.

SM: Many have commented on how badly *Barbarosa* was handled on its US release.

FS: The company I was making it for went broke, and Universal took over the distribution, along with a number of other films. One was *The Legend of the Lone Ranger* (1981), which they thought was going to be sensational. But any fool looking at it could have told them, "This is a total disaster." And it was.

By the time Universal got around to releasing *Barbarosa*, they weren't interested. In fact, Bob Raimey, who is now with New World, said to me, "This picture isn't going to work, and we're not going to spend any money on it." His reasons were that it had Willie Nelson, who had just failed in *Honeysuckle Rose* (1980), that it was a western, and that it had Mexicans in it. Great, huh?

I said, "Look. Westerns aren't working, so you have to treat it as an ordinary movie. You should release it in New York and try to build up a reputation over a two-month period. Let people discover it as a film, then release it everywhere else. What you're planning to do will cost $1.5 million, and the film will just disappear. Instead, why don't you spend $200,000 and find out if you can make it cross over?" But he said. "No, you won't get the New York critics." So I countered, "If I get the New York critics, will you reconsider?" Bob said he might and might not. "Furthermore," he added, "if you don't get the New York critics, I won't release the film at all."

Finally, I convinced them to have a screening in New York, meaning Manhattan. So where did they screen it? In Yonkers. The film then broke in the projector and all sorts of other things went wrong. But I did get the critics and great quotes from Pauline Kael and David Denby. I even had one critic who hated it go back and see it again; I managed to convince him he liked it. Despite this, Bob Raimey still ignored me and released it the same way they had released *Honeysuckle Rose*. Work that one out.

So, in answer to your question, not only was it dumb to make a Western, it was also dumb to make it with those people. But I like the film; I like it a lot.

Iceman

SM: After *Barbarosa*, which gained you a considerable critical reputation, you went off to do a film that struck many people as an odd choice.

FS: After *Barbarosa*, I was supposed to do *Partners*, a tap-dancing musical we were going to shoot in Chicago. But there was a change of management at Lorimar, where I was doing it. Half-way through shooting *Barbarosa*, they rang me up and said, "We want to make this film for $8 million, instead of $15 million." "How do you think you are going to do that?" I asked. "Oh," they said, "we want to fly down to talk to you about it." I told them I couldn't do that in the middle of production. So they said, "Well, we want to do without this number and that number," and so on. I replied, "That's good, you can do without the director as well. I'll see you later." (Laughs) And they took everything that was of value out of the film.

I then tried to get up a number of other projects. One was set in Taiwan and written by James Goldman. I felt it was as good as *The Manchurian Candidate* (1962), but we couldn't get it made. Another great project was *The Consultant*, about a guy who manipulates political images for the media. It had Roy Scheider, and Jacqueline Bisset as a documentary reporter who gets mixed up in some killings. Just as all systems were go, we found out they weren't. As it turned out, Jackie Bisset and I didn't get on too well, anyway.

While I was in the middle of all this disappointment and nonsense, my editor from *Barbarosa* [Don Zimmerman] called me and said he was working with [producer] Norman Jewison on a project called *Iceman*. He shot the script over to me. I read it and then went and begged Norman Jewison to let me do it. I didn't think it was the best script in the world and I had to do a lot of research work on it, but it is a very authentic film. It is literally on the "what if" basis, and if you take just one leap of faith it all works. *Iceman* isn't the world's most intellectual picture, but it has real heart about what it's examining.

SM: The film has the feeling of being made by people who applied more care and intelligence than the script deserved.

FS: That is probably right. I think the original writer, John Drimmer, had some good ideas, but he wasn't capable of carrying them through. Then Universal hired a guy who had written a great script for something or other, but he was neither very intelligent nor hardworking. So we were always behind the eight ball.

Norman Jewison, whom I like, also insisted during the audience-testing period that certain things be removed. I think those cuts took away a bit of the edge and some of the explanation. I wouldn't allow that to happen again, but I had no choice at the time.

I am not having a shot at Norman. He did what he felt was right, and I think he was in one respect: some of the scenes were a bit boring. But sometimes you have to have those boring bits because they are the rock on which everything else is built. You often find this in a good play. During the first act, you often wonder, "What the hell am I sitting here for?" But it all pays off at the end.

The problem with *Iceman* was that it was always perceived as el cheapo science fiction by the public, who stayed away in droves. We should have been wiser to that possibility, but we weren't. Still, it has had an extraordinary life on video. I get checks from video—how's that for a real surprise? And if I am getting checks from video, somebody got rich.

Plenty

SM: Your next film, *Plenty*, is a leap forward in assurance and control.

FS: I love *Plenty*. I felt I was able to apply all the things I had learned beforehand on my other films. Where things are said becomes as important as what is being said. The locations are a genuine character in the film.

SM: *Plenty* was London based. Was it English or American financed?

FS: The financing was very complicated. That's [producer] Ed Pressman's doing!

We ended up being financed by RKO, which had just been rekindled in America, and then opened up in London as well. So it was American money but an all-English production. Unfortunately, the revitalization only lasted a couple of years.

Both Sam Cohn, my agent, and Steven Tesich, a very good screenwriter in New York, had talked me into doing *Plenty*. I had enjoyed the play but had a couple of problems with some of it. I agreed to meet with David Hare, the writer, at the Sherry Netherland in New York.

The first step was to decide if we should cast Meryl Streep or Kate Nelligan, who had done the play on Broadway. Personally, I wanted Meryl, for the reasons of getting more inroads into the character. She was also important in terms of getting the amount of money I believed was necessary to do the film. Kate had the reputation on stage at that time, but Meryl had it on film.

Ed Pressman then started running around trying to get the money. As soon as I smelled he had some of it, he found me on a plane to England. I had him about $400,000 in the hole before he had a chance to blink. He had to make it work! (Laughs)

SM: How was it working with David Hare? He has a reputation for being very precious about his screenplays and not allowing a word or an emphasis to be changed.
FS: Such stories would have come from the film he did in Vietnam [*Saigon: Year of the Cat*, 1983] and from people like Frederick Forrest, who wanted to ad lib his dialogue. You don't ad lib a playwright's dialogue! Of course, David wanted his words said in a certain way, as does any great writer. There are rhythms and motors and emotional undercurrents in those words.

David and I actually spent a lot of time transforming *Plenty* from a stage play to a film. There were eight or ten drafts done on that screenplay. I would savage David; he would savage me; then he would go away and make it his own again. I would then savage him again, and he would show me what I'd not seen. I'd suggest another way of doing it, and we would work something out. Then he'd go away and make it his own again. It was a real process.

I believe we succeeded in fixing some of the flaws of the play. In fact, David and I laughed a lot when one critic said, "It's just like the stage play. They haven't changed anything at all." The critic thought that was a slight, but we felt that was a fantastic compliment because more than a third of the script is new material.

Even though the script differed significantly from the original play, I always felt I was interpreting David Hare's work. It is great work, and I wasn't about to go off and make some other film. In fact, during the filming, if there were moments we felt were still not working, we kept talking about them while I shot other stuff. That way we could hopefully fix things before it came time to shoot. And by David's having that involvement in the process, the film stayed in his language and was pretty much as he wanted it.

Plenty was a great experience for me on an intellectual and craft level, as well as a personal one. David and I got on very well. As with all really good people, we found frank exchanges the best way. If you can put aside ego and be frank, you are able to see how your own limitations may have prevented you from seeing something earlier. In my case, there were psychological things going on in the play or script that couldn't readily be perceived because they were in the mind of the writer. David wouldn't necessarily think of saying to you, "That's why I have done it," but, in the cut-and-thrust of the challenge, he will come out with it. You will then see things in a completely different way.

SM: What have you thought of David Hare's work as a director?
FS: I know he is quite controversial, but I really like *Wetherby* (1985). I think it's great. I also love his early television work, like *Dreams of Leaving* (1980). Fabulous!

When he directs, David is a bit like David Mamet: he lights so that you concentrate on faces and the words become all important. But I don't think, like some, that they're only illuminated stage plays, because he really stages them as film. He tries to be original in his cinematic language, and he is learning all the time. Sometimes, I think he is a bit what I'll call "self-conscious," though I don't mean it as strongly as that. He will do something from a literary or theatrical consideration, but it will come off as a self-conscious camera movement. But he has a completely original approach and is really exciting.

I also like *Paris by Night* (1988), but I think I would have done a better job of it. I loved the script and really wanted to do it. I would have done a real film noir with a lot more bravura in the visuals. It would not have been David's film: it would have been David and Fred's film, quite different. But it's still a challenging and different experience.

Roxanne

SM: After the success of *Plenty*, you moved to comedy with *Roxanne*.
FS: I had actually been trying to do comedy for quite a while. Before *Iceman*, I had been involved with a physical comedy based on [*The Adventures of*] *Robin Hood* (1938), which I was going to do in the style of *The Three Musketeers* (1973) but hopefully even better. I was really looking forward to that, but it never came to be. I also had a Judith Ross script called *The Other Man*, which I thought was very funny.

In the meantime, I took two writing jobs. I did an adaptation of the book, *Meet Me at the Melba*. Interestingly, it is a lot of actresses' favorite script, but I couldn't get it made for love or money. Then I wrote an original comedy called *Misconceptions*, which I believe is very funny, but again couldn't get it made.

As well as these, there were two Steve Tesich screenplays, both comedies of tone and character. They are very funny, but I couldn't get anywhere with them. I got so depressed by this that I actually shot twenty minutes of one of them on videotape. The company which had put the project into turnaround thought I had created a miracle and changed their minds completely. Then, two weeks later, when we went in for the final meeting, they changed their minds again. I think that had to do with Kirk Kerkorian playing around with money and not the script.

So, it seemed as if no one would let me do a comedy. Then a friend of mine, Martha Luttrell, had her agency bought out by ICM, where Sam Cohn is. Suddenly she went from a friend who gave me advice to one of my agents. And it was she who sent me *Roxanne* and who convinced [producer] Dan Melnick that he should meet me.

When I met with Dan, I rather arrogantly gave him my theories on comedy and life and acting. But he seemed to like all that and my work. Steve Martin also turned out to be a great fan of *Plenty* and was looking to take an acting step. So we had dinner with Steve, and I took the bull by the horns and said, "Steve, your script doesn't start until page sixty-one. What are we going to do about it?" (Laughs) Fortunately, Steve agreed, and we got stuck into it. Then the guy who had been resisting me at Columbia left for another job, and I was in.

Roxanne was a great experience for me and a breakthrough. You see, something happens when you start refining your aesthetics: you begin to censor yourself without knowing it. I saw a good line the other day: "You become good taste, looking over its shoulder." You start to over-intellectualize and you eliminate all sorts of possibilities from your work.

I hadn't fully realized that until *Roxanne*, where there is a lot of wonderfully silly things happening. For example, I had the idea of putting "The Blue Danube" at the start of the scene where the firemen practice with the hose. Then I thought, "Heh, I could do this whole sequence to 'The Blue Danube.' I can shoot it with that in mind, just knowing I might do it." But then I started to have doubts and decided it was corny. But hold on: Why is it corny? Who says it's corny? And even if it is corny, what's necessarily wrong with that? Shouldn't I just be free and mad?

Then I remembered all the things I used to do at Bruce Clarke's Jingle Workshop, back when I was doing documentaries. I'd invent *musique concrete* things. I even did a whole film with just five voices. I orchestrated all these sounds and words and supermarket conversations, then electronically treated them so that they became like metal-pressing machines. I used to be very free and experimental, going out and pushing the borders.

But as you get into features, there are certain things you get rid of because everything has to be in the service of the story and the characters. Then one day you realize you have locked away something you'd forgotten you had. *Roxanne* opened all those doors for me.

It was very strange, because here I was doing a comedy which was forcing me to be far more conventional than I would have liked. There is always only one place to put the camera, and the minute you plan to have an alternative joke or you want to drop a line, you are forced into coverage. You can't afford to do it in one shot. Against that need to be conservative, I had to fight to adopt a style and keep it in the film. Suddenly, I was required to bring out a whole armory of stuff I'd forgotten I had.

So *Roxanne* was a very freeing experience for me, and I have had a renewed attitude ever since. If something works, it works. Don't get too intelligent and overimpose information in the photography and the music and sound. Don't get stultified. Do all the work beforehand, then let go and be free and emotional. Don't crush things to death intellectually. At the same time, though, there are areas of yourself you can't put into what are essentially conventional stories.

SM: Did that sense of freedom gained from *Roxanne* contribute to the "home movie" style of *Evil Angels*?
FS: Absolutely. Wobbly-cam! "What is this guy doing with wobbly-cam?" I used to be so perfect with all my camera moves and make the audience quite unconscious of what I was doing. If I moved, I crept. But now I ask myself: Why? Who says? You must find what the picture needs, then do it. And, yes, the "home movie" style is definitely there in *Evil Angels*. It governs the whole structure of it, crossing as it does to people around the country for comments.

SM: One stylistic element common to all your films is the abrupt changing of perspective on people in the landscape. You cut from very wide to very close and even through ninety degrees, which almost no other director does. The opening of *Iceman* is quite extraordinary in its use of ninety-degree cuts.
FS: That is my grammar. Each film is different, as we agree, but there is a basic grammar about cutting on line and shocking scale changes. These are stimulus things: I hate those miserable little thirty-degree changes and boring over-the-shoulder stuff. Cut around strongly, go ninety degrees if you want.

I like to work with modular-pattern filmmaking. If you find you have a flaw in the development or something, it is actually easier to unplug and shift things around when working this way than if you are using a more conventional system. That is something I learned many, many years ago and is partly why I do some of what you mentioned.

But it is also more than that. If you go in on line, you are concentrating on one thing and not introducing extraneous information in the background; you are not distracting the audience.

SM: The scene at the beginning of *Roxanne*, where C. D. Bales (Steve Martin) comes down the steps with his racquet and walks along the path before meeting the two hoons, is almost the classic sequence of Schepisi patterning.
FS: Yes, it is. Absolutely.

SM: Another stylistic element is the sense of community detailed in each picture. In *Roxanne*, for example, there is the strong feeling for the town and of the relationships between people.
FS: Yes, Bill Hurt actually expressed it a little differently, and I think more accurately. He said, "You fill in the corners." Most people don't. They concentrate on main characters, and everyone else is peripheral. For me, every character who appears in a film, from every bit part right up, has to have an inner life. Many times they play things that are not immediately perceivable. And I give as much information about who they are as I do the main actors. That is part of what builds that sense of community: they are all fully realized people, interacting in a very real way.

SM: The perception of you in America must have changed greatly after the success of *Roxanne*. Did you feel that?
FS: Absolutely. Up till then I was just an interesting filmmaker, straddling the majors and the independents. There was a lot of pressure from the good independents, and particularly writers, to do their work, and I still had the possibility of working for the majors. But then *Roxanne* made money. More than that, it was funny and warm. It could have been just a conventional comedy, but it became more than that. It made the studios appreciate my skills more, and it also made money. I am not sure in which order that goes, but I have an idea. (Laughs)

SM: Steve Martin had been tried in other films and not really succeeded, so the fact that he worked so well in *Roxanne* must have been seen as proof of your abilities as a director.
FS: I think that's true. But there is a certain irony in that because what people haven't picked up on is that Steve actually had something to act. This wasn't just a series of vignettes or one-liners. There was a story, a character, and a depth beyond the simply comedic approach, and a romance that had an emotional storyline.

SM: Presumably Steve Martin wrote it that way to give him what he felt he hadn't been offered before.
FS: I don't think he did that consciously. It was just the story he picked [*Cyrano de Bergerac*]. But he might have. I can't properly answer that, though I'm sure he was looking for a good vehicle, yes.

Evil Angels

SM: After *Roxanne*, your reputation was at a high with the major studios. But instead of trying to consolidate yourself in America, you came to Australia to make a film for Cannon. [Schepisi chuckles.] Once again you went off in a surprising direction.

FS: Well, I don't want to repeat myself. I want each film to be a challenge and a new experience. I don't want to go back over where I have been, unless I can find a different avenue of approach. I'll certainly do more comedy, but there is a hell of a lot of other things I want to do as well.

Quite frankly, I didn't want to do *Evil Angels*. I thought it was going to be too hard, but [producer] Verity Lambert just drove me mad about it. Fortunately, I was able to do it—and this will sound wrong—on Hollywood terms. I don't think I could have done it without Meryl. With her name, I was able to get the money to do it properly. She was an enormously helpful collaborator on every level. She gave me the confidence to believe I could do it. I couldn't, wouldn't, have done it without her.

SM: What did you think was too hard about it?

FS: Outside of the controversy, and the amount and importance of the information, was the fact I couldn't take any license. I understand now why people twenty years after an event combine characters and cheat on a few things. What they present dramatically can be closer to the truth in an emotional way than if they were strictly hidebound by the facts. I don't think we ended up being hidebound, but that's what I was frightened of.

As it was an on-going case, there was also the danger the film could negatively affect the lives of people involved. I didn't want to take it on if there was any danger of my doing that. Verity felt my hesitation was because I didn't know how to make the film, and that was true . . . at first. Then I did find out a way of doing it. But I had to tell Verity that I couldn't guarantee the film's commerciality if I went in that direction.

I'm glad she talked me into it because I think it is a bloody good film. It has been successful in many places, and in the oddest places it hasn't. In America, it wasn't, but that is a whole other story.

SM: When directors go to a foreign country, they often bring a fresh perspective to issues that local directors have missed. That is certainly the case with *Walkabout* and *Wake in Fright* (both 1971), which could not have been made by Australian directors. It seems to me that in *Evil Angels* there is a freshness and objectivity in looking at Australia that might have been influenced by your time working overseas. Would you agree?

FS: Yes, I do. There was one thing I didn't say when you asked why I went overseas: to gain a better perspective and balance on my own country and culture. I wanted to see things in world terms and experience other similar situations. You definitely get a better appreciation of your own country if you can get away for a while and experience things on an international level. Of course, things can get distorted as well if you are stupid.

The Russia House

SM: How did you become involved with *The Russia House*?
FS: Sam Cohn sent me a manuscript of the book just after Christmas [1988], asking me to read it quickly. There were other people up for it at the time, and Sam, who was also representing David Cornwell [John le Carré], wanted to know if I would be interested in case it didn't work out with these others. I read it, responded well to it, and said I'd be interested.

I was on my way to LA when he rang and said to go to London. So I went there and met David Cornwell, telling him how I felt about his book and what I thought I could do with it. I knew that he hadn't been happy with any of the previous films based on his work. We talked for a while, and then he suggested I meet with Tom Stoppard. Tom had been put forward by Mike Nichols when he was being considered for the project. We got on very well, and then both met with David to see if the three of us wanted to make the same film. We did and came to an agreement, forming a little pact amongst ourselves.

Then I flew to New York and rang Jerry Rappaport, the guy who had distributed *The Devil's Playground* there. He is the biggest distributor for the Eastern bloc in films and food. He told me that Elem Klimov, head of the Filmmakers Union in Russia, was coming the next day and set up a meeting for me. Elem and I hit it off, and we opened up the lines for the arrangement that we eventually adopted.

Then I went around with Sam and tried to sell the project. Sam thought it would sell a bit more easily than I did; I knew it was a bit intelligent. Then Tom joined me in Los Angeles, and we went and did a "dog and pony" show at a few studios. Eventually, we talked Alan Ladd Jr. at Pathé into it, and he gave us the money to write the first draft. (Incidentally, Laddy was president at Fox when I had first started there.) One of my conditions was that I also be given enough money for the production designer, the DOP, and me to do a location survey. Unfortunately, Ian couldn't come in the end because he was working on another film.

I became the producer, but I asked for someone who had worked in Russia before. Paul Maslansky is an American who had worked a lot with the Ladd Company and who'd made two films in Russia. He became my co-producer.

I went England for discussions with Tom on the second draft. While he worked on that, I shot off to Russia and did an eight-day survey in and around Moscow and Leningrad. I then sent the designer on to Lisbon and Maine and a couple of other places.

The second draft came in June, but Pathé wouldn't make the film unless I got Sean Connery. This was after long discussions about who, how, and why. So I flew from London to New York, and then on to LA airport. I met Jay Kanter, who is Alan Ladd's right-hand man, just before he got on a plane to Malaysia. I gave him the script, had a chat and a couple of drinks, and off he went. I then walked to another section of the main terminal and met with Sean Connery for an hour in the lounge of some airline or other. I gave him the script, talked like hell, and tried to convince him to do it. I laid down my terms; he laid down his. Then he went off, and I headed to yet another terminal to pick up [daughter] Ashley, who was coming in to spend some time with me. We then drove into town and delivered a script to Laddy. That was on a Saturday, and on Monday Sean rang me and said he wanted to do it. Boom, we were up and running!

Everyone had kept thinking there was no way we could get it off the ground. Even my own agent still can't work out how we did. From a book to a film takes a long time. But Moscow, Leningrad, London, Lisbon, and Vancouver all in that time: pretty good!

SM: Did this speed have anything to do with the changes looming in Russia and Eastern Europe?

FS: No. I wanted to go in September before the weather conditions in Russia became too difficult. But the bloody lawyers took a bit long negotiating Tom's contract, and we lost a few weeks. I knew that October was the latest we could start, and, if I missed that, I'd have to wait six months. So we went like stink to do it in time.

That was the main driving force. At that time, nobody knew what was going to happen in Europe. Regardless of what might happen to Gorbachev or the system, there was no guarantee that the benevolent moment of free enterprise would continue.

SM: During the making of the film, was anything changed to take account of altering circumstances?

FS: No, the book is a moment in time. I felt it would always be relevant and that there was no point trying to chase current circumstances. In fact, the film stayed pretty well where the script was originally, even maybe back-pedalled a little.

The Russia House is an anti-spy film. It is about how the very people who should have known things were changing didn't know. They don't want things to change. There are economies and ways of life based on the arms race. That is what we are really examining; that is the underbelly of the film.

It was during production that the Berlin Wall came down, and Hungary and Poland came out. Tiananmen Square happened the day before we went to Russia on our second survey. It became very clear that nowhere in Russia had there been any reporting whatsoever on any of the events in China. I found that quite shocking.

SM: Le Carré's book is based on very long and precise conversations. From a Hollywood point of view, there isn't much action in it. Was that ever a studio concern?
FS: Alan Ladd's original fear was that it would be a talking heads picture. I kept saying it wouldn't be, but rather something that would take you inside Russia and let you really experience it. Nobody thinks of it as a dialogue picture now. They think of it as an extremely involving story with an incredible sense of scale. It is a dramatic story that sucks you in and keeps you there. The love story is very strong, and you don't need the other stimuli of car chases and shooting round corners.

Basically, all the Russians are Russian, except for Michelle Pfeiffer. But you believe she is Russian. Where Russians should speak Russian, they do so. There are only one or two places where a translation is needed, and how that is done becomes part of the story. It wasn't a real problem.

A Cinematic Gallant

Stephen Schiff / 1993

First published in *The New Yorker*, December 20, 1993. Reprinted by permission of the author.

Fred Schepisi is probably the least-known great director working in the mainstream American cinema—a master storyteller with a serenely muscular style that can make more flamboyant moviemakers look coarse and overweening. He has never been a self-promoter, and his films are difficult to pigeonhole. Even so, his obscurity is perplexing. Perhaps it has something to do with the fact that Schepisi (pronounced Skep-see) not only comes from Australia but still lives there—and not in Sydney, the traditional center of Australia's film culture, but in Melbourne. Then, too, his interests have not always coincided with those of the box office. He has directed ten features, of which nine have been extraordinary pieces of filmmaking (and even the sole exception, last year's *Mr. Baseball*, was about as good as a Tom Selleck picture can be), but only one has been a hit: *Roxanne* (1987), the elegant comedy in which Steve Martin played a contemporary Cyrano de Bergerac and gave his most inspired—and limber—performance ever. "Fred has chosen odd material," says the Hollywood producer Scott Rudin, who is working with Schepisi on his next project, a comedy about Albert Einstein called *I.Q.* "He hasn't handled giant hit movies, so that's why people don't talk about him—this is a town where grosses are the whole game. But he's a major, really important filmmaker—definitely A-list. I'd think of him for any good piece of material I had. And when he says no, don't ask again. He's very decisive about what he likes. You never can predict what's going to grab him."

Usually, what grabs him are stories that pit a spirited outsider against a tinyminded establishment, an educated half-caste against the white agrarian society of turn-of-the-century Australia, for instance, in *The Chant of Jimmie Blacksmith* (1978); a newly thawed Neanderthal against the beady-eyed Arctic scientists who want to dissect him, in *Iceman* (1984); a dour Seventh-Day Adventist against the media-crazed Australian public that thinks she killed her daughter, in *A Cry in the*

Dark (1988); a hard-drinking British publisher against the spy networks of three countries, in *The Russia House* (1990).

Schepisi tells stories about storytelling. Myths and legends whisper through his films, and he has a taste for the epic. He likes a wide screen, a vast setting: vertiginous distance shots pin his characters against daunting landscapes. Yet he often cuts away to examine nearby insects and animals, as if to remind us that the tale he's spinning isn't the only one in the world. You can be swept along by a Schepisi movie without ever grasping what it is that is sweeping you. His films feel smooth and patterned even when they're jumping hectically between flashbacks, time zones, geographies; they move in mysterious ways. Schepisi's directorial approach is that of a ballroom dancer, feinting and then embracing, throwing you off balance momentarily and then breaking your fall a second later. He has an urbane, almost flirtatious style. His movies hold doors open for the audience, guide our gaze, position and reposition us so that we see what we need to see and then, when we tire of the view, examine something new. Schepisi is a kind of cinematic gallant. Watching one of his pictures, you feel yourself in attentive hands.

"You have to understand your audience," he explains, cramping his vowels in the Australian manner. "You can't take the film wherever you want to take it if that means screwing it up for people. A film is about being in a boat going down the river. You can kind of go over to that bank and then nip around to that bay, but basically you've got to stay on the river. And eventually it comes to a waterfall—boom!—and you've got to just go over that waterfall. You can't suddenly say, 'Oh, well, before we go over the waterfall let's go up that little creek there.' Too late. Because the emotion has now taken over, and you've got to just go straight to the target. Otherwise, you screw up everyone's experience."

As Schepisi talks, his hands play along: they're the nipping boat; they're the foaming river; when they clap, they're the waterfall. He's not a tall man, but his billowing midriff and cowboy swagger convey an impression of size. His hair is long and lank and strawberry blond, and he's currently making one of his periodic stabs at a beard: it's growing in little red islands. Schepisi is fifty-three now, but his frisky, ingenuous demeanor makes him seem much younger. He has a great, probing snout and merry little eyes, and these things, along with an enormous, face-splitting grin, put you in mind of a dolphin inviting you in for a splash.

We are sitting at the dining room table in his cluttered New York pied-à-terre; the walls and halls are full of paintings—soft, abstract ones by his third (and current) wife, Mary Rubin Schepisi, and red, labyrinthine ones by contemporary Aboriginal artists. There are pencils and loose sheets of typing paper everywhere. Schepisi scribbles as we talk, drawing what he can't quite articulate, and as he chatters and sketches I begin to see what makes his films so fluid and rich: they are the product of a remarkably disciplined, almost musical mind, a mind that has trained itself to break stories down into their tiniest components and then reconstitute them again, without losing the emotion that makes them sail. The apartment is, more or less, his American office, and nothing like his airy Victorian house in Melbourne, where he plays lots of tennis and spends Sundays cooking opulent brunches for a brood that includes seven kids (the youngest nine, the oldest thirty-two). Here in New York, the phone never stops ringing. No matter who is on the other end, Schepisi calls him "mate."

"He is, I think, a genuinely happy person," Scott Rudin says. And so he seems—especially now, having just finished his exhilarating adaptation of John Guare's hit play, *Six Degrees of Separation* (which opened in New York last week). Guare had picked Schepisi after interviewing several other prospects for the job. (Barbra Streisand and Norman Jewison were among those reported to be interested.) "Fred said he loved the way the play was structured," Guare says, "and he wanted to find the cinematic equivalent of it. And everybody else I asked was saying, 'Oh, wouldn't this actress be good in it, and that actress.' Well, I wanted Stockard Channing, who was so great in it onstage, and Fred did, too. Also, I had seen *The Chant of Jimmie Blacksmith*, about this young Aboriginal man coming into another culture, and it was devastating. And with *The Devil's Playground*, Fred was like an Australian Louis Malle, the way he dealt with young people in that seminary—he was so sympathetic. And I felt the way that he used the setting in *Roxanne*, not as just a picture postcard, but that town exerted a force on all the magical things that happened in that movie, and I wanted New York to have the same feeling." As for Schepisi, he had long yearned to make a real New York movie. "I had wanted to do *Bonfire of the Vanities* when that was coming around," he says. "And before that I was interested in *Billy Bathgate*. I definitely love New York. It's the atmosphere, the energy the place has."

Guare once wrote that when he and the director Jerry Zaks first began staging *Six Degrees* in 1989, "all I knew about the play was that it had to go like the wind." Onstage at New York's Lincoln Center, it did: it had a breathless, wait-till-you-hear-this air. The characters spoke their story directly out at the audience, as if we were sitting across from them at a dinner party: Flan Kittredge, an art dealer, and his wife, Ouisa, just had to tell us about the night this preppy young black man named Paul burst into their posh Fifth Avenue apartment claiming that he had been mugged in Central Park, and how he proceeded to charm and awe his unwitting hosts by cooking dinner, spinning eloquent theories about *The Catcher in the Rye* and the nobility of the imagination, and, mostly, convincing them that he was not only a dear friend of their college-age children but the son of Sidney Poitier—none of which turned out to be true. From this scrawny premise, based in almost every particular on an actual incident, Guare brewed an amazingly rich thematic stew: the play was about liberalism and race, the ambiguity of relationships, the illusory nature of status and celebrity and wealth, the use and abuse of experience, and a dozen other weighty matters, all roiling around together. Watching *Six Degrees* was like swallowing an intense decoction of New York life. You didn't need to see the wine and pasta to feel the dinner party's hum; you didn't need to glimpse Central Park to sense its splendor and menace splayed just beyond the play's imaginary windows.

You might also have felt that you didn't need a movie version of *Six Degrees*—that its buoyant theatricality could only be diminished by the kind of literalization that inevitably accompanies film adaptations. But Schepisi's version is, in most ways, as good as it could possibly be: theatrical, yes, but exuberant, witty, and poignant—the final fulfillment of Guare's vision. It also goes like the wind. Ouisa and Flan Kittredge (played by Stockard Channing and Donald Sutherland) still spend the film telling their story, but Schepisi and Guare have placed them where the play never could, where one really would find them blabbing away—at New York art galleries, at Lincoln Center between acts, at Mortimer's Restaurant, and the Gotham Bar & Grill and the dinner table of Kitty Carlisle Hart. Schepisi staples the characters against their surroundings the way he always does, but this time those surroundings aren't the awesome mesas of the outback or the ice mountains of the Arctic—they're the canyons of Manhattan. The camera swoops around street corners like a runaway taxi, hurtles through the Strand used-bookstore, helicopters in on the Metropolitan Museum—always on the trail of Ouisa and Flan and the growing gaggle of cronies whose world "Paul Poitier" (played, somewhat awkwardly, by Will Smith) has penetrated.

Pretty soon, you feel the pace of these lives in your blood, and you sense the way Paul's presence has thrown a monkey wrench into the works, jamming the gears and conveyors that keep New York on the go. Like so many of Schepisi's characters (and like Schepisi himself), Paul is an outsider, a kind of sophisticated barbarian. But the outside he personifies is many-headed: he is black, he is poor, he is young, he is homosexual, he is homeless—all the things that make cozy urban liberals like the Kittredges feel morally insufficient. And one more thing: he is make-believe. Paul has cobbled a convincing identity out of thin air; his invasion of the Kittredges' life marks the intrusion of fiction into the world of seeming fact. I say "seeming fact" because Paul's appearance sets off a chain reaction: suddenly, the Kittredges' relations with their children, Flan's career, even the marriage itself come to seem unreal, a sham. Fiction infects these lives like a virus, and Schepisi's camera charts the germ's progress. It's as though we were scuttling with it through the circulatory system of the city—through streets and lobbies and hallways, through museums and restaurants that are like the organs and nerve centers of some gigantic metabolizing creature. Even when Schepisi parks somewhere to shoot a long conversation, the camera rarely stops moving. It breathes forward and backward, a predator rocking expectantly on the balls of its feet.

"That came out of a sort of panther thing," Schepisi says. "I wanted Paul to be completely enchanting, but I wanted you always to be asking, 'Where's the threat? Where's the danger?' And I remember saying to Will Smith, 'I want to feel that you could spring at any time.' I knew that that would be very hard for him, so we did it with the camera a bit—quite a bit. And somehow it sort of grew into a real thing for the film. The camera doesn't go in its prescribed path. It moves, and, before you quite realize it, it goes in another direction. And it might be lifting slightly and then moving around slightly." Schepisi's hands form a glider in flight. "It's a pattern across the whole film, to give it the right kind of drive-through energy."

The camera movement in *Six Degrees* is the freest and most invigorating that Schepisi has ever tried, but experimentation of that sort is not new to his work. In *The Russia House*, he perfected a kind of ominous glide that made you feel as though you were being followed or spied upon, as though there were always something lurking just out of view. The glide had another function as well: it felt swoony and romantic. And in that way it reflected the movie's central irony—the American and British spies may think they've launched an espionage operation in Russia, but what they've really launched is a love affair between their operative, Barley (Sean Connery), and his Russian contact, Katya (Michelle Pfeiffer).

"The film itself is really what dictates your camera movement," Schepisi says. "I'm very strong in thinking that a film should have a style, design, and discipline that are all true to it. You have a personal grammar and certain things you want to have a bit of cinema fun with, but it's always got to be completely in the service of the story." In *Iceman*, when the Neanderthal (played by John Lone) escapes from a vivarium and starts rampaging through the scientists' labs, Schepisi's camera leaps in and out of the creature's point of view, first observing him with a stalker's cool surmise and then peering through his eyes with a movement that's quicker and more feral—the thrilling fear of a hunter on a mythic quest.

"That's a thing I call subjective-objective," Schepisi says, "and I do that all the time." In *The Chant of Jimmie Blacksmith*, for instance, the title character is a half-Aborigine who spends the first part of the movie grinning sweetly as his white employers pelt him with abuse. Then he erupts, taking an ax to a houseful of white women and children, and instantly becomes a legend in the process—an outlaw feared and reviled throughout Australia. The massacre is the most horrifying scene in any of Schepisi's films, and one of the most horrifying acts in all cinema—not because Schepisi shows spurting arteries and gaping wounds but because of the way his subjective-objective technique captures the ghastly dance between terrified victims and their equally terrified killer. "When Jimmie jumps into the house, we jump in as his point of view, and then we change; we become one of the other people in the room, watching Jimmie ducking and weaving, and then we go back and become Jimmie's point of view again. Back and forth, subjective-objective. We're being both him and his victim, and, because we're changing the perspective all the time, it creates an unsettling panic."

Techniques like these aren't taught in film schools; most of them, in fact, belong to Schepisi alone. He seems to have made them up as he's gone along, inventing something new with every picture. And he likes to break the rules. If the film schools tell you you're not supposed to jump-cut, Schepisi jump-cuts—and he does it in a way that, far from jolting the viewer, creates an unexpected intimacy. If they tell you you're never supposed to flip-flop the camera angle in a scene (it's called "crossing the line" and is thought to disorient the audience), Schepisi does it all the time. In the opening shots of *Roxanne*, when Steve Martin goes tripping down a sidewalk in one direction, Schepisi has him zipping into the next shot from the opposite direction, and then, in a third shot, zooming right toward us. Those reversals kick off a pattern of suavely zigzagging motions that run throughout the film, jacking up the comedy, and eventually limning the characters' star-crossed romance. "There's a whole conventional pattern for cutting, and that's what you see in most movies," Schepisi says. "And I just don't like it. I don't think it's right. I don't think it's got any magic to it at all."

Schepisi began developing tricks of his own when he was still in his twenties, pursuing a career in advertising and documentary production back in Melbourne. He had started out poor, the second of four children; his father was a fruit dealer and his mother an aspiring concert pianist who wound up working in the fruit store. Fred was sent to boarding school at the age of eight, and then, at thirteen, to a monastery whose Dickensian rigors he would document in his first feature, *The Devil's Playground*. He likes to say he wasn't much good at school, but he skipped two grades nonetheless and found himself, at the age of fourteen, a year away from graduating from high school. Instead, he dropped out. "I hated school anyway—hated it, hated teachers. So I didn't finish, and I didn't go to university. But somebody told me that you could earn a lot of money in advertising if you were good at English. So I went into advertising at fifteen, as a dispatch boy."

At twenty, he married his first wife, Joan Ford. "She actually helped me settle down because I was a rage of emotions in those days, mostly because of boarding school. I need a lot of loving, and my parents were not big on affection and tenderness. She helped me get through all that. We had four kids together. Also, she got me to reading really good books."

By the mid-sixties, he had established his own movie company, called The Film House; it remains one of the most successful production firms in Australia. "This is something I strongly relate to in *Six Degrees*," he says. "The thing about a young person getting a chance. Paul is just starting out in life, and he needs a chance, like I did. And when you first start out, you're so vulnerable and easily crushed, especially when you're just starting to think you might be good at something. You feel very strongly that you could prove yourself if given an opportunity, and I remember that feeling—it touched me very deeply in the play."

Now he began to experiment, directing commercials and documentaries in order to teach himself how to work with actors, how to manipulate lenses and layer soundtracks. "I used to try techniques that nobody had ever done anywhere," he says. "I've got reels of these things, with high-contrast black-and-whites and hand-painted-on films, and all that. My friends were kind of mad and avant-garde and out on the edge. We would get students involved, and we went out and got novelists and playwrights who had never worked in films before. It was a real workshop situation, which is very peculiar to Melbourne. It was all just completely free, exciting, experimental stuff, none of which you can do in Hollywood films."

One of his mad collaborators was a singer-actress named Rhonda Finlayson, who became his production manager, casting director, and second wife. Then, in the early seventies, Schepisi met the novelist Thomas Keneally, who wrote *The Chant of Jimmie Blacksmith* (and, eventually, *Schindler's List*, the novel on which Steven Spielberg has based his latest film). Schepisi and Keneally collaborated on *The Priest*, a rather dreary half-hour movie, which nevertheless won a Silver Award from the Australian Film Institute. Encouraged by its success, Schepisi went to work on his dream project, *The Devil's Playground*, a surprisingly deft and witty study of the sexual repression and self-loathing engendered by seminary life. The movie took five agonizing years to make, but Schepisi used the time to develop a set of techniques that were unique to him—the bedrock of his style.

"I didn't really know what I was doing in terms of budget and all that," he says. "So I needed a film to use as a model, something that was similar in size of cast and story and locations to *Devil's Playground*. Finally I picked *Morgan*. And I broke *Morgan* down scene by scene, wrote down what all the shots were and how many cuts there were, and figured out how long it would have taken to shoot everything. Then I charted a graph of all the actors. You can do this with any film."

Schepisi stops, grabs a sheet of paper, and begins to scribble. What he draws looks something like this

	1	2	3	4	5	6	7	8	9	10
John	•	•	•	•		•	•	•		•
Jim						•	•	•	•	•
Jack	•	•	•					•		
Sean	•	•	•	•						
Joan			•	•	•					•
Jane					•	•	•	•	•	•

"It's funny," he says. "If you take the scene numbers on the horizontal here, and you put the actors' names in on the vertical and just put dots in the scenes where they appear in the film, you can tell in one second, without the emotion you get from reading the script, what impact the actor is having. Someone will say to you, 'There's a problem with your film. This character just disappears.' And you'll say, 'Bullshit,' because you're really involved in it. But if you actually just lay it down you'll see that on a chart this character disappears for that long. And one thing I have discovered is that if the audience falls in love with somebody, and you take them away from that person, even in the most complicated film, they'll hate you. It's a purely emotional thing, and I understand it. It means that there's a primal something there that you've got to account for."

Now he shunts that piece of paper aside and doodles on another. "Look at this," he says. "One of the other things we did on *Devil's Playground* was we said, 'Let's check to see if the film's interesting'—not too depressing and not too boring. And we did a graph, like this

"Okay, development is the incidents that make up your story—that's the base of the chart. Above the line are what I would call the 'values,' all the things that have a lot of sit-up-and-take-notice impact on the audience—sex, action, violence, argument, character revelation. And each of those is a 'boom.' Below the line you have the other things that aren't booms—they're gloomier, but they still have an effect. The farther away from the line you are, the bigger the impact. Right? So now you go and look at each scene, and you say, 'That's a boom; that's not a boom; that's a boom; that's not a boom.' And if you get a whole long section with no booms above the line and lots of dots below the line or too close to the line, you say, 'Oh, shit. Something's wrong.' That's when you have to transpose some scenes."

In many ways, *The Devil's Playground*, which was released in 1976, presages the rest of Schepisi's work. The young seminarians and their teachers spend their lives scourging and denying their bodies, but their bodies refuse to capitulate: they still desire, swell, discharge—they still win. This is Schepisi's great theme: the return of the repressed. That which is kept down in a man or in a society returns to invade and test it and attempt its overthrow—as the Iceman does, as Paul Poitier does, as the title character does in Schepisi's great second feature, *The Chant of Jimmie Blacksmith*.

Jimmie Blacksmith cost about a million US dollars to make, and, though that sounds modest by American standards, it was the most expensive film that had yet been shot in Australia; its creation even became something of a media event. Nevertheless, when it was finally released, in 1978, the Australian response was mixed. Many people thought it had cost too much; others found it squirmy, uncomfortable viewing. Certainly it was strong stuff—the most potent indictment of Australian racism that that country had ever seen. But it was something more as well. In *Jimmie Blacksmith*, Schepisi had directed a masterpiece, a passionate, deceptively smooth shocker that deplores Jimmie's savagery even as it condemns the white bigotry that has driven him to it. The movie is anything but a message picture. It builds its world molecule by molecule, from the soil to the sky, using the wide screen to explore not only Jimmie's grim deeds but the quality of the light that plays upon them and the flight patterns of nearby birds. In the end, the film feels as fated and strange as a Greek tragedy; the drama it portrays seems to emerge from the earth and air of Australia itself.

By the time *Jimmie Blacksmith* was finally released in America, in 1980 (to enthusiastic reviews), Schepisi had found himself an American agent—the formidable Sam Cohn, of ICM—and was fielding dozens of directing offers. The property he chose, a quirky yet hypnotic western called *Barbarosa* (1982), allowed him to explore his favorite themes against an American West that has never looked wilder, more majestic, or more surreal. *Barbarosa*, too, is about the return of the repressed: the title character (played by Willie Nelson) has been expelled from his own family—banished by his father-in-law, Don Braulio Zavala, on his wedding night. Repressed in person, though, he returns as legend. Barbarosa's putative crimes become the campfire lore of every Zavala child; assassinating him becomes the obsession of every Zavala youth. Like *Jimmie Blacksmith*, *Barbarosa* is about a man who must live with his own myth, and it works the way most of Schepisi's films have worked: by contrasting the outlaw with the story that a society spins about him and demonstrating, as *Six Degrees* does, the havoc that fiction wreaks on the world of fact.

Yet Schepisi's view of fiction isn't simple. In his movies, fiction is also the thing that glues a society together: the fiction of religion in *The Devil's Playground*, of racism in *The Chant of Jimmie Blacksmith*, of the Cold War in *The Russia House*. Fiction is the tie that binds—but it binds in more ways than one. In *Iceman*, where the constricting fiction is science, Schepisi encases his characters in antiseptic tunnels that resemble a rat's maze and, then, with a whoosh that feels like a rebuke, leaps to a shot of the magnificent ice peaks that the scientists have shut themselves away from. His 1985 adaptation of David Hare's play, *Plenty*, is about the stultifying fiction of British hope and glory that culminated in the Suez crisis. Schepisi makes every stately London building and street lean in and squeeze his heroine (played by Meryl Streep); he shoots her in offices through imprisoning layers of glass until you can feel her spirit bumping at the edges of her life like a fly in a bottle.

Fiction has power in these films, but it is also oppressive, unjust. And never more so than in Schepisi's most searching exploration of the subject, *A Cry in the Dark*. The movie was based on a case that electrified Australia during the early eighties: Lindy Chamberlain, the wife of a Seventh-Day Adventist minister and the doting mother of two sons, claimed that in 1980, while she and her family were camping near Australia's spooky Ayers Rock, a dingo, or wild dog, had crawled into their tent and made off with their nine-week-old daughter. The Chamberlains weren't pretty, and they weren't good on TV: they seemed curt and impatient, and they kept talking, rather bloodlessly, about how the disaster that had befallen them must have been God's plan. In the movie, you watch public opinion ineluctably turn against them until, in a sequence that is all the more harrowing for its lack of sentimentality, Lindy is tried and convicted of her daughter's murder and sent to prison. (The conviction was later overturned.) Badly marketed by Cannon Pictures, *A Cry in the Dark* was a flop in America, but it is a great film and Schepisi renders its intimidating complexities with the vigor and ease of a master. Meryl Streep's portrayal of Lindy (which she has called "almost the thing that I'm proudest of") allows her to be chilly and cynical, and even physically repugnant, but it also displays the character's wicked savvy. And Schepisi uses her performance with an unusual kind of integrity. Streep earns our sympathy as the story demands that it be earned—not because Lindy is likable, not because we fall in love with her, but because she's innocent and her conviction by innuendo is monstrous.

A Cry in the Dark is distinctive in another way as well: in it Schepisi perfected a technique he had been developing ever since *The Devil's Playground*—the meticulous cinematic construction of a community. As he tells the story of Lindy Chamberlain, Schepisi cuts away to barrooms, dining tables, patios, cafeterias—he ranges all over the continent to catch the gossip about the case as it develops. The cuts are so fluent and the patterns they make so seductive that they never feel jarring; instead, by the film's end Schepisi has built a disturbing and deeply felt portrait of Australia itself. "I love doing that," he says. "I do it in *Russia House* and in *Six Degrees*, too. It's a kind of mosaic. But you have to be very careful, because it has to be designed. You need a principle for why you're doing every shot the way you're doing it. I learned a lot about that shooting *Plenty*. In that film, whenever Meryl goes into a new apartment we always shoot it the same way. Whenever she stands by a window, you always hear similar sounds, and we always approach it the same way because they're the déjà-vu moments where she's remembering when she was young. We do that with sound, too. The sound of parachutes opening at the beginning I use again all through the film, when people are opening tablecloths and curtains, because it brings back a certain feeling."

Schepisi tinkers with sound in the editing room as well. "What I did in *Six Degrees* when I found that things weren't getting laughs, I actually mixed the sound of the joke line ten percent above the rest of the dialogue in the scene. And it worked. Another thing I do is steal sound from other takes. I print takes I know I'm not going to use except for sound. Because maybe the actors have done a great take, but they just lost energy on a word, or mispronounced, or bobbled, or put a wrong emphasis. And I'll just use three words from a different take and edit it into this take. I do it all the time. Probably at least ten percent of what you see in my films has words from a take other than the one you're watching."

Schepisi is known for demanding a lot of takes, but he gets what he wants from his actors: they transcend themselves. The performance that Stockard Channing delivers as Ouisa in *Six Degrees* is a knockout, funny and touching and exquisitely observed, but he has frequently sculpted marvels from less promising clay—from nonprofessionals like Tommy Lewis and Freddy Reynolds, the Aboriginal leads in *Jimmie Blacksmith*, or from stars who were not, shall we say, previously known for their expressiveness, such as Daryl Hannah in *Roxanne*. He genuinely likes actors, and, though he would never put it this way, he knows how to manipulate them. "Normally, I don't tell them technical things," he says. "I give them an emotional reason for standing where I want them to stand rather than saying, 'Hit your mark like this.' But then, with somebody like Sir Ian McKellen"—who has small roles in *Plenty* and *Six Degrees*—"he's always a little nervous on early takes on film, and it's better to give him something technical to concentrate on, like 'I need you to stand here, and then why don't you give her a look,' and his whole concentration goes to that, and then he lets himself go for everything else. That sort of stuff. Sometimes with Meryl you don't need to say a word all day. Someone like that, when she's great, don't fuck it up. And don't go in and say, 'That was good,' either. Because then she's going to go, 'What was good?' She'll check herself—like she's taken flight but she suddenly looked down. You don't want to screw it up. It has to come from inside. It has to come through the eyes."

And here we arrive at the limits of his prodigious technique. All the planning and analysis in the world cannot account for what really catches fire in a Schepisi film. They can account for its formal beauty, they can account for its clarity and for the way its narrative moves, but they cannot account for its passion and intelligence and humanity. That mystery—the mystery of how technique gives rise to something beyond technique to create art—is at the heart of Schepisi's work, and it reaches a kind of apotheosis in *Six Degrees of Separation*. For Paul Poitier is himself a sort of artist—an artist whose medium is identity. He has invented a simulacrum of a marvellous and fascinating person, the way a painter creates a simulacrum of a landscape or the way Michelangelo, in the Sistine Chapel ceiling (which Ouisa and Flan inspect in one of the movie's most jubilant scenes), concocted a simulacrum of the cosmos. Paul's technique is to lie, and, for most of the movie's characters, to expose the lie is to extinguish the light it sheds. But Ouisa refuses to dismiss Paul as a mere phony. She refuses to cheapen the effect his fiction has had, refuses to let it pass into the realm of chitchat and anecdote. For her, Paul is a passageway into another world, just as she has been for him. Far more than her art-dealer husband, Ouisa understands what art is: it is greater than the sum of its techniques and effects; it continues to resonate as experience; it is both the thing perceived and something that transcends the thing perceived. "Art keeps vibrating," Schepisi says. "It tells you things in ways that you can't be told otherwise. That's what this experience has taught Ouisa in the film, and it's a lesson I've learned, too—that when you're dancing through life and trying to make a buck and get established and keep up with your friends, you need something to stop you. This incident with Paul has stopped her, opened her up. That's what art can do."

He stops for a moment, sighs rather loudly, and runs his fingers through his floppy hair. "I'll tell you why I talk about technique and structure and all that stuff," he says. "Arthur Koestler once asked if our great scientific discoveries were accidents or the product of work and preparation. And his own answer was that maybe they are accidents, but they wouldn't happen unless you first did all the work. Because otherwise, when you come across something great, you won't recognize it. You can't cynically calculate what you want to get across. You just create the situation where it can happen, and then it just appears. I believe that. What *Six Degrees* says about art touches me: that you never put on a brushstroke unless the brushstroke means something; that you never use a color unless that color vibrates with itself and then with the human soul. So that's why I go on about all the technical stuff. Because if you do that stuff right, the spirit bubbles up through it."

Last Orders: An Interview with Director Fred Schepisi

Cynthia Fuchs / 2001

Posted for popmatters, 7 December 2001. Reprinted by permission of the author.

At first glance, Fred Schepisi looks like a quiet fellow. But he turns quite effusive when he starts talking: sharply observant and possessed of a dry sense of humor, he's comfortable expressing himself. At sixty-two, he's been around the movie block more than once. From his early work in Australia—*The Devil's Playground* (1976) and *The Chant of Jimmie Blacksmith* (1978)—to his bigger-budgeted US and UK projects—*Plenty* (1985), *The Russia House* (1990), and *Six Degrees of Separation* (1993), his greatest critical success—the writer-director has established a varied and mostly impressive resume.

Yet Schepisi still struggles to get pictures made. To his mind, this is a function of economics: he's not keen to make huge action pictures but neither is he looking to make a tiny picture that won't be seen or pay the rent. All this makes him especially happy with his new movie, *Last Orders*, despite the fact that he made it under less than ideal circumstances: lousy British weather, allotted money that didn't come through, a tight schedule. No matter. The result, based on Graham Swift's novel, traces the complicated shared history of four East Londoners: Jack (Michael Caine), Vic (Tom Courtenay), Ray (Bob Hoskins), and Lenny (David Hemmings). Their multi-decades story unfolds in flashbacks, following Jack's death, as the remaining three spend a day driving to the beach where they will fulfill his "last orders," to scatter his ashes over the water. At the same time, Jack's widow, Amy (Helen Mirren), takes her own journey, to the institution where her fifty-year-old retarded daughter lives to say goodbye one last time before Amy starts another life, apart from her family.

Cynthia Fuchs: How did you come to make an accessible layering of voices and points of view from Graham Swift's novel?

Fred Schepisi: The novel has a structure that's broken up, not in the same way, but with the same effect—each chapter was headed by the name of a character. Within those chapters, while they were advancing the story, they were reflecting on the past and expressing their hopes for the future pretty much in monologues. The way I chose to interpret that was similar to what I've done in other films and used to do in documentaries; (it's) kind of like a mosaic technique, if you like. Say, in *The Russia House*, there's a point where Sean Connery and Michelle Pfeiffer meet in the tower, and all those beautiful Russian churches are outside. And you think you're just watching them, but actually you're watching five different time zones in the story: you're watching them and the tensions they're going through; you're watching a spy watching them; you're watching the spy's report back to his bosses in the form of a tape a number of days after the event; and then you're watching two sections of the past as Michelle Pfeiffer tells a story.

I think that's how we tell stories. It's how memory operates—how our thoughts operate—because we go on memory, we go on apprehension of the present, and we go on hopes or expectations for the future. When you tell a story, you're throwing other lights on it, which makes the story richer and more interesting. We can't stop saying, "Yeah, but don't forget the time you did such and such . . ." To that end, I did not ever try to pick up on the time periods (in *Last Orders*). By that, I don't mean that the time periods aren't accurate; they are incredibly accurate. But I don't come into them and waste time going, "This is where we are," because why is that of interest? What's of interest is you or your story of what's happening, and it's all about your emotion and your understanding. So I've got to follow you, and then it's the pleasure of the audience to pick up on all that other stuff that's going on in the background, if they want to. If you do it accurately enough, they accept it without thinking about it. So that allows you to move from 1935 to 1979 to 1950-something to 1989, which is our actual present tense. I didn't do all that conventional stuff where you go to the old-fashioned poster or the lady with the pram to tell you what time period it is, and I didn't play songs or music from the period to set you up.

CF: That's a common device now, to use the compiled soundtrack that you can then sell as a CD.

FS: Well, yes, but then you get pulled by that. You go, "Oh I remember that song," and your mind starts to go to details evoked by your memory. But, in a picture like this, that makes you lose track of where you are. There is some source music from within the eras, but it's more background to help you accept where you are without having to think about it. The score of the movie is kind of a pop-jazz-classical structure, that's got three themes going through it. The role of the music corresponds with a particular belief I have, which is that characters have themes and, when they come together, you're hearing both those themes at the same time. The theme helps because, even as I change its presentation or blend it with something else, you're feeling an emotion, and you're not even aware you're feeling it because I've trained you to feel it throughout the picture. Of course, when I say "I," I mean the composer (Paul Grabowsky), the editor (Kate Williams), and so on.

This helps you understand the characters' inner life, what they're feeling, even if it's not exactly what they're saying. It gives you pause for thought, other information. Probably the boldest move in the film is the love theme, as it becomes that, the theme of Ray and Amy, when you find out that they've been unfaithful—him to his best mate, her to her husband—and, within thirty seconds, I'm playing the love theme of Amy and Jack, her husband, because she says, "He loved me, and he always did."

CF: The music does help to bridge the many storylines.

FS: Yes, there are sort of three journeys going on at once—two are going on in our present time: Amy visiting her daughter (June, played by Laura Morelli) and the men's car journey. And the third, which is Amy and Ray, is actually taking place a week before the other two.

CF: Many films deliver characters in a present moment, and the story is about their movement from that point. Your films tend to be more about how character might be shaped by past experiences.

FS: Yes, and this film kind of takes that to the nth degree. Everybody thinks that action is what it's all about, but the real action for me is the way characters interact with one another. Somebody said that this is a film about ordinary lives that proves there are no ordinary lives. When I was casting the young people, they would read the script and say, "Oh my God! Is this what we're going to have to go through?" It's so complex, what a struggle.

CF: The sections of the film showing the characters as their younger selves almost become another movie, though you know they're headed somewhere specific.

FS: Exactly. I like the way you're drawn into that past part of the story and almost forget the other one for a minute. You throw a whole other color on the emotion that you're experiencing—from both the older person remembering and the younger one experiencing.

CF: The pub culture is central here, with so many of the characters' memories tied to it. But those memories seem to be mostly the men's, though Amy and other women do appear in the scenes.

FS: I think the way it works in most of those pubs is that the guys go over there and the women go over here. So, the guys stand around the bar and do guy stuff, and the women sit at tables. It's very family-oriented too: kids go as well. I don't think the US or Australia has an equivalent. In Australia, women weren't allowed in the men's bars until 1976, when I think two women actually chained themselves to the foot rail.

CF: How do you see class working in the film?
FS: Well, the characters are all from East London: they're of a lower class—though the distinctions are sort of changing. It even happened in acting. Michael Caine, Terence Stamp, and Tom Courtenay were probably the first to be allowed to use their actual accents. All the actors there are taught what's called received English, the proper way of talking, and that's how all English films were, before them. That's made it possible for a whole generation of actors to act in films and plays about their own lives. Margate, for example, or Southgate, another resort, is where the working class go; the rich go to Brighton. The people who retire to Margate seem to go there quite young, at sixty-two or something, though they look like they're seventy-five. They're out to get the sea air, and you see them, dressed in woolen clothing, sitting in their deck chairs. And that's part of what the film's about: that's where they go for their Sunday outings, if they're lucky enough to have a car. That whole business of picking hops, that's something they all did, but it's their holiday. Not the picking, but it got them out in the country and kind of camping. So, for him to want to go to Margate is pretty creepy.

CF: To do anything other than work, they have to travel.
FS: Yes, well, their life is contained in that one area, but to go to places like Margate or to the home (where June lives), that's definitely a schlep.

CF: The journey back in time takes us to World War II. How were you thinking about the war as backdrop?
FS: Oh, that memorial! That's one thing I didn't actually do in the film, show the difficulty of finding that memorial. It's so perverse. There's no beautiful sweep up to it; you have to go through twenty suburban streets, and then you're lucky if you can find it because there're no signs. In the book, there's this whole thing that they can keep seeing it but can't get to it: in the sweep of the film, that was like one frustration too many. That generation was defined by that war, having fought in it, and having friendships bonded and friendships lost, only going through plenty—I made a film called *Plenty!*—in 1953. It took that long before England started going through good times again.

CF: How has your understanding of the process of filmmaking changed over the years?

FS: If I do an autobiography, it'll be called "The Films I Didn't Get to Make." And that could be more interesting than the ones I did. For a while I was able to make films that were not seemingly commercial in the mainstream. But over the last nine or ten years, that's not possible anymore. That's because of the general attitude of the studios, and specific individuals no longer being there, leading to corporatization. Now the costs of marketing have become more expensive than the film in some cases. Therefore, that's almost negated a whole area of filmmaking. So it's gone to $80 million and up (international, high action, not hard-to-follow dialogue), or each of the companies has formed what they now call "classics" divisions, where they make films for $12 million or less. The more they can make them for less, the more they're actually doing that.

So, any time that you're in a middling budget picture with interesting subject matter, they're not doing those pictures anymore. If you're making a $25 or $30 million picture, you're still going to have to spend $50 million, or whatever the figure is, to release it. That's one of the factors that has sort of made those pictures disappear—and me with them! If I was making *Six Degrees of Separation* today—which I made for $16 million (in 1993)—I would not get $16 million. I would get $8 million, if I was lucky. And so I wouldn't be able to make the picture.

So I have to go straddle two worlds, go back into independent filmmaking. I've found one or two mainstream films lately, but they almost always come crashing down. I was going to do *Don Quixote* with John Cleese and Robin Williams, but it was $16 million. And so, although we got money from foreign sources, we couldn't get any out of America because, they said, it was "episodic."

CF: Most US movies are episodic.

FS: Shhh! Don't tell them that! In fact, I was doing *The Shipping News* for a while, but I was doing it with John Travolta, and with his expenses, it was up around $55 million. But they didn't want to do that book for that money; they wanted to make a more conventional story if they were going to spend so much. Or, I was doing *I Was Amelia Earhart*, a script I had done, a beautiful piece. Even working very cleverly, it would have cost about $30 million. It needs a romantic sweep to show her joy of flying. You don't pull that out of a hat: you've gotta wait for the light and the conditions (to shoot). But they wanted to rewrite the script for $20 million. No, then it's not *that* script; it's *this* script. Then that went away. The trouble is, if you don't hook them in on a certain scale, they can dispense with a picture too easily. They put it out there and put a minimum amount of advertising into it. If the public picks it up, as you're witnessing with *In the Bedroom*, suddenly it's terrific. But for an *In the Bedroom*, how many pictures did Miramax dump? They put all their eggs in one basket. That breaks your heart: if you get to make the picture, then it gets killed in theaters.

The world I want to go back to is one much like the one I had (for *Last Orders*). I had complete control. Yes, the money didn't turn up when I was shooting, and yes, I only had $9 million, and yes, I only had forty-two days to shoot it. But I had great actors who came and wanted to act: they were playing parts that were in their very souls, and they were excited to act with one another. Even the young people: they're going to be the Michael Caines and Helen Mirrens of the future. They came so full of energy. It was raining and cold, and, when a bit of sun peeped out, there they were in their thin summer shirts and dresses. They'd plop down in the mud and pretend it was hot out. And I was able to give what I can give.

When I did commercials, I was quite arrogant. I thought of it as: when you came to me, I always knew that I was able to take you to the best place you could go, and you wanted to go there; you just didn't know it existed. As I know there are plenty of places that exist that I don't know about, that are beyond my ability or knowledge. I'm always sort of scratching to get up there. I know that, but a lot of people (in the film business) don't know that. And they're so scared of it that they try to pull you down to their level. Although they hire you, they don't let you do what you do. I kind of vowed never to do that again, and, to that end, I've written a number of projects, two originals, two from novels, and one from a play, all of which I'm trying to get made.

CF: It sounds like you have a lot in the pipeline.
FS: Well, the other thing is, you've got to live. In the last nine years, since *Six Degrees*, I only did two (films) for which I really got paid, and then you go and do a project like *Last Orders*, which you love, but you don't really get paid much for that. If the opportunity comes along to get a bit of money and it's a good thing, then you sort of take that chance because that's going to buy you the time to do the other stuff. The stupid thing to do is someone else's passion project, where you don't get the money or the power, but that's another story. The joy of doing something like *Last Orders*, it's fantastic. You can feel it on the set every day.

Fred Schepisi on *Last Orders*

Tom Ryan / 2002

Previously unpublished. Printed by permission of the author.

Tom Ryan: There's a line about you in the *Sight & Sound* review of *Last Orders* which describes you as "an Australian-born Hollywood director."
Fred Schepisi: (laughs) Really?

TR: Is that how you see yourself now?
FS: No, I live in New York. I try to get back to Melbourne as much as I can. I used to do postproduction here when I could. It all gets very confusing sometimes. You're here because of personal reasons . . . But really you are wherever your films are being made. And I think that, in a strange kind of way, we're the modern circus people.

Michael Caulfield wrote a wonderful little song called "Celluloid Gypsies" for a party we had on *Jimmie Blacksmith*. It's a good song. But that's about the truth of it, and it's hard for it to be any other way. It's hard on everybody, your family especially.

TR: Why *Last Orders* at this point in your career?
FS: I was preparing for *Don Quixote*, and Elisabeth Robinson, who was working with me, said, "You should read this book. I think it's right up your alley." I did and together we set about trying to get it made . . .

The humanity of it is what appealed most to me. I don't see it as about the end of life. I see it as a celebration of life in all its wonderful complexity. It's as much about them when they're young as it is about them at this stage of their lives.

I like going into little worlds. They don't always have to be little. Bermondsey is not a place we all know. We think we do because we've seen all the characters as comic figures or gangsters or cockneys or something, but we haven't really got into the heart and soul of the reality of that place. If you do, you get to discover a world you really didn't know about. And what do you always do when you discover that?

You discover yourself. You always get a surprise at the commonality of things. I guess I saw a lot of that in this.

TR: You picked a really difficult book to . . .
FS: I did, didn't I?

TR: It goes all over the place. It must have seemed daunting when you took it on?
FS: The first thing was to find a film equivalent to the book's structure. The book is accused of being another *As I Lay Dying*, but that's nonsense.

TR: But Graham Swift cites that as his inspiration, doesn't he?
FS: He does, yes. It's structurally similar, but that's all. The book's very internal, and each chapter has a different character's name. It's from his point of view, and it's his musings. It's a little difficult to get into until you get used to it. It took me a long time to find a film equivalent. I wrote many drafts. Swifty and Elisabeth Robinson gave me notes, and we talked about it a lot. In that case, it was probably fortunate that I didn't get the money too early because I could put the script down for four or five months and go away and do other things. And then rediscover it. It was not easy at all.

The approach we took is like what you and I were doing before you started the interview. We were sitting and talking. You said you were wondering on the way here what my new place is like compared to the place I lived in before, in the street next to yours. And then I brought up Peter Beilby [a former Schepisi colleague at The Film House and a former editor of *Cinema Papers*], who is now living up the road from you. And you were at university with him. So basically, in telling one story we went into five or six time zones which were all informing the story we were telling, but it didn't seem like we were not telling a straightforward story.

The whole film is based on that principle: it's the verbal storytelling principle. That's why I don't play music from the period unless it's generic to the scene. I don't show you period prams or posters to tell you where you are because it's not important.

What's important is what happened in the past which is what's influencing the present. Everything's accurate, so accurate that you don't even have to think about it. You get on with it; you stay in the emotional life of the story content. That was the principle I followed. Once you find that, then you can go somewhere. You can start to play games.

But that's not enough either. You've gotta have some tensions running through; you've gotta have some mysteries, some things to pull you through, and I hint at them very early. Not overtly necessarily—like, somebody says *that*, so you know *this* . . . boom, boom! . . . like you would in a mystery. But you see people behaving strangely. What you're hearing isn't what's actually being felt. Like cutting to Tom Courtenay when David Hemmings is speaking or by watching Tom Courtenay go "Uhhhr!" when Ray Winstone starts to say something. You go, "What's going on here? Will I find out?" And then there's the thing about the money and Amy and the kid. Then there's the surprise with the Ray Winstone character . . .

TR: Except that in the book, you know about Vince early on. Is this another one of the mysteries you're talking about?
FS: It's completely restructured from the book so that you've got something pulling you forward, something you want to know. You know there are clues being tossed out, and you've got to listen and keep listening . . . I think there's one or two scenes by the riverbank in the book—I can't really remember—and that's one of the three through-lines in the film that give you a lot of information that you can't otherwise get. But really what it's doing is telling you about those two people, and you can see what they mean to one other.

TR: It's the first film you've done without Ian Baker. You must have felt like you were being unfaithful.
FS: (laughs) He'd had a rough journey. We had six pictures go down on us, six major pictures. And it wasn't like they just didn't happen: we were working on them. We were actually fourteen weeks into preproduction on *Don Quixote*: design and costumes, set designs, we were already on location. The same kind of thing with *The Shipping News*: we did all the location surveys and worked out a whole attack on the picture.

So he lost a lot of jobs because he was hanging out for me. He'd ring me up and say, 'Are we definitely happening?' and I'd say, 'Yes, we're happening,' and so he'd drop the job he'd been offered and then, of course, we wouldn't happen.

Queen of the Damned was being shot in Australia, and he was going to get "full money" for it—there is no such thing as full money, you know—and I couldn't stare him in the face one more time and say, "Look, I'm telling you, this is happening," because the financing was coming from six different sources and it had changed three times in a month. I was pretty nervous and while it was alright for *me* to go and take another risk, I said, "If I were you, I'd take the other job and make a bit of money."

TR: The other side of that is that you're working with a new cinematographer and that positive things can result.
FS: Well, I can tell you that, right across the board, with one exception, there's nobody working on the film that I'd worked with before, aside from the editor, Kate Williams, who had been assistant editor on *I.Q.* and a very assistant editor

on *Six Degrees*. She'd done a number of independent films in the interim as an editor.

Elisabeth chose a company in England to help get the money. I went with it because these are people who work in that much lower budget area. So I figured that they would know how to do it and that I'd better get dragged back into it if I was going to get to do all the projects that I wanted to do . . .

My line on the film was always, "We're making a $23 million picture. I don't want anyone to think we're making a $9 million picture, which was what it was when we started. So you're not gonna cut costs. You're gonna work out how, with the missing millions, we can make that picture at this price."

That was the attitude at all times. Tim Harvey, the production designer, did a brilliant job. Really brilliant. If you look around the picture, you might say that it looks pretty small—you know, four guys going to Margate. But you're also at war in the desert; you're on ships exploding; there's stuff going on all over the place. You're in nineteen different time periods, and they all just flick by. But if they're on the screen for just one second, you still had to create all that, build it all. If you'd shot eight minutes of film, it wouldn't have cost you much less than doing fifteen seconds. So it was quite an enterprise.

TR: What kind of look overall were you after?
FS: Always in the now! Neither with sound nor photography did I want to be playing gimmicks. You know, saturating the film or desaturating the film, making it brown to do different time periods, 'cause you'd go bloody nuts in the end. But, subtly, it is the lighting of the period, not the cinema lighting of the period but the actual lighting of the period. You know, all those old globes that had the shades over them. It doesn't affect daylight; daylight hasn't changed, unless there's smog or something.

So there were subtle differences, but it was the reality of every situation that we were after, the reality with a bit of an artistic touch.

TR: There's a real emphasis in the film on group shots and the emotional effect that goes with that: like the shot of them all at the bar or in the car . . .
FS: Yeah. It's 'cause they're all equal. Actually, I usually use CinemaScope, or anamorphic, or whatever the hell you want to call it, 2.24. The only film I didn't use it for was *The Devil's Playground*, where we used just ordinary wide screen. Because you can do that, you can do whole groups and you can narrow down to one, by how you move the camera, how you move in or slide over (gesturing). You're editing without editing. You can open the screen right up, or you can pull it right down to that side or that thing or behind something, or adjust the focus of the lenses. It's a dynamic frame, but more than that it's an emotional frame. A lot of people don't

use it, particularly on dialogue films because they don't know how to use the other space, but if you're using it emotionally it's a great thing to do.

In *The Devil's Playground*, we shot a scene that was a wake. Everybody clapped at the rushes. This often happens. Then they see it in the cut and they say, "How boring!" And you have to sit back and go "What the hell did I do wrong?" What it was—and I kind of knew it at the time—I knew that Arthur Dignam, the guy who was having the trauma at this wake, was the force of the scene. And you must never leave him. So you start close on Arthur [Schepisi cups his hands to make a screen shape] and you come out and you discover all the others, and the camera moves all around and comes in close to you and goes away from you and then goes all the way back and sits down again. But there are one, two, three, four, five other characters—I can't remember how many—who are all important because what he's saying is having a major impact on them, and the impact it's having on them is telling you a lot about him.

It was my first film, and I wanted to be sure. So I shot his reaction and the reaction of two guys over there and one over here. The editor, Brian Kavanagh, and I were seduced, because they were fantastic reactions and absolutely important. Using them punched the whole thing up. You don't use them much, but the scene died—the force of the scene was taken out because we were watching what the peripheral people were doing. So when you kept it in one shot as a group, you stayed in this guy's anguish and agony and your view could pick which person you wanted to look at and see how this was affecting them without ever losing that person. Then they clapped again.

Probably that lesson is with me all the time. A film like this isn't about individuals; it's about the group and how necessary the people in the group are to one another. It's the currents that are flowing between them at all times. It's never about what's being said, as Johnny Guare said about *Six Degrees of Separation*.

TR: When I think of *Six Degrees of Separation*, I actually think group shots and moving camera as well. The people in the apartment, the things around them . . .
FS: You can do really close group shots with anamorphic, can't you? You can do a close shot with four people. And you can just see the electric currents running between them across the screen. He's saying that, and these two are looking at one another. This one's going, "Oh, my God!" And it's a fantastic thing, although probably not so good for television. That's why I'm waiting till we get that great big, flat widescreen.

TR: Why didn't *Last Orders* do the kind of business it deserved at the box office?
FS: It did alright here in Australia, where it was released exactly the way it should have been, with a reasonable amount of publicity and at a time that made sense.

In England, it was part of a sale-and-release-date arrangement, which came with the distributor who, frankly, had very little experience [Metrodome Distribution]. I found out recently that as part of the arrangement, someone was supposed to pay them 600,000 quid and they didn't. So I guess that had something to do with the way it was released.

They wanted to release it in January, and I said, "Why would you want to do that? You've got *Gosford Park*; you've got *In the Bedroom* . . ." There were four films that came out at the same time, all competing for the same audience. They said, "Oh, this'll make a million pounds." I said, "Well, why are you excited about that? In England, the film should take five to ten million pounds. Why don't you release it in April and get rid of all this other competition? Don't compete for an audience that only comes out rarely."

Oh, the reasons! The PR people said this, the PR people said that. It was bullshit. You have to educate this audience to come out of their houses. I'd helped them design the advertising campaign; I'd helped them design the poster. But what they did was so off the mark, it was unbelievable. I could not convince them to change the date or their attitude. I said, "Why are you doing this?" They said, "Oh, when we come out, we'll get the overflow from the other films." Why would we want the overflow from them? Why don't we get the whole thing? Then I saw a memo they put out saying, "Oh God, we're up against the juggernaut of *Gosford Park*." Wasn't this a picture you said didn't matter? "The juggernaut"!? I honestly didn't get it.

In the week we opened, the marketing manager went to Universal in America for a study program. The head of distribution went to France for two weeks, and the head of the company took elective surgery. That was, like, in the week leading up to the opening.

TR: So they'd decided that it wasn't going to work?
FS: Ah, I think they're just very small and very English. Really, it makes me angry. You've only got so much power. You know you're right, and there's only so much persuasion you can use.

In America, they wanted to come out in February. Why would you do that? You've got an ensemble piece that's got no specific stand-out performance that you hang your hat on. Why not wait until April, when all the big stuff is over and you're the only picture in the market-place? Why would you put yourself into that competition? Then they decided that they would go for Academy Awards. To which I said, "Why would you do that?" Then they said that, because they'd done it with *Pollock* (2000), they would release only in California for one week to qualify. I said, "If you're gonna do it, if you really believe in it, then you should do it in New York and California and maybe Chicago, and put money behind it because money's what gets you to the Academy." "No, no. We know the strikes." "But you're ignoring the differences between the competition last year and this year." "No, no. We're right." They did it.

We won an award in Los Angeles, the National Board of Review Ensemble Award. End of story. Now we are no longer eligible for anything. So the New York awards come out. Nothing about us. So people go, "Oh, well. Must be a fluke." And they start to ignore you. Helen Mirren starts to win for *Gosford Park*. Now we are negated. I had critics ringing me up going, "What the fuck's going on? We can't vote for your picture. We want to vote for it, but you're not eligible." Pssshhh. Gone!

So then the perception is you're a dud, and you're gone. Now of course they go, "Well, we're not gonna spend any money because we're not gonna get an award." And you go, "What the fuck is that about?" Ah, honestly.

Fred Schepisi on *It Runs in the Family*

Tom Ryan / 2003

Previously unpublished. Printed by permission of the author.

Tom Ryan: The screening of *Last Orders* at Toronto led you to *It Runs in the Family*.
Fred Schepisi: Yeah, somebody involved in the Douglas company was there, saw the film with all the older people in it and, you know how it happens, suddenly I was the old geezers' director. You know, "Kirk Douglas: old geezer! Fred Schepisi: good idea." (laughter)

TR: So Michael Douglas has the script. He's approved you. You come on to the project. The cast is already in place?
FS: No. Not entirely. There was the suggestion that his son might be doing it. I've also gotta go and meet his dad to find out if he can speak clearly enough and if he has enough strength to do the picture. Meet his son, test his son, see if he's okay or if there's enough potential there for me to bring him up to scratch before we start. It was all done on that basis. If it was an Olympic event, I'd have to get ten points for degree-of-difficulty: a guy who can't talk, a guy who can't act, and a guy who's the producer. From the outside, at least, that's really how it would have seemed.

TR: Did you do much rewriting?
FS: There was a lot of rewriting. When I was sent it for Michael and Kirk to play, I said to Michael, "Where's your part?" It was very minimal. Most of Kirk's part was there and all of Cameron's, so I said that, if they were all going to do it, it needed proper balancing-out. "You and your dad need to be put into situations where we can play with it. Otherwise, what the hell are we doing? And how will we get people to want to go to see it, apart from the fact that it's an interesting story in general?" So there was rewriting to spread the story across all of the characters.

TR: So, for example, did you write the Seder scene, or was it there to begin with?
FS: No, no. There is some rewriting in the Seder scene, but it's basically what it was.

TR: I'm just trying to pin down the stuff you might have added to flesh out the Michael Douglas role.
FS: Right. I think the scene in the park. The rent strike scene was new, some of the scenes in his office. The incorporation of Cameron into the fishing boat scene was new.

TR: So was Jesse Wigutow involved in this too?
FS: We were doing it together.

TR: So you were following your usual method of sitting around the table and . . . ?
FS: And another writer came in for certain things, like writing the funeral speech.

TR: Can I ask who?
FS: Yeah, you can.

TR: And will you tell me? [Donald Sutherland, a Schepisi house-guest in Melbourne at the time of the interview, enters room left and plays disbelieving: 'You got to make another film!?' Banter ensues.]
You were talking about the other writer and were about to tell me his name.
FS: Donald Margulies [a playwright who wrote *Dinner with Friends*—turned into a telemovie directed by Norman Jewison—and worked on the TV series, *Once and Again*]. There were bits from all of us.

TR: You also brought in Ian Baker and editor Kate Williams . . .
FS: Yeah.

TR: To what extent did you feel like a director for hire in a way that maybe you hadn't before?
FS: Well, I have before. When you take less money and you take on a passion project, that's when you should have control. In this case, I kind of figured this going in and realized as I went along that what my role here was to interpret their dream.

TR: I really meant the question more in relation to your coming into the project and maybe being stuck with things that you might. . . . You don't have to answer this if you don't want to.
FS: I wouldn't have done the film if I didn't believe that Kirk would be clear and strong enough to do it. I wouldn't have done the film if I didn't believe that Cameron would come up trumps. I wouldn't have done it because I think it wouldn't have been fair to Cameron. It would have been absolutely cruel to him because he was going to be compared to two of the most polished actors of their generations.

You can get somebody to be good and raw, but he had to be more than that. I wouldn't have done it if Kirk was diminished. I just think that would have been ridiculous.

Beyond that, or when I knew that was achievable, while I knew that I was putting a lot of myself into it, I knew that I was also really interpreting their dream.

TR: It's hard to resist the sense that we're watching the off-screen Douglas dynasty meshing with the on-screen one. Were you conscious that there might be problems with the audience confusing these?
FS: I think every one of us was aware that there could be pitfalls. Everyone spent time examining what they might be so as to try to avoid falling into them. Just having the family together alone for that long, even without the extenuating circumstances of making a film is a pretty big ask. The extraordinary thing is that there was never one cross word the whole time. It was extraordinary.

Somebody said at the end of the first week, "This is too much family." And everybody began to run to their various corners. But the expression of it or the recognition of it took away whatever might be the problem. As the producer, Michael was very nervous about his dad's strength, very nervous about his son's newness. So there was a lot of pressure on him.

TR: There's a sense in which the film really does draw upon the talents and off-screen reputations of each of the members of the family. Like Cameron Douglas, who I understand does a lot of DJ-ing in New York.
FS: Yeah. A lot of people misunderstand this. Most of what's in the film was written way before the Douglases ever saw it. The whole part for Cameron is completely as it was before any Douglas became involved. Much of the part for Kirk—including the Viking funeral, which several people seem to think is some kind of homage to the fact that he was in a film called *The Vikings*—was written way before Kirk Douglas ever came into consideration. The only part that's dramatically changed is, in fact, Michael's part.

Every one of them understood that what they were doing was playing fictional characters and, like all good actors, they drew on themselves, their own experience and research. In this case, the research was very close to their own lives to a certain extent. But none of them made the mistake of confusing it with real life or of taking any cheap shots, and it just brought another reality to the film. Not *the* reality. They were playing fictional characters. Always. There's a really strong differentiation.

TR: You've got a large family. When you say there's a bit of yourself there . . .
FS: Sure.

TR: . . . so quite apart from structuring it and whatever, emotionally you must have been seeing your own world as well?
FS: Absolutely. Difficulties within a family that reach through all the generations. I think everybody has it and you've gotta put yourself into something like that. There's a little bit of writing from me in there, here and there.

TR: Did you ever have any problems with the cast—or the producer—over the way a sequence should be shot? I mean, beyond the normal?
FS: No. That doesn't mean that the producer didn't have a number of ideas. And it doesn't mean that Kirk didn't have fifteen pages of notes every day. Absolutely. That kind of enthusiasm at eighty-six is admirable beyond belief, but it's kind of great to see the way he kept wanting to contribute. I really like that.

TR: When I hear that, it blows me away. This man is eighty-six, and he's conscious of posterity. It's obviously really important to him.
FS: Yeah.

TR: What is it that "runs in the family"?
FS: High energy, nervous energy, personality similarities. There are differences between them; they're quite different characters who come from quite different places but are very reflective of the difference between the generations. So a lot of the work is done for you.

TR: I understand that the film was going to be called *A Few Good Years* . . .
FS: Yeah. It started as *A Smack in the Puss* and everybody misunderstood that. Then it became *A Smack in the Kisser*, which I liked a lot. Then it was *A Few Good Years*, which is kind of plaintive. But research made that appear to mean that Kirk only had a few good years left, as opposed to you only getting a few good years in life. Then we tried a couple of other titles that weren't available. And *It Runs in the Family* was an available title.

TR: I guess the TV series *All in the Family* is old enough now for an American audience not to be confused by the similarity . . . I mean, *It Runs in the Family* has a bit of a sitcom sound to it.
FS: Ohh. Yeah, but what's a good title? The title of a successful film.

TR: Your last two films convey an overarching concern with mortality. *A Few Good Years*, like *Last Orders*, catches that in a way that the other titles don't.
FS: I think so too. The world and America misconstrued that.

TR: All of your films have a strong sense of location. Now this is a New York film and you get a sense of where the characters live, but you seem to withhold information about precisely where they do, although maybe a local would recognize the signs better than I do?

FS: I think the important thing is that one's a genteel world—generally upper East Side; one's a kind of downtown, bohemian world—a loft-living world, although these days that can be anywhere; and one's a university world—downtown, although Hunter College is uptown. I think the look of the worlds is clearly delineated. Time spent physically locating them is time we didn't have. They are actually located, but it's not important. The contrast is what matters.

TR: And the Claremont County is in Connecticut? Does such a place exist?
FS: Claremont County? Where did you get that? (disbelieving)

TR: There's a sign above a building as they drive into the place for the Claremont County Library.
FS: Oh, yeah. That's in Connecticut.

TR: I know you spend a lot of time in New York. Do you feel like a New Yorker? Are you comfortable, at home, there?
FS: Absolutely.

TR: Michael Douglas talks in the press materials about the way the project was fuelled by the events of September 11. Did you talk about that at all during the production?
FS: Oh, yeah. And whether the specific subject should be included in the film. Ah, it's a slice-of-life film about generational differences between families. It's not trying to be about anything more than the humor and the heartache, and that's what it should be.

TR: But when you see New York now, it resonates differently. Especially when you know a film was made after the event. There's nothing anybody can do to change that.
FS: No, no.

TR: So you look at the city and it's poignant in a way it hasn't been before, which lends a dimension to *It Runs in the Family* that might not have been there were it not for September 11. You've got the feeling there, but it adds another layer.
FS: Oh yeah, I'm sure that's true.

TR: I get the sense that you've organized the film around a series of rituals, which you also did with *Last Orders*. That it's there that one can find a structure for the film.

FS: No, not really. It's just a family story. It's not the same thing. Yes, there's a Seder dinner, which could be Christmas dinner. It's meant to be any family dinner: Christmas, Easter, it could be a wedding. Any time you bring a family together. ... The whole point of the first section is to slowly take you through who all these people are and bring them together. And you identify with whoever you most relate to in the first scene. Then you wonder where it's going to after that, and whoever you identify with is who you'll probably follow from that point. There are all the things that just happen in real family life. Everybody's just trying to be themselves in their own world, and in the end you should be coming to terms with who the rest of the family is.

TR: Yes, but the way you use the baseball game suggests a ritual. The game itself is a ritual and so is watching the game on TV or going to it.

FS: And the son who should have gone too. Yeah. He'd said he was busy. That's meant to point to a similarity between all of them. They all like to do that. But they want to do it themselves, in their own ways. It's not so much a ritual as an everyday reality of their lives. It's like the [Australian Rules] footy here in Australia.

TR: Yeah, but that's it. The baseball is like the footy. It's central to the culture of the place. It's like a walk in Central Park means something specifically New York. You can go for a walk in the Tuilleries, but it's not the same, or that opening shot of the skyline, instantly recognizable. It becomes as if the city as a place defines its inhabitants and what I was wondering with that question about rituals was to what extent your sense of New York was defining the way the characters behave or who they are—you know, like the shot through the window in Michael Douglas's office is unmistakably New York, or the glimpse of the river through the window in their apartment . . .

FS: The film's very New York and the sense of place is very important to who they are. And where they are is too. He works in that area up there but lives downtown because that's where he wants to live. He doesn't really want to be in that other world. It's a very important element of it. The worlds they're trapped in as opposed to the worlds they want to be in is very much a part of it.

TR: Music is a really strong presence in the film as well, defining the generations. And you get a sense of the characters locking themselves inside their own music. Is that you choosing it?

FS: Actually Michael and I and Paul Grabowsky and Sue Jacobs, the music supervisor, were involved in that. It was always very generational—four generations rather than three—and it tells you a hell of a lot.

TR: Is the fact that you're using the Diana Krall version of "Where or When" over the end credits a way of you privileging that era?
FS: No, not really. In fact, we had a number of ways to go at the end. But it's such a powerful and emotive piece. We used it for the waltz, and it was, in fact, Kirk's idea to be singing it. We thought it was such a good idea that we picked up on it at the end with a contemporary version. It just felt like the right thing to do. We certainly weren't picking one period over another. But we also planted music all over the film, so we could have actually gone out with Paul's composed music as well. So it was 50/50.

TR: Just listening to you while you were talking then, it became clear that it's as if there's two of you when you work. There's the you that's really rigorous and concerned with structure and the way things lock together. And then there's the you that says, 'It just felt like the right thing to do.'
FS: Oh, yeah. It's always gotta feel that way. Always. The structure, the style, the discipline are the rules you run by and that you judge things by, but the heart has always got the last say. Always. Must be. Only by understanding all the rules can you set your feelings free. That's very important.

TR: There's a sense of things left unfinished in the film.
FS: Absolutely.

TR: I don't think I've ever seen a film where so many threads are left dangling. If there were one or two, you say, "Somebody got careless there." But this is like a theme. What happens to Kate, for example? She's picked up by the cops, but I don't remember seeing her or hearing anything about her after that.
FS: You actually hear a hell of a lot about her. A hell of a lot. When she's arrested, he's saying, "I'm sorry. I'll do something about it. I'll help you." And she says, "I never wanna see you again." When they're in the jail, he says to his parents, "There's this girl. You've gotta help her." The parents say, "Don't worry, she'll be alright. There's no warrant. She'll be fine." The mother says, "Don't worry. We'll take care of her." All of that is there. But the strength of everything else that is going on is pulling your attention. You would be amazed if you actually studied how much of that information is there. But there's a lot going on.

I did not want to wrap up every goddamned thing. I did not want to have resolutions because that's not slice-of-life. Yes, the girl was going to be okay, but do we have to go and see her being okay? The guy says, "Jesus, I wish I'd looked after her the way that you looked after your girl." Should he pick up the phone to find out if she's alright? She wouldn't even fucking talk to him. She never wants to have anything to do with him ever again.

But the story there is that he blew it. The real story is: does he recognize that? What happens is that you as a viewer go, "I'm interested in that girl. And I wanna know what happens to her." Not to be tough about it, but it's not the movie's problem. It's yours.

TR: Fair enough.

FS: A lot of people haven't noticed that by the way . . . Is the marriage resolved? No, it's not resolved. But it is resolved. They're both saying, "I love you," but you know they're in deep shit and they've gotta go and work it out. What's gonna happen with the old man? Is he going to make it a permanent arrangement and hang around the house? What are they gonna do with him?

That's the point of the picture. You can come to some kind of accommodation of your family, but it isn't gonna be all neat and nice and fabulous. It's bloody gonna be tough to keep that accommodation going. You're all so different, and you're all gonna still irritate the shit out of one another and still demand things out of one another than none of you can deliver. That's the whole rationale for the film.

TR: In another film, there might have been a scene where the Michael Douglas character confronts Susie about how the panties got into his jacket. In this film, you leave it enigmatic.

FS: Well, he's like, "Don't come near me." He's worked that out. And she only did it in a fit of panic. It's amazing. You know, once again, if you ever look at the film again, you'll see what she does with the panties. She's rubbing them up his back, rubbing them on his head, practically rubbing them in his face. The guy comes in the room; she's, like, juggling the panties, "What the fuck do I do with them?" You're watching that, and I'm telling you—I do the cardinal sin of distracting you with the panties and all you're lookin' at is the bloody guy's face. She even goes (reaching out to simulate the action) and puts the panties in his pocket.

TR: I missed that.

FS: But it's there. I can choose to go "eliminate, eliminate" and zero in on that. But if I zero in on that, you're gonna say, "Oh, hang on, I know what's gonna happen here."

TR: Because you've laid it on.

FS: Yeah, I'd have laid it on. And there was no way of emphasizing it any more than going "ugh," you know. What I do is do it in a way that you kinda know that something like that might've happened. Do you deal with it? No, you don't deal with it. He's going, "Back off." He's really saying the same thing by not going, "What the hell did you put the panties in my pocket for?"

TR: Who wrote that great line that he has: "Guilt is stronger than lust"? There's no comeback to it.
FS: That was Michael's own.

TR: Little details. During the Seder, why the cutaway to the shot from outside—which you also use on other occasions—but this time with a siren?
FS: It's the city of New York. Just reminding you where you are. Downtown, New York at night, lights going on, all these microcosms happening, one here, one there, one over there.

TR: So it's the *Rear Window* principle at work?
FS: Just putting you in a location, reminding you of where you are . . .

TR: I found it a really touching shot. The siren did it. The shot from outside like that has been done before to establish the warmth of the family environment, whatever else is happening inside. But that siren is kind of plaintive . . .
FS: But it's New York. Downtown New York. [imitates siren sound, or at least I think that's what he's doing] It's what's going on. The world is going on, helter skelter all of the time while that small family is together.

TR: There's a fragility in it, though, that's reminding us as we watch that as soon as one of them steps outside they're back into this wilderness. I find little things like that really touching, and I'm interested in chasing the reasons why you did it that way rather than some other way—'cause it seems just right.
FS: Yeah.

TR: What about the name of the boat they go fishing in? Arbitrator.
FS: Aha. It was in the script. Jesse did that.

TR: In my naivety I think, "Oh, maybe it was just the boat they chose." You need a boat; you get one from nearby, and it happens to be called Arbitrator. But it's actually that kind of attention to detail.
FS: [laughs, patiently] It was in the original.

TR: Was the "ask me anything scene" in the original script?
FS: Yeah.

TR: Do you like the Grombergs?
FS: Yeah. I just find them like a normal family.

TR: Yeah. But some people you like and some people you don't. Are there things about them that you have a personal investment in, if that's not too personal a question?
FS: Um. Yes, there are. Are they me? No. Are there elements of me or elements of my family? Absolutely. There are lines from my life that have been incorporated there. But I don't know how to answer that question. They are your family. So you've got to learn to deal with them and understand them and tolerate them. But also you like them at the same time as they annoy the shit out of you. They are who you are. You're part of them.

TR: I haven't seen it, but I've read that the trailer for the film makes it look a bit like *Grumpy Old Men*.
FS: I didn't think so. It's been changed a couple of times since I saw it. It should really be for all the generations.

TR: Do you ever get any say in it?
FS: Oh, you get a certain amount, but . . .

TR: Because your background is advertising.
FS: I know. I know. I had some say at the start, but then they made changes. . . .

TR: So now it's on to *Empire Falls*?
FS: Yeah. It's a three-hour film made for cable in the US . . . I can tell you're really at odds with my movie.

TR: I'm not really at odds with it. I . . . Okay, I said to Debi [my wife] straight after I saw it that it didn't move me on the first viewing, but I really admired things about it like the way it was structured. And I loved its generosity towards all of the characters. But I wanted to be touched by it a lot more, and I reckon there are two scenes that pushed me away. The one I mentioned before with Cameron Douglas, for whatever reason. The other was that I didn't believe the wife's reaction to the perceived infidelity.
FS: Oh, but people never do what you think they'll do.

TR: Okay. And I like that. But she's a psychologist. So she knows that you have to allow people to speak. She passes judgement . . .
FS: Psychologists are, first of all, absolutely the worst with themselves. Always. So

I think that's truer than any other reaction would have been ... I find people react to this picture entirely subjectively. They relate it to their own particular experiences or expectations. I've had audiences—after the previews we did—saying that Cameron's character was bullshit, that no kid reacts like that. And then we had others stand up and say, 'What? Are you fuckin' crazy?'

TR: So is there anything you would do differently?
FS: There's one key fault. The film opens up with a series of scenes in which you meet each of the main characters. Then that's repeated with scenes where more information comes out about them, all leading up to the Passover Seder. You get the sense that nobody's been looking forward to it.

I thought that would work, but it now seems to me that the apprehension about the dinner isn't enough and maybe gets lost a little in the process of introducing all these different characters. What I should have done was have a little more specificity in there. "If I talk to him tonight, I'm gonna thplzz!" Or "If he brings up that shit, thplzz!" So that you build a bigger expectation and tension as you move towards the dinner.

TR: So it's about the set-up not working as well as it might have ...
FS: It would all be the same, except the content would express the apprehension more clearly and increase your curiosity about where it's all leading. And to bring out more of the family tension, just in small remarks, so that you want to get to the dinner. And you're thinking, "This is gonna be a beautie," as opposed to more passively, interestingly but passively, getting to know each character. It should have had the double thing to help people to know where it's all going, to appreciate why they're watching it. It makes audiences more comfortable if they know they're going somewhere. And within that, you can surprise and delight.

TR: And that would then affect the entire film.
FS: Yes. One should learn these things before you do 'em. (laughs)

Shooting Dialogue as Action: An Interview with Fred Schepisi

Fincina Hopgood / 2011

First published in *Senses of Cinema*, October 2011. Reprinted by permission of the author.

Fred Schepisi has been writing, directing, and producing films in Australia, America, and Britain since the 1970s. Along with Peter Weir, Gillian Armstrong, and Bruce Beresford, he was a key figure in the renaissance of the Australian film industry at that time, although his latest feature, *The Eye of the Storm* (2011), is his first shot in his home country since the award-winning *Evil Angels* (1988).

Adapted by Judy Morris from a 1973 novel by Nobel Prize–winning author Patrick White, the film stars Charlotte Rampling, Geoffrey Rush, and Judy Davis and features an impressive ensemble of supporting actors including Helen Morse, Robyn Nevin, John Gaden, and Colin Friels. The film depicts the dying days of the wealthy Elizabeth Hunter (Rampling), a domineering and charming matriarch, who has summoned her expatriate children, Sir Basil Hunter (Rush) and Dorothy de Lascabanes (Davis), to her bedside in a lavish mansion in Sydney. Basil is a fading star of the British stage, while Dorothy is a penniless princess, divorced from her French husband. Tended around the clock by nurses, the bedridden Mrs. Hunter slips in and out of lucidity as she revisits moments in her past, including her experience of a destructive tropical storm.

Fincina Hopgood: What attracted you to *The Eye of the Storm*? Patrick White has a formidable reputation, and people have tried to adapt his novels before but without success.

Fred Schepisi: I had read some Patrick White: *The Tree of Man* (1955), *The Vivisector* (1970), *Voss* (1957). Not easy reads, sometimes quite rewarding. But when they came to me to talk about this film—Anthony Waddington, the producer, told me about it—I said "Patrick White—why? It's not exactly easily accessible material." He explained why, (and) I said, "Alright, that sounds fair." I like to be challenged; it gets the creative juices going. I like to learn something: if you don't know enough about something, you learn something in the process. It takes you into uncomfortable areas sometimes.

So I read the novel and really dug in. When you dig right inside Patrick White, you get an appreciation for his skill. He does sometimes—and this is heresy to some people—he does repeat himself a lot: he gets on a theme and bangs the drum a fair bit. Then he goes off into reveries and surrealist inner-life raves. They're kind of marvelous, but when you're looking at it from a film point-of-view, you're thinking, "Is that a road I'd go down, or do I take information from that?"

When they asked if I'd write it, I was fairly busy at the time, and I thought it may take me a while (and that) I didn't have that kind of time. Also, I'm not inside the material. I'm not from Sydney. Most of that world is strange to me. I felt it needed to be written by somebody who knew that world, and since he goes on a lot about (how) everybody's an actor, everybody's putting on a performance—this kind for their family, this kind for their friends, this kind for the people they work with—I thought of Judy Morris because she's an actress. She's been involved in some quite commercial projects. She's from Sydney; she's from that world. She knows the upper class and the lower class—she knows them both—and there would just be some instincts she'd be good with.

FH: Particularly since she's had that commercial aspect in her previous work [co-writing *Babe: Pig in the City* and *Happy Feet*] because one of the things that struck me is that White isn't necessarily a commercial film proposition, particularly the reputation he has for being rather misanthropic and cruel towards his characters. How does that work when the basic rule of thumb in commercial filmmaking is that one should empathize with the characters?

FS: Yeah, I hear that all the time, and I think, "Why? Who made that rule up?" Okay, it might have value, but sometimes you get engaged because somebody's the complete opposite of what you want them to be. I describe it as like going into a bar in Texas and there's a snake in the jar going "bang!" against the side of the jar, and that's fascinating (to watch) too.

FH: You've worked with leading American, British, and Australian actors. Given the caliber of the casts in your films, I suspect you must be an actors' director. Can you talk about your technique as a director, or how you work with actors when you've got such luminaries as, in this film, Charlotte Rampling, Geoffrey Rush, and Judy Davis?

FS: I've found the very best actors all want to be directed, but what they really want isn't always to be told what to do. What they really want is a sounding-board they can trust. In a way, they want someone to hold a mirror up so that—obviously they don't want to watch themselves—they know what they're doing and what direction they should be going.

They can pick up within the first set-up of shooting whether you are a sure hand and if you know what you're doing and they can trust you: that this person's going to look after me, this person's not going to let me do anything over-the-top or silly. So they can be quite relaxed and push the envelope, they can take chances, they can go further than maybe they should in the scene, knowing that, once they've gone past a certain point, I will talk to them about bringing it back so that they can find the proper height they can get something to. You find it by going past and coming back.

In regards to having a technique as a director (working with actors), that's difficult because it's absolutely different for every person. Some people need different things. Paul Newman, for instance, hated psychobabble: you know "You're a tree, let's do an improv here, let's go into a whole psychology session . . ." Paul's desire was "faster, shorter, quicker, look over here, don't do that, that's fantastic." You might say, "Your character at this point, have you thought that he might do such-and-such?," and he'll either go, "Ah yeah, great!" or he'll say, "No, no, no, but . . ." It's very, very direct communication.

FH: So you must be very good at reading people then, to work out what style's going to fit what personality?
FS: Well, it kind of comes to you. Say with Meryl Streep: you can't keep going "that's wonderful." She might have done something terrific, but another actor hasn't come up to scratch in that take, so you go over while stuff's happening and you talk to that actor. Then you just go over (to Meryl) and, as I say, stand next to her and you just shimmer! We're in this together . . .

FH: You've made two films with her, *Plenty* and *Evil Angels*. In both, she plays rather prickly characters, brittle and potentially unlikeable, so they strike me as quite brave choices for her. You talk about providing that safety net for the actors . . .
FS: Some actors you joke with all the time, some actors you don't . . . You're not always going to get on perfectly well with everybody. They can very easily (reject) your suggestions and very easily put you in a bad position, so the thing is to try to create a situation where they can give it their absolute best. But your other role is to focus all those efforts in the one direction, the world that you've created and where it's going to go, so that everybody is going in that (same) direction, not over here, not over there. No matter how brilliant it is, it's gotta be in that direction.

FH: Another significant aspect of your career is your ongoing collaboration with cinematographer Ian Baker. Is there any film you haven't worked on together?

FS: Only one: *Last Orders*. We were having a rough trot at the time, not between ourselves, but we'd had six films in a row fall over, like *Don Quixote*, (where) we were well into pre-production.[1] Then there was *The Shipping News*.[2] They were a bit soul-destroying for all of us because there's a point where you emotionally commit (to a project). You try to hold back as long as you can, but there's a certain point where you go over that line and then, when you get killed on it, it's pretty hurtful.

This film, *Last Orders*, came up and the finance just kept changing and changing and changing. It changed three times in preproduction. And Ian was offered a film at very good money, a Hollywood film, and I said, "Honestly, take the money. You've been loyal to me this whole time and lost jobs. I can't guarantee you that this film is going to happen, and I'd hate to do it to you again."

FH: So it's wonderful that you've come back together on *The Eye of the Storm*. How would you describe your working relationship with Ian? You've worked together since the 1970s. What's stayed the same; what's evolved?

FS: You should not work with the same person all the time unless they're trying to improve themselves, unless they're pushing themselves and you, and then vice versa—you've got to push them. We have, I guess, an unusual relationship. We have lots of chats beforehand, and come up with images and stuff. We used to go and look at paintings. We don't have to do that so much now, as we've done it so often. We talk about style, and so Ian likes to help get a texture across the whole film. I tend to basically pick the shots, the way things work, how I see it being edited and put together, helping things emotionally. We talk about that, but you don't know all that in advance. Then when we get there on the day, we've both got monitors, although I don't look at the actors through the monitor. I'm dealing with set-ups and he's dealing with lighting and textures across the film.

In *The Eye of the Storm*, you're in the bedroom a lot, but not too many people notice it; otherwise, it might get boring. We came up with camera moves and things that are about bringing together and then separating or irritating or reflecting. We're doing camera moves that you shouldn't do, but I'm doing them to unsettle you as the audience because that's what's happening in that room. It's giving life to what would otherwise be incredibly static.

It's under discussion all the time, and Ian gets on with the lighting while I work with the dolly grip and all of that. He'll come up and (discuss shots with me). Meantime, he's trying to change the times of day, the way the lighting is in the room—with reason, not for anything stupid. So we're working like that all the time. Then he'll come up and say, "You're behind schedule. Isn't it time for one of your famous one-shotters? This scene would be a good one to do it with."³ And I'll say, "Yeah, thanks!"

FH: So he has that pragmatic side as well as his artistic side.
FS: Exactly.

FH: *The Eye of the Storm* is a quintessentially Australian story about the legacy of the nation's colonial relationship with England, the squattocracy, et cetera. How do you see the film speaking to an international audience?
FS: I've actually run it for a few people in Los Angeles and New York. (They had) exactly the same reaction as we got here. Their train of thought went something like this: "I didn't think it would be funny. Why am I sitting here watching these assholes? Then without realizing it, I've been drawn into them and who they are, then all my emotions are being chucked up and in turmoil. I'm being taken to places I never expected to go, and I was riveted all the way." And then they talk about things in the film and very quickly they're talking about their own families. It's the same reaction in both places. If I can get that across to people, to get them to go to the film, that would be great, but I'm not sure how you do it other than word of mouth.

FH: Yes, the film taps into quite primal emotions about family, the machinations of family, and you don't have to come from an upper class family to relate to that. I think audiences will be attracted to the film because of the cast, but then there's a universality to the story once you get in there. What are the plans for an overseas release, following the film's September release in Australia?
FS: It's in the Toronto Film Festival. We've got a distributor in Canada but nowhere else yet. These days, you've got so many films being made that bloody distributors in America want to wait—see how many festivals you get in, what your reviews are likely to be—so they don't have to take a risk. And they say, "Look, it's so hard to individualize a film for an audience unless there's a real gimmick or a hook in it. So you need the reviews and the festival cred to help you sell it." But couldn't they go on their gut instinct?

FH: Toronto has been a great launchpad for Australian films. For example, after Scott Hicks's *Shine* (1996) premiered at Sundance [in January], they held it over until Toronto [in September] and got great word of mouth from there.
FS: Some festivals haven't really jumped on *The Eye of the Storm*. A French friend of mine (says that) the attitude out there at the moment is to (select) what (the festivals) think are modern films, and what they actually are is modernist films. (As opposed to) films that are, let's call them, classical, although I think this is

not at all classical, but it appears classical because I try to keep everything pretty smooth. Even though I'm thumping you into the past,[4] because it's about the characters and you're concentrating in on the characters, it seems like a classical approach no matter what I'm doing.

FH: That reminds me of a comment Geoffrey Rush made at a forum about the film at the Melbourne International Film Festival (MIFF), that your directorial style is not to leave your fingerprints on a film. As you say, you're drawn into the characters: you're not thinking, "That's a nice flourish Fred's put in there," you're actually immersed in the story. Whereas a lot of festival films are about showing off the flair of the director . . .
FS: Exactly, with shots and movements which, if you ask me, are not as good as what we're doing.

FH: And a lot of the time their technique is really sloppy.
FS: All that avant-garde bullshit, they don't know what they're doing. And it's sound too. . . . People are not quite aware of what we're doing with the sound. There's a fine line where (you think), "Do you run music through the storm, or do you just go with the storm effects?" Both were equally good. It's an extraordinary piece of music where [Mrs. Hunter, Rampling's character] starts to break down. When we got the level right, with the effects and the music all working together, every one of us who'd seen the film probably fifty times, the hair went up on the backs of our necks. We got it right; it was the right decision.

FH: That shows you how important the soundscaping is to that sequence that's completely free of dialogue.
FS: Absolutely.

FH: This is your first feature film in Australia since *Evil Angels*, although I know you've been trying to develop other projects here for some time. Do you now see yourself as being based in Australia, or would you go back overseas for the right project?
FS: My next film is in America—at least, for this week! It's *Words and Pictures*, an original screenplay, with Clive Owen. We had Julianne Moore, but, because we had her, we've now delayed the film twice, and I've said, "I'm not delaying it anymore; it's not right. We'll have to get someone else." Shooting starts in January.

I'm also working on an adaptation of Kate Grenville's novel, *The Secret River*, writing with Jan Sardi on that.[5] We've had some disagreements about approach, but the bulk of the script is there. It was just a couple of methodology things early on.

FH: There are a number of adaptations in your filmography . . . [*The Chant of Jimmie Blacksmith*, *Plenty*, *Evil Angels*, *Six Degrees of Separation*, *Last Orders*, *Empire Falls*].

FS: It takes three years to write a novel, so a lot of thought has gone into it. A lot more than what goes into most screenplays.

FH: Is there a richness to the screenplay that comes from being adapted?

FS: Yes, a complexity. A lot of people just want narrative drive. When I was showing *The Eye of the Storm* early on to some of my colleagues, they suggested taking things out because what they wanted was narrative drive. But (the essence of) Patrick White is an engagement with a whole world. I do that by not cutting to the street outside, then to the stairs, then to the room, then to the characters. I want to know what that character's thinking, what's the next moment in the story, and so I go from them to (the settings), and then you discover where (the character is), or you go to someone who's affecting them or (being affected by) them.

FH: That maintains an emotional through-line that takes you through different time zones.

FS: Exactly. How often do you see a bloody film where they cut to (for example) a circus, and there's fires, and there's jugglers, and Ferris wheels and music, and shit like that, then you finally get to the actor. I say, cut to the actor!

FH: [Local critic] Peter Craven described that really well, at the MIFF Forum, where he likened your style of filmmaking to Visconti's: one that maintains a connection with the character's thoughts from one moment to the next and isn't concerned with establishing shots.

FS: If everything is apt, absolutely apt and correct for the period and the character—you don't see anything that doesn't help that out—then you're not even conscious of it . . . That is definitely the way I work.

FH: Given that yours is such a diverse body of work across the Australian, American, and British film industries, do you see any continuity in your films or recurring themes that you are attracted to? For instance, I've described you as an actors' director.

FS: Well, I do a lot of character stories. I don't shoot dialogue the way most people shoot dialogue: you know, the medium shot, wide shot, close-up, close-up, reverse shot. Filmmakers lose their bravura when they get to dialogue scenes. I like to do things that people don't notice you're doing, bringing things into the background. I shoot dialogue as action, or probably a better description, I shoot it as emotion. In the same way that in theater you draw attention to some things and not to other things, I'm doing that all the time. It's about connections and disconnections. This whole business of "keeping the other person alive," they call it: only go to them when it actually matters. Stay on that person if that person's the force of the scene. If you want this person, you move to a position where you can bring them in or take them out. That's called grammar. That's why people don't make dialogue films: because they're boring, because they're so static. And the trick is to make them not static.

I used to be obsessed. *Plenty* has only four shots that are repeated in the whole film. I used to be that obsessed, but it's too hard. No one really gets that. But you still work on the same kind of principle to keep it alive. And character films are deeply engaging.

But you have to subjugate all the things you do to whatever the particular story or event is. *Don Quixote*, which I was going to direct, would have been a whole different experience with vistas, action, and madness. As would *Shipping News* have been, not the bland thing it ended up being. With *Last Man*,[6] I want to take you to a place you've never been in a war film. I want to put you inside that experience in a whole other filmic way, which is why we're not getting the money, because I need more money to do that. I don't want to just make a bloody war film. In a way, it will be just as much a character film.

FH: Is that project still on the table?
FS: (sighs) I'm going to give it one more run. Jonathan Shteinman, I hope—who was executive producer on this film—might help us with that, but it's a tough one.

FH: Finally, what are your thoughts on the current state of the Australian film industry now that you've come back to it after a period of time?
FS: It's become quite bureaucratic—and I'm not talking about the funding bodies—in what you're allowed to do, and not allowed to do. Rules, regulations, safety officers. There's a lot of nanny-state stuff happening.

FH: Is that different to America?
FS: Yeah, it's a little more rigid here, although some of the American scene is going that way, too. Outside of that, the crews work a couple of hours less per day than I'm used to in America, but they get as much done. Their enthusiasm and the skills they bring are really conducive to making films. I was quite thrilled with that experience, and things like make-up and hair. Those people, they work horrible hours, way longer than anyone else. But they work in collusion, also with wardrobe, because everything they do when the actors go in, that's when the character happens. I like to go to wardrobe when things are being tried on: when a dress goes on or a jacket goes on, half the character goes on. So you better be around for it.

And the people in Australia are just so helpful in pushing things forward in the right direction. That went right through the crew. I had the sound person coming up to me and saying, "That was a great take," and getting excited or letting me know when the dialogue wasn't clear . . .

FH: So everyone's looking out for the whole film, not just their own department.
FS: Yeah, which is great. The whole experience was fantastic.

Notes

1. In 1997, Schepisi was working with US producer Elisabeth Robinson on an adaptation of *Don Quixote*, with an old screenplay by Waldo Salt, starring John Cleese and Robin Williams. While this project was never realized, Robinson introduced Schepisi to Graham Swift's novel, *Last Orders*, which Schepisi went on to adapt and direct in 2001.
2. In 1998, Schepisi was originally slated to direct the adaptation of E. Annie Proulx's Pulitzer Prize–winning novel, *The Shipping News*, for Columbia Pictures, starring John Travolta, but he and the studio disagreed over key aspects of the adaptation. See Anita M. Busch, "'News' Break: Travolta Is 'Earth'-bound," *Premiere*, January 1999: http://www.reocities.com/xenu2000/archive/Premiere9901.htm. *The Shipping News* was eventually directed by Lasse Hallström, starring Kevin Spacey, and released in 2001.
3. By "one-shotters," Schepisi is referring to his preference for filming scenes—particularly dialogue scenes—in one unbroken shot, with the camera often moving slowly in, towards, and around the characters. As an example, see the extended conversation sequence in *Plenty* between Susan Traherne (Streep) and her future husband, Raymond Brock (Charles Dance), in the British embassy after the death of Susan's "husband," Tony (a fellow member of the Resistance during World War II).
4. Schepisi is referring here to the flashbacks to the island beach house and the tropical storm in *The Eye of the Storm*.
5. Jan Sardi wrote the Oscar-nominated screenplay for *Shine* (1996) and adapted Bruce Beresford's *Mao's Last Dancer* (2009) from Cunxin Li's autobiography. Sardi's screenplay was eventually developed in collaboration with Mac Gudgeon and *The Secret River* was made in 2015 as a two-part TV mini-series, directed by Daina Reid.
6. Schepisi has long been working on the Vietnam war film, *Last Man*, based on Graham Brammer's book, *Uncertain Fate*. Originally scheduled for filming in Queensland in late 2008, the film—which was to have starred Guy Pearce and David Wenham—fell over the day before production was due to begin. See Karl Quinn, "Schepisi Hoping for the Perfect Storm," *The Age*, 22 April, 2010: http://www.theage.com.au/entertainment/movies/schepisi-hoping-for-the-perfect-storm-20100421-sy7r.html. For the background to this project, see Daniel Ziffer, "Fred Schepisi's New Local Venture," *The Age*, 4 April, 2008: http://www.theage.com.au/news/film/fred-schepisis-new-local-venture/2008/04/03/1206851111212.html.

All against One and One against All: Fred Schepisi's Outsiders

Dan Callahan / 2014

First published in *Sight & Sound*, February 2014 (on-line). Reprinted by permission of the magazine.

The Australian director Fred Schepisi has been making movies for over thirty-five years, but there has been little serious analysis of his fifteen feature films either thematically or on a technical level, maybe because they seem like an impenetrably eclectic group in terms of genre. Yet Schepisi's visual style is unmistakable, and his interest in individuals facing off against a hostile world has been consistent across a wide range of genres, from the western (*Barbarosa*) to science fiction (*Iceman*), from romantic comedy (*Roxanne*) to espionage thriller (*The Russia House*) to high comedy of manners (*Six Degrees of Separation*).

Schepisi's new film, *The Eye of the Storm*, is an adaptation of Patrick White's novel headlined by a trio of tough-minded actors: Charlotte Rampling, Geoffrey Rush, and Judy Davis. It is Schepisi's first feature since maybe his lowest ebb as a director, the misguided *It Runs in the Family*, which brought together the Douglas clan, Kirk, Michael, and Michael's son, Cameron, for a kind of on-screen vacation. This film offered clear proof that Schepisi has sometimes been at the mercy of his material; he could also do nothing to salvage the misbegotten comedy, *Fierce Creatures*.

But when there is enough meat on the bones of his subject and appropriately unsentimental performers involved, Schepisi is one of the rare directors working today who can put you right inside the consciousness of drastically troubled characters. He's often at his best when looking at milieus that are slightly outside his own experience, and he flourishes with collaborators who can give him some of the specific social information he needs to illuminate the wide worlds his films take in. "I hadn't read this book, but I'd read other books of Patrick White's," says Schepisi, speaking about *The Eye of the Storm* from a conference room in New York.

He's a big, bear-like man who talks slowly and calmly, as if he has all the time in the world to get things right.

"Everybody has tried to do White's novels on screen and failed. They wanted me to write it, but I said they needed somebody who was more in that high-class Australian society and that world and all of that to write it. I can help. White sort of goes on in the book about how everyone's an actor or an actress, so I suggested they get this actress, Judy Morris, who's also a writer, to work on the script with me."

White's novel is close to six hundred pages, and at least three hundred of those pages are comprised of the thoughts of the three main characters, Elizabeth Hunter (Rampling), a rich, ruthless hedonist, and her two disappointed children, Sir Basil (Rush) and the Princess de Lascabanes (Davis). "I don't think there's any such thing as a family that isn't dysfunctional in some way or another, major or minor," says Schepisi, who cast his daughter Alexandra in the important role of Elizabeth's young nurse. "Australians have always claimed that an elite society only existed in England, but that's nonsense. There are those entitled people like Elizabeth in our world, too."

No director working today uses the widescreen 2:35:1 frame as often or as well as Schepisi. "The reason I use very wide framing is that I can shut things down or I can open things up," Schepisi says. "I can go wide to show you where you are. You can get so much more information onto the screen that affects what's going on in the scene." When he films two people talking, Schepisi almost never does a standard shot–reverse shot sequence but sticks his people together in the corner or the middle of the frame and cuts at strategic moments to long shots that make you aware of their environment.

A pertinent example of Schepisi's method is the scene where Susan Traherne (Meryl Streep) goes to speak to a diplomatic official (Ian McKellen) about her husband's advancement in *Plenty* (1985). Susan is a disturbed, self-indulgent person, and Schepisi keeps her and the official together in his composition at first as they sit down to talk at the top of the embassy stairs. But then he gradually begins cutting away to shots of the grand, impersonal trappings of the embassy as she starts to get restless and agitated.

Given a major actress, Streep, and major, difficult material by playwright David Hare, Schepisi makes his own contribution to *Plenty* with cumulative, intuitive visuals that express his heroine's interior disorder, which gradually begins to seem like a reasonable or at least understandable response to the complacent English society around her, a society she is determined to destroy in her own small way.

"With *Plenty*, (the setting) *where* something was being said was as important as *what* was being said," says Schepisi. "Because it often belied what was being said, or it often exaggerated what was being said. Using the wide lens, again, without making a big deal out of it, you could show all that; you could show all the monumental things pressing in on Susan."

Plenty, like many of Schepisi's other films, is about the fluidity of time and memory, and Schepisi makes wholly original choices to make us feel the way time can collapse. At one point, at a tense dinner party, Leonard Darwin (John Gielgud) is speaking with some distress to his colleague, Raymond (Charles Dance), about the Suez Canal crisis, and the other guests are still dining while they have their private chat in the drawing room. Schepisi gives Gielgud an extreme close-up to voice his displeasure about Suez and then makes a very hard cut to Susan sitting in a chair. The cut is so hard that it momentarily feels like she has been in the room listening all along, but actually this is a jump forward in time of only a few minutes, when all the other guests have again assembled in the drawing room.

This is the kind of deliberately disorienting editing Alain Resnais attempted, in a much more jagged, self-conscious fashion, in films like *Muriel* (1963). But Schepisi achieves effects like this almost invisibly, so that most audience members will feel them only subliminally. "The editing has got to be in the writing," he says. "You don't leave that for later. You finesse it later, you shift it around a little bit, but basically everything, the intent, the way the sound goes through, the way the words go through, things that pull you through the progression when you're in a different time zone, all of that is scripted. And it takes a lot of consideration."

In his subsequent films, beginning with *The Russia House*, Schepisi has often used distinctive camera movement to make you feel what his characters are feeling. In *The Eye of the Storm*, the camera in Elizabeth Hunter's bedroom is almost always moving slightly, which gives you the sense of her wandering consciousness and also the effect she has on other people. "We actually stuck big cranes in the bedroom," Schepisi says. "I'm going in, and I'm closing in on two people who are kind of uncomfortable with one another. Now, by my movements of the camera, I'm making you uncomfortable with them. That's the intention. The moves are all a little concentric, they're a little odd, and it's to make you have the same unease that they have. And when it looks like they're coming together, I use the wide frame by pulling away, and I actually separate them. With the wide frame, you can stick them very far apart like that."

Schepisi favors the same kind of fluidity found in his framing and editing right from the planning stage. "I don't storyboard," he says. "I write shot lists, but I don't storyboard because I can't draw. I used to be very . . . I'd write down the shots, and I knew what the images were going to be. You've got to be careful because you can get locked into things that are not necessarily helpful to the actors. And when you get to the location, they're not necessarily going to work that way."

His engagement with actors has often been revelatory, right from his first feature, *The Devil's Playground* (1976), a film based on Schepisi's own youthful religious background. "I was called a junior because of my age, but I was in a monastery for a brotherhood, not a priesthood," he says. *The Devil's Playground* is a thoughtful, fleet, generous, highly sensual film about the pressure of lust on an all-male community pledged to renouncing worldly pleasures and concerned with the ultimate outside judgment of God.

Schepisi's second film was *The Chant of Jimmie Blacksmith* (1978), based on a novel by Thomas Keneally, who had played the priest in *The Devil's Playground* where he gave a speech about what it's like to burn in hell. The main character of Jimmie (Tommy Lewis) is a half-white, half-Aboriginal boy who tries with all his heart to please his white bosses until the pressure becomes too much for him to bear. "The boy who played Jimmie Blacksmith wasn't an actor," Schepisi says. "We discovered him in an airport. I had a guy who had some relatives who were Aboriginal; he was a good actor's coach, and I had him work with Tommy for ten weeks. He worked with Tommy through music, through mime, through straight-out yelling and screaming, and he was getting Tommy to lose his self-consciousness about emotions, getting him to free up to be able to express emotions, to be able to yell and scream. Most amateur actors, if they yell, they're too embarrassed to yell right out, or they're too embarrassed to let emotions out. Tommy did that work for about ten weeks, and then he would come and work with me once or twice a week."

Lewis's Jimmie Blacksmith is a boy who's so desperate to impress others that he winds up at war with them because he can never do enough to get their respect or even their attention. The tragic and cathartic *The Chant of Jimmie Blacksmith*, one of the most insightful and far-reaching movies ever made about racism, is probably Schepisi's masterpiece, and it remains far too little screened and discussed today.

The Devil's Playground and *The Chant of Jimmie Blacksmith*, both made in Australia, acted as calling cards to work elsewhere, and Schepisi took Hollywood offers on his own terms, patiently waiting for the right material. "On *Iceman*, I still did shot lists, but we developed more of the philosophy of why we were shooting every shot," he says. "In *Iceman*, we did a lot of movements through tunnels and things to show these scientists in their own rats' mazes. We shot things always through glass or reflections so that the scientists are always surrounded by their technology."

Having delivered a second masterpiece with *Plenty*, Schepisi worked again with Streep on *A Cry in the Dark*, an overwhelmingly wide and detailed view of the notorious Lindy Chamberlain case, a trial by media where the entire country of Australia turned against one supremely tough and ungiving woman who had lost a child to a dingo at a campsite. "I wasn't in Australia at the time of Lindy Chamberlain," says Schepisi. "I was travelling around, and then I became quite alarmed at the brouhaha that was going on with this case. The producer, Verity Lambert, kept asking me to do it, and I didn't want to. I thought it was difficult, and it was an ongoing case that would probably affect people's lives. She got on to me and said, 'Listen, you're not doing this because you don't know how to.' There had been a script. So I sat down for a week and a half and worked out the picture the way I did. Then I rang Verity up, and I said, 'This is how you do it.' I told her to fuck off and hung up!

"Six weeks later she rang me up and said, 'I have someone to talk to you.' It was Meryl Streep, and she said, 'We're going to do this picture.' I knew with Meryl, and then subsequently with Sam Neill, that I had collaborators that would help get the picture made. So I was very relieved about that, and that gave me the courage to do it."

In all of Schepisi's best work, individuals who are seen in some way as outsiders are forced to deal with the hostile world around them. Jimmie Blacksmith cares only about what other people think of him and make of him, and his eagerness to please eventually destroys him. Susan Traherne and Lindy Chamberlain, on the other hand, don't give a damn what people think of them, and their indifference to public opinion eventually destroys them too. These three movies, *The Chant of Jimmie Blacksmith*, *Plenty*, and *A Cry in the Dark*, represent Schepisi in his most penetrating and unsparing mode, and no one has made stronger films on the theme of a solitary person marked down as different by society and forced to pay the heaviest price for their difference.

On the more comic side of this issue, the large-nosed C. D. Bales in *Roxanne* turns the perception of himself as different into a kind of victory of wit over matter. And Ouisa (Stockard Channing) in Schepisi's note-perfect film of John Guare's play, *Six Degrees of Separation*, is a secure, cosseted Upper East Side wife who learns not to care what people think of her, which acts as a kind of liberation for her.

Finally, in *The Eye of the Storm*, Schepisi has two weak characters, Basil and Dorothy, who care so much about how they are perceived that their lives are an extended agony of failure and self-consciousness, and one masterful character, Elizabeth, a woman so selfish and so indifferent to what others think of her that not even a climactic tropical storm can wash away any of her serene self-absorption.

Schepisi's career constitutes a steady progression from Jimmie Blacksmith's confused rebellion against society to Rampling's Elizabeth Hunter emerging almost unscathed from a below-sea-level hideaway after an annihilating storm. Not only does Elizabeth triumph over other people, as Jimmie, Susan, and Lindy cannot, but she even has a key and unforgettable triumph over hostile nature itself.

Of his films' main characters, Schepisi says, "They're the cutting edge for seeing what's good and bad about everything. A single person up against the world or society, that's good for drama, and it's good for comedy, too. You can treat that as both drama and comedy, generally. But mostly it's about humanity and looking at humanity and seeing how people relate or don't relate to one another. Outsiders are a great way to look at the world, aren't they?"

Fred Schepisi on Making Movies—"What I'm Most Interested in—Always—Is the Humanity of the Piece"

Tom Ryan / 2015

Previously unpublished. Recorded between December 2015 and March 2016. Printed by permission of the author.

Tom Ryan: What's the key difference between Frederic Alan Schepisi as a filmmaker today with seventeen features behind him and the bloke who shot *The Priest* more than forty years ago?

Fred Schepisi: I'm older. (laughs) I dunno. I think I'm still coming from the same point of view. I guess that when you don't know any better, you can be very gung ho and fearless. Now I do know better. But it hasn't always helped. I suppose when you get bashed about enough, you lose a bit of that blast-through energy that you wish you still had.

As far as filmmaking goes, when I did *Devil's Playground*, I had a very specific approach: don't move the camera unless you're following somebody. A viewer needs to be "inside the picture" all of the time and not noticing the techniques it's using. That's changed for me over the years, I guess because I've kept learning. I still don't want you to notice: I only want you to notice what's happening *inside* the film. You're being drawn in naturally by your wish to know something. But now the moves are motivated not only by the characters' movements so much as by a wish to gain access to them emotionally. So you're using the camera, and the editing, to bring you inside the people and their interactions and emotions.

A sense of place has remained very important for me, as in *Plenty* or *Russia House*. And, a project still has to excite me, fill me full of possibilities from the start, and make me nervous too. Will I know enough or be able to do enough to pull it off?

I've never done anything before like *Andorra*, a film I'm working on right now. It's based on Peter Cameron's book and has a central character who's a lot different from what he initially appears to be. There's something of *The Talented Mr. Ripley* to it. As before and even more than in the book, the peripheral characters all have lives of their own, not just in the way they intersect with his.

TR: To go back to the beginning: was your work in advertising a means to the end of making films or was it simply a way to make ends meet?
FS: A bit of both. Some history will help to explain that. After I left school, I needed a job, and I went to Carden Advertising not long before television was launched in Australia in 1956. Because I was a pushy little bugger, I ended up with the responsibility for television and radio production. At that time, the State Film Centre was a great resource, and we were always borrowing films made by the Canadian National Film Board from their collection, in particular Norman McLaren's wonderfully experimental shorts, as well as reels of advertising stuff.

Phillip Adams, my colleague at Carden, got me going to the Melbourne Film Society screenings and then, obviously, the Melbourne Film Festival. Another colleague, Alex Stitt, also got me involved in Moving Clickers at Moggs Creek [a Victorian coastal town on the Great Ocean Road]. And, around that time, we all started making our own satirical shorts, like *The Mild One*. Sometimes we were picking up on McLaren's techniques and looking at how we could apply them to ads, and sometimes we were using them as a springboard to go to a better place. I remember thinking, "You know, I could do that, and I think I'd like to do that." All of which coincided with my becoming a little disenchanted with advertising and the fakery of it. The insincerity, if you like. Even hypocrisy.

I followed Phillip from Carden to Paton Advertising, where I became the head of television production. At some point, though, the agency got so large that it had to be split it into two streams. There was a credit squeeze in 1961, and everything went to shit economically. The company lost a lot of revenue, so the easiest thing for them to do was to get rid of one side of the agency, which, of course, was the side I was on. (laughs)

I got a handshake of £500. At that point I had three kids, so it was a bit tough. I sat waiting for the phone to ring for a while (laughs). It didn't ring. Then I heard about Cinesound needing a manager and knew that was the direction I wanted to take.

TR: So at that point you became completely focused on getting into filmmaking?
FS: Yeah, around about then. I put my age up a few years, got the job, and found myself on that road. I'd been doing a bit of writing before that, but then I began taking it seriously. I hated the way industrial documentaries were being written. You know: "It takes nine hundred pounds of steel and two hundred thousand

pounds of pressure to turn out seventy-five. . . ." Who cares? There's gotta be a better way of doing it. I thought. It can't be done any worse, so I might as well see if I can do it any better.

Through people like Walter Lassally and Robert Flaherty, I came to see how the process could work. What I was taking from them wasn't what they did but how they got to do it: you get a sponsor to back what it is you want to get across. So we didn't wait for companies to come to us; I went to them.

For example, with *People Make Papers*, I went to *The Age* [a major newspaper in Melbourne] and asked, "What is it that you're missing in your area that a film would help? How might you enlarge your circulation?" They said that the only long-term change they'd make was concerning school leavers. So I proposed a film about the excitement of the paper and the way it was all put together.

And we tried to do it differently. There's no music in it; the score is just the sounds of the printing presses. I'd arranged for Frank Smith, who was a great saxophonist who'd been composing jingles, to come in and do the soundtrack. He said, "Nah, you don't need any music for this. It's better as it is." Brian Kavanagh cut it. We'd shoot commercials during the day and then go out with my cinematographer, Peter Purvis, and a very small group at night. I think I got six thousand bucks for it.

TR: So where was it shown? How was it used?
FS: They'd send it to schools and other places where people might be interested.

TR: How much freedom did you have to do what you wanted to?
FS: I'd script it and cost it, and they'd say, "Yeah." And then I'd do it.

TR: There's one I looked at called *A Hundred Odd Years from Now*, a crazy futuristic thing about an all-female world and a male whom they stumble across, take as a prisoner and show how good dried fruits can be.
FS: Really? (Laughs) Oh, yes. The male is called Yockoo.

TR: My first reaction was to wonder how on earth you persuaded anybody to approve this.
FS: (Laughs) Well, because it showed the worth of dried fruits and how to use them in cooking in an entertaining way. I think Alex Stitt wrote that one.

TR: I presume *Tomorrow's Canberra* was government-funded?
FS: Yeah. This was, of course, before there was the Canberra [Australia's capital city] that we have now. I went to the National Capital Development Commission

and said, "What do you need? Why do you need it? What are you tryin' to say?" I actually wrote three different scripts for them. I said, "Here are three different approaches. Each'll cost sixty grand."

Since the city was still a work in progress, we had to create what it would be, which allowed me to make an impressionistic film, to use suggestions to tell our "story." One sequence I absolutely love was the one where we're right in on people's faces, and you're hearing noises from offscreen. You never see what's making them, but you can tell what they are.

It was a film that we could have a helluva lot of fun with and, at the same time, show the processes that would need to be followed in order to achieve the vision. The top guy at the commission cried when he saw it: "That's what we're doing," he said. It was enormously satisfying. A lot of the techniques I used in that film later came to fame in *Koyaanisqatsi* (1982), not that it was copied . . .

TR: Given all of this, why no documentaries in your filmography? Did you simply not have the inclination?
FS: Aaaah! I think I was just heading towards feature films. I wasn't all that enamored of documentaries. But I rue the fact that I can't really do in features all the stuff I used to be able to do back then. Because you've got to subjugate the pyrotechnics for what the story is and what the subject is and for the style, logic and discipline of the particular story you're telling. I miss that, the room to be inventive in that way. You try to think that way the whole time you're working, but you still have to bend to the needs of the project.

TR: What kinds of experimentation are we talking about here?
FS: Well, first of all, learning lenses. We were often to the forefront working with new lenses. I think we were the first people here to use a 1.8 aperture, but with quite a wide angle, which Stanley Kubrick used on *Barry Lyndon* (1975). Along with Alex Stitt and Bruce Weatherhead, who worked on design, I was opposed to the use of backlight and sidelight. Sometimes it'd look good, but there was a formula for lighting that was "glowy," shall we say, and that was really boring.

We were influenced a lot by still photography lighting. Some of the reason you couldn't do that on film was that the stocks just weren't fast enough at that time. But certainly when 4X came in, you could really play with it. So we were doing what was called "open-eye lighting," where you take the Fresnel lamp out of a big 4K, which makes it softer and less hard direct. We also used polystyrene to bounce light. Basically we started using the techniques of the great American still photographers, like Richard Avedon. We were looking at that stuff and trying to get that on film.

There were a number of commercials that we shot in color, where I wouldn't allow any lighting at all. We'd look for locations where we could use the existing daylight.

It's very difficult to do that for a whole film, particularly a structured one because, if you're doing different angles, it's impossible. From this angle the sun might be there [Schepisi gesturing off to the right], but then it moves and doesn't match the light in the next angle. *Cleo from 5 to 7* (1962) is a good example of a feature getting it right. There's a quality of immediacy that comes out of that. I think we did it for the Park Drive ads, among others. Our whole attitude was no lighting, one shot.

TR: Watching the ads one after another at the National Film and Sound Archive, I was struck by the sense of fun that comes through them.
FS: Right. It *was* fun. We did some wonderful things [laughing with pleasure at the memory]. We were one of the first to use front screen projection. There was no CGI in those days. It was just us playing with possibilities.

I did a commercial for Alcoa and the whole thing was on packaging. Toothpaste tubes, how they were made, how they sat on the shelves. We used *musique concrete* as our guide. It was all kind of abstract, where I was taking conversations in supermarkets and turning them into rhythms and turning those rhythms into music [Schepisi clapping in time], turning the music into standard machines pumping out so many things, turning that back into music. Bruce Clarke was with us, and we were all having so much fun experimenting.

TR: Melbourne was quite a place back then. On one side of town, we had Arthur and Corinne, the Cantrills, doing their thing; on the other there was Film House plying its trade—all experimenting. Despite your differences, you had so much in common.
FS: Yeah. They're terrific.

TR: In your commentary on the *Libido* DVD, you talk about learning how to "get the camera where it needs to be." Where is that?
FS: That's dictated by what you're trying to do. When I did *Roxanne*, I didn't want to be conventional. Steve Martin didn't want a comedy director; he wanted "a real director," as he put it. So I was always looking to be inventive and surprising, and that was always dictated by what was going on. In rehearsals, he'd give me lots of unexpected things to work with.

But with comedy, sometimes, there's only one place the camera can go. You might need to put it up in the corner over there because, if you don't, you won't see all the elements that are making the scene funny. There's one shot in *Roxanne* where the fire truck comes out and goes down the hill, and, as it does, all the shit comes flying off it. The joke requires that you see all that happening. When we went to set it up, Ian [cinematographer Ian Baker] put the camera low because he wanted to see the hill and all the wonderful hills beyond. He was composing a nice shot. Well, the bloody fire truck comes out alright, the stuff comes off and drops behind all the other stuff, but you couldn't really see anything. The camera needed to be up high looking down. Screw the hills in the background. Mind you, it was totally my fault for not making clear in the first place what I was after.

TR: So it's the same situation as when I'm telling you a joke and I leave out a line. It's not funny anymore. You're talking about that visually.

FS: Yeah, and it has to be the same for drama. The camera has to be in the right place for what you want to show, both in terms of its placement and movement. The reason I love CinemaScope is that you can get a lot of information about the situation that you're showing on the screen, or you can give it a different context. You can do a small movement and include something else. Or you can move behind an object on screen and start to shut down the frame. In the olden days, they used to do that with an iris. And just as you can close in, you can open out.

What's going on absolutely dictates that: What's the force of the scene? What are you trying to put across? In *Devil's Playground*, there's a scene where a boy has drowned, and we're showing people's reaction to that inside the monastery. We put the camera low in a doorway because it was the only place we could use to get the shot I needed. We showed this glorious room with people at the windows, sitting on a desk, et cetera, just five people standing. And I said to everybody, "Silence is king." It was group guilt that was the force of the scene.

Because I wasn't sure, we also shot the scene going in on everybody, and they were beautiful shots, bloody beautiful. But they weren't right. We needed to stay on the group and let silence do the work. That's what I mean about finding the right place for the camera to be.

TR: You make me think of Andre Bazin's notion about how staying back in a wide shot and allowing the viewer to choose where to look is the only honest filmmaking, a truly democratic way where the director, allegedly, isn't telling us what to look at.

FS: He can go and get fucked. (laughter) I think that's relevant if it's right for the situation. But as a filmmaker, you've also got the advantage of being able to get right inside your characters' emotions by moving close to them and letting their faces do the work.

TR: That's interesting because in the commentary on the *Libido* DVD, you're talking about *The Priest*, and you say, "I used to like to get incredibly close on things," as if it was a bad thing. Stylistically it's also true of your early short film, *Party*, which, like *The Priest*, is effectively a one-act play. Is that necessarily a bad thing?

FS: I don't remember why I might have thought about it like that . . . Maybe I was going through a stage.

TR: (laughing) "But you said thirty-five years ago . . ."
FS: I remember on *Devil's Playground*, we never did a move unless it was motivated. We never did moves just for the sake of moves. You weren't conscious of the camera specifically. I want to be in with the people. In a way, I kind of agree with your mate, Bazin. But you always learn and change with the projects you're doing. In *Plenty*, I was interested in the way the English locations looked: all the terrace houses with columns outside them, statues, stone things everywhere, a little bit like their personalities. I worked to put the characters inside a constraining environment. When the Meryl Streep character meets with Charles Dance and John Gielgud in Brussels, what's going on outside the window is all these refugee camps, while here you are in this opulent, almost decadent, British officialdom.

Along similar lines, all the shots when she comes into her apartment were done in exactly the same way with one movement. The years pass and the apartment has been refurbished along the way, but the camera move remains the same. So, throughout the movie, there's this déjà vu effect, which is what she's going through.

Sound has a lot to do with it too. The sounds of the parachutes in the opening are replicated when she's laying out tablecloths and things like that, which take her right back. And it takes audiences back subconsciously too.

With *Russia House*, we often moved back and forth between being right in there with the characters and using a long lens to suggest they were being observed, even if you don't know at the time who it is.

TR: When did you adopt that strategy of the prowling camera? Even when two people are sitting opposite each other, conversing like we are now, your camera is almost always on the move, sometimes almost subliminally.
FS: I think directors are often very bravura when it comes to shooting action sequences, but when it comes to dialogue it's all flat: shot, reaction shot, bang, bang, bang, bang [Schepisi gesturing in sync]. Close-up to close-up to close-up. David Lean described that as getting on the characters' faces and watching their thoughts whizz around. Editors call it "keeping the other character alive" when somebody else is talking. I hate that. I'll do anything to avoid it.

I have arguments with editors because I don't like cutting backwards and forwards. Who should I be on? Again, who's the force of the scene? Who's the conversation affecting the most? I'll stay on them until it's important that we see what the other person is doing. To add to that, the movement creates a little bit of unease or maybe brings in something in the background that tells you something else.

I don't use a zoom like Vilmos Zigmond in the Altman films, because that closes things down. I want to vary the perspective, even if just a little bit. I don't like zooms, even if I occasionally use them a little bit to help out.

TR: In *Words and Pictures*, the camera moves almost unnoticeably during the exchanges between Clive Owen and Juliette Binoche. You only see it if you're looking for it.
FS: I'm trying to draw you in. In the sequence where he comes to her house and they sit in her studio, we moved the camera while staying close to them. What I want to do as the conversation's progressing is to suggest they're psychologically being drawn into each other: he's casting a web and she's considering it. But then I go wide to remind you that they're still in their own spaces. Then he moves to look at the pictures, we follow him, and when he chances his arm, you go with him.

TR: When you're setting up that exchange between them with Ian Baker, how do you talk about it? Or, because you've worked together for so long, does he just know?
FS: He knows why we're doing it . . . I used to shot-list the whole film before starting. I don't do that now. We have a philosophy about how we go about things, why we're shooting this way rather than that. I now only sit down and shot-list something the night before we shoot. He reads it and doesn't know what the fuck I'm on about. (laughter) He can never read my writing. Then we talk about it. He gets on with the lighting and works out the spatial parameters inside which we're going to need to work. Maybe we need to shuffle things around a bit, but we keep talking to one another the whole time. And meanwhile you've got to work it out with the actors and make sure they're comfortable with it. We're all getting on the same page. It's organic. You're problem-solving all the time.

TR: Is he involved in picking locations?
FS: He might be. Economics don't always allow for it. We joke about how I always seem to go for difficult locations . . . like that beautiful apartment we picked for Juliette Binoche's character in *Words and Pictures*. Somebody had built that at the end of a warehouse, and we got permission to widen one room and then knock through to connect it to a studio outside of that. The front room with the lovely view outside was long and narrow, and very difficult to light. But he's very good at coping with all of that.

TR: Do you have conversations with him about the overall look of a film before you start?

FS: Yes. I like to get him on very early, and we have lots of preliminary discussions before it becomes official. But, because of the economics, I usually can't keep him on. Then the production designer and I talk about the different colors on set and the way we're going to be lighting it. And we talk about attitude. If the movie dictates it, we get into talking about the philosophy behind how we're going to go about shooting it. We send people out to survey specific locations, and I'll do a lot of research. I'll be sending Ian pictures throughout all of this, then he comes back, and we go out and look at all the prospective locations. He'll talk about the difficulties for him, and we'll work them out.

TR: My general memory of *Russia House* is what you've said about the sense of somebody always watching but also of small figures surrounded by massive statues and buildings, tiny people buried inside history. Would you have a conversation about that kind of thing with him beforehand?
FS: Yeah. What are the things we want to see? Why do we want to see them? Yeah, absolutely. In the end, I might pick most of the shots, but he's in my ear at the same time. 'Cause how you shoot something is like how a writer writes novels. His vernacular and his grammar is what makes it work. And it's the same for us. At certain points, Ian will say, "You've already done that. Don't do *that*." Sometimes he'll come up to me quietly and say, "Isn't it time for one of your one-shotters? This sequence could really benefit from it . . . and help us catch up on the schedule." (laughs) That's not the only motivation, but it sometimes triggers the choices you make.

There's the scene in *Words and Pictures* where the kid in the car is giving cheek to the girl coming down the street. We didn't have a lot of time. We were wondering if we should lay tracks. I'm trying to get it clear in my head about why exactly I'm doing the scene, how it's gonna fit. He came over and said, "You go and sit down. We'll just do it with a steadicam." "But how are we gonna see her face? And how are we gonna get from here to here?" "Just fuck off and sit down." (laughs) And they came up with that fantastic shot you can see in the film. You can see all that you need to see. That's how we work.

By the way (laughing), if you want to amuse yourself, watch the kid driving. He never looks where he's going.

TR: I'm not trying to put you out of work or anything, but could Ian go away with a script and shoot it the way you'd shoot it? Does he know you well enough for that?
FS: I don't know. But I don't think he wants to have to direct. He tried all that in commercials, and what he's interested in is the art of the shot and creating a consistency throughout. He *could* do it though. He'll come to me and say, for example, "You don't want to do that. You're just compromising on time."

TR: Do similar kinds of things happen when you're working with an editor or a composer?

FS: Yeah. They keep trying to do what you want as well as push you towards a better place. They have their instincts, and that's why you're working with them. They know that I like to cut according to the dramatic interest of a scene rather than who's delivering a line. So sometimes, they'll be cutting something, trying to keep up with the schedule and work in line with what I like. I'll sometimes come in, and we'll realize that the cut is *never* on the person who's doing the talking. The rhythm and the center of attention are all wrong so we have to rejig the scene until we get it right.

My general view is that you shouldn't do close-ups anyway, unless you need to, because a close-up is an emphasis. I know that with television and everything else operating on a smaller visual scale, you're in there all the time. And a lot of actors like it like that.

TR: You've collaborated primarily with three composers: Bruce Smeaton, Jerry Goldsmith, and Paul Grabowsky. Have you formed the same kind of relationship with each of them, or are they three very distinct individuals whose talents you've drawn on in different ways?

FS: Probably the latter. Bruce Smeaton did some fabulous stuff for us on films like *Devil's Playground*, *Jimmie Blacksmith*, and *Plenty*. All great scores.

Our final project together was *Evil Angels*. I didn't want the music to color your views about Lindy Chamberlain or anyone else in any way. I just wanted it to evoke the passage of time, to give energy and create tension. Not to take sides. And it was extremely difficult.

We had a couple of goes at it, and it wasn't really working. I think we recorded some of Bruce's score, and Verity Lambert agreed with me. So I pushed harder to get more nondescript-in-a-way music, music that actually worked in line with what I was after. I guess I took him to a place that was very frustrating. I believe he rang my business partner at the time wanting to get me locked up because he thought I was fuckin' insane. (laughter) That seemed to finish our relationship.

TR: [I show Fred the item from IMDb about *Iceman*, offering an alternative version of the breakdown of his relationship with Smeaton] Do you wish to correct the record here?

FS: [reads the entry, looking increasingly mystified] That's all bullshit. "I was fired and then brought back on to the project for postproduction"? "I tampered with the film after it was locked"? Well, first of all, I wasn't fired. I don't know where that comes from.

TR: IMDb puts quote marks around that, but it doesn't directly attribute all of that to him.
FS: . . . and anybody who knows me knows I don't believe in locking a film. It's an ongoing thing, and it often changes when you get the music and the sound effects.

TR: But there was trouble on *Iceman* with Norman Jewison, wasn't there? About the final cut?
FS: No. That's not the right way to put it. We did testing and coming out of the testing there were things that Norman or the studio wanted. I'm not sure Norman wanted them, but the studio did. And there were some wonderful things that disappeared.

TR: Jerry Goldsmith?
FS: I found with Jerry that he seemed to get on to why I was doing what I was doing very quickly. You know, things change over time. When I was working with Bruce, he'd play themes on the piano, and you'd have to imagine what it was all going to sound like, what the orchestration would do, and all of that. It was difficult for a composer to get all that across. So there was always uncertainty on both sides. Then that started to change. Electronics came in and easy recording devices, so you could sample what you were dealing with.

By the time I started working with Jerry Goldsmith, he could go to his studio and show me. He had a whole set-up in his house. He could record something, play it, change notes on the computer and so on, and run it up against the film. You got a quicker and better sense of where you were headed, and you'd talk about it. If you criticized Jerry in the wrong way, things mightn't go so well (laughs). But he seemed to twig quicker to what I wanted and what the overall attitude of the film was. He would sit down and play a couple of different approaches that you could consider, and you could talk about which one might be best.

You might have a theme for particular characters and for the film, although you mightn't use them as directly as that. When two characters get together, you might work their two themes together, all on the principle that the music should say what the film couldn't say otherwise. Not just to push the movie along in general and not just to color the emotions, to say that now you should feel this and now you should feel that. You should do something that enhances the film and that informs the audience in another way. If possible.

But if you do a suite across the film, by the time you get to the last third of the film, you only need to bring in a dusting or a memory of that stuff, and it immediately informs what you're now looking at in a richer way.

I had that with Bruce too. It was always our idea, and Bruce would always put that idea forward as strongly as I did. He was very good about how to use music.

So, if you look at *Mr. Baseball*, for which Jerry did the music, there was the obvious organ thing, and then there was a theme for Tom Selleck and one for Aya Takanashi. But when they get together in the bath, have a listen to that because it's the bringing together of everything: as these people come together, the music comes together. It's such a beautiful piece of music, for all the right reasons.

Jerry also understood sound effects and how they fit in and where the music should be in relation to dialogue. He did a lot of good stuff.

TR: With the kind of work he did on *Russia House* and on *I.Q.*—those endless, jazzy variations on "Twinkle Twinkle, Little Star"—he seems really inventive.
FS: He was really inventive. This is the thing he used to get to more quickly than anybody else: this is what we're gonna do, this is why we're doing it. Like the tango that opens *Six Degrees of Separation* comes from a piece of music later in the film. We plan all of those things and somehow we just got on the same tram very quickly. Once we were on that tram, you might have a little difference about something or other, but it would all come together fairly quickly.

You'd talk through where all the music's gonna go and why, and where it shouldn't go too. I had a very good relationship with him and—his wife will tell you this—he said he had two meaningful partnerships with filmmakers: one was me, the other was Franklin Schaffner.

It's all about being simpatico, enjoying what one another's doing.

TR: He'd come aboard when the film was finished or . . . ?
FS: No, no. I'd talk to him way back at script stage. In a different way, I have the same kind of relationship with Paul Grabowsky. We talk *a lot* before we do the film, and I show him cuts all along the way. He'll come in with some ideas, and we'll knock 'em around. We're pretty open with one another. We've got a directness and a frankness in how we talk that gets us to a better place. *Last Orders* is one of those films in which everybody gets a bit of a theme, and then it's all gradually wound together. Like Jerry was, Paul is musically diverse.

TR: Some writers hold the view that putting up their work for adaptation to film is like having someone pulling out your teeth and stuffing money into your pocket at the same time. Have you had happy collaborations with writers on screenplays?
FS: I've worked on the screenplays for most of my films: call it "script editing," if you like. And some of the best times I've ever had were spending five hours in a room discussing a script with Tom Keneally, John Guare, David Hare, Tom Stoppard, and the others, going, "Well I don't get this. Should we be thinking of such and such?" And they'll either go, "Okay, that *is* a problem," and you'll work

together to come up with a solution. Or they'll explain what they meant in such a way that illuminates the subtext for you. Then this leads to that, and so on. It's a joyous kind of give-and-take.

David Hare was great like that. For *Plenty* on stage, they used little cinematic projections for the sets, and it was very clear that *where* things were taking place were as important as what was taking place. So it wasn't that difficult to do the same thing cinematically. But, at our first meeting, I told him that I thought there were some holes in the play, some things I didn't follow. And that Kate Nelligan was dazzling, but played the role with a shield around her; and that, for the film, I wanted the character to reveal little fissures, not too obvious, but there. "So, if you don't agree with that, I understand, but I wanted to be honest right up front."

He came back, "Actually, I'm glad you said that because there's some things in the play I wanted to fix." So we got on from then on. In fact, almost a third of the script for the film is all new, and we always chuckle when people say that it's almost the same as the play. It means you've found the cinema equivalent of it.

With John Guare, a lot of people had been trying to do *Six Degrees*. My agent and great friend, Sam Cohn, had been shopping John around. He was telling me about how people were coming to him proposing ways of unravelling his "little play" and putting it in chronological order. They'd all been blowing it.

He eventually went with me after I found the key to open it up. It kept the surface fun that it had on stage in a filmic way, but we also opened it up so that, without actually having to say anything, we could see this world that the characters were operating in, how they were clinging to it and why. After we started working on it together, John felt absolutely free and wrote like hell. I'd edit it and reshape it and give it back to him.

TR: I haven't seen it on stage, but you never could have made the kind of chronological leaps there that you do in the film, could you?
FS: Well, in the play, the characters would tell their story to the audience, and their friends would come up out of the audience and do their thing and then disappear back to their seats. And Will Smith's character would sometimes appear in a panel off to the side. Almost everybody doubted that you could make it work on film because it was so locked in to theater conventions. So it did play with time too, but in its own way.

There was a time when I thought I might have the characters telling their story directly to camera, but then I rejected that. My approach was to put the camera in among them, like you were sitting at the table or that party or event with them. As always, finding the key makes all the difference. Basically, structurally, it's the same. But that's what happens when you're working with really good people.

TR: Was the collaboration with Richard Russo on *Empire Falls* a happy one?
FS: Yeah, it was fantastic. He's a good guy. It always starts with the writing. Good writers like him are always great to work with because they're rarely defensive. When you're working on a screenplay with them, you can ask questions about their work and their guards won't always be going up. You can criticize something that you think doesn't work, and one of two things will happen . . . no it's three: (1) it is wrong or (2) it's not wrong, you've just missed the point or (3) it seems wrong, but actually the problem lies elsewhere. Once that's sorted out, then the thing you're talking about no longer seems wrong. Whichever of these applies, it helps you understand the material, or it highlights something for them that needs fixing.

TR: So you get the sense that they're prepared to let their original material go and start again via you?
FS: No. When it's work of that quality, I'm trying to find a way to realize it on film that absolutely preserves the integrity of what they've done. I don't try to use it as a springboard for me to just go off into other places. My intent is to go deeper, get a better understanding of it.

TR: Were there any significant changes between the script you started with for *Words and Pictures* and the one you shot?
FS: The first task was to modernize it. From the time it was written to the time we were doing it, things had changed: cell phones, tablets, the electronic board, the general use of technology in classrooms, all that stuff didn't exist. So we had to find a way to incorporate it. When the boy harasses the Asian student, that was originally done with pictures stuck up around the place rather than via an iPhone. That was one of the big things we had to do. It was all done in collaboration with Gerald Di Pego, and it was ongoing . . . Twitter being the new haiku.

The one thing that was missing in the discussion the characters had about words and pictures, I think, was what you can't express that way. And music is the vehicle for that, as in the music file the Clive Owen character sends to Juliette Binoche when he's in deep trouble with her.

TR: To what extent did the casting shift the thrust of the original screenplay for the film?
FS: Well, it was all flexible. Obviously, we had to give the character Juliette plays a French background, but it didn't matter. She could have been from anywhere. This is the whole thing about multicultural countries. Look at our own: how many people do we know who are Arab or French or Italian or Chinese? Half the people

we know are, yet we don't put 'em in movies in that way. So where a character comes from should be irrelevant at the start to the story you're telling, although it can obviously then affect it in subtle ways.

The best bit of casting in that film is the headmaster. Navid Negahban is Abu Ben Nazir [the al-Qaeda leader from *Homeland*], and nobody casts the poor bastard. But in *Words and Pictures*, he's the head of a school and an Iranian . . . and why not? That's the reality of it, and I'd like to see much more of it. I didn't see the need to explain it. Fuck it, that's what it is. So, to answer your question, the casting didn't really change much.

TR: I love the way you've answered that question: by referring to the texture of the film as a whole . . . The characters are all there for you: background, foreground. They're all part of the way you think about it.
FS: Quentin Tarantino picked up on that too when we did that talk session in Sydney a little while back. He was referring in particular to *A Cry in the Dark*, and I really like the way he talked about how everybody is so *there*. But it drives me nuts when they're *not* because I'd like you to be able to look at the film again and again. I don't expect that anyone will, but if they do then I want them to notice something that they didn't see before. You've got the front energy, but you've also got all this other stuff that's enriching it.

That approach probably comes from all the bloody commercials I did. People are going to see 'em a hundred times, so you want to make them in a way that there's enough going on that it's a little bit fresh when you see them again.

TR: Was there ever anymore about Swint (Adam DiMarco) in the script? It's as if he's banished from the film as well as the school . . .
FS: No.

TR: Jack's betrayed his son in a pretty horrible way and is given a chance for redemption. Shouldn't Swint be too?
FS: (laughing) No. He's a little shit.

TR: Yes, but shits are part of humanity too.
FS: Yeah, I know. But there were too many threads going on, and, in that world and their lives, he would have just been *out*—gone. Particularly in this day and age in America.

TR: But isn't that what could make him interesting?
FS: Maybe.

TR: You are very harsh on bullies in your films: *Jimmie Blacksmith*, *Empire Falls* . . .
FS: I am. I got beaten up at boarding school because I used to wet the bed. I'd come around the corner, and they'd be waiting for me with a whack. It wasn't fun.

TR: Once you've started shooting, do the writers stay on the job or move on?
FS: Some stay; some move on. I'd be happy to have them there at all times. They can see as things are changing what might be needed or what might be a potential problem. Sometimes you come across a simple scene, and you can't work out why the hell it isn't working. You almost inevitably come back to there being no solid subtext to it for the actors: that the scene is only there to be a transition. And that's not good enough. It's not moving the story or the characters forward in any useful way. My job is to jump in and invent some motivation, but it'd be even better if the writer was there to cast a fresh pair of eyes on what we're doing. No matter how much you've studied it and worked on it, you don't realize beforehand that there's a problem there.

John Guare was always on the set—and having fun. I used him to help with Stockard Channing, who, after doing the play on stage for years in New York and London, described doing *Six Degrees* on film as like putting the toothpaste back into the tube. She was the guardian of the piece, and she was having a bit of trouble. And I got John to keep talking to Will Smith, explaining to him why his character was behaving the way he did. He gave him background, biography, and confidence, while I was busy elsewhere. Some writers can do this; some can't; some don't want to.

With *Last Orders*, I kept Graham Swift involved. It was a very difficult screenplay to write, and you needed to keep that surface fun again. I'd get fifteen pages of notes at the end of the day from Graham, and it was great. When you're working with people of that talent, you owe it to them to preserve the integrity of what they've done and give it the best interpretation you can. That's how I think of it.

TR: So nothing's changed since you said, "Forty-five years ago," about the making of *Barbarosa*, "I was not trying to make Fred Schepisi's film; I was trying to realize Bill Wittliff's film"?
FS: Yeah.

TR: What about if you're working from an original screenplay, as you were say for *I.Q.* or *Iceman*?
FS: Ah, man. Some writers are not as good. Some writers have been given an idea and not realized it very well. Some writer might have a good idea . . . but having an idea and making it work are very different things. To a large extent, you keep

them involved as much as you can, but at a certain point you've got to work out whether they're helping or hindering.

I.Q., however, was an entirely different matter. (long pause) People kept trying to change it, the studio, actors . . . We had a writer, the original one, who was doing well—Andy Breckman. He was the best. He got shunted out. I wanted him back, couldn't get him back, so went to another writer, Michael Leeson. We were doing very well together, but then he got pushed out by various people and, for the sake of his sanity, we let him go.

We started filming, and they brought in Marshall Brickman, who's a lovely guy. But I was warned that he'd agree with something and go off to write it, but, as he was writing it, would get inspired and come up with something completely different. Which was fine, except that we'd started shooting and it became a nightmare.

TR: He's not credited, is he?
FS: No. It was one of those Hollywood mishmashes where they hire a writer who only comes on for three weeks, gets paid a fortune, and goes away and doesn't do anymore work on the project. Some of them don't care whether it's completed or not.

Which reminds me: on *I.Q.*, we had this wonderful typist. We'd be sitting in a room and getting ideas, writing them down, and giving them to her. And sometimes we discovered, because of her very honest reactions, whether something was working or not. If we were in doubt about a scene, say, we'd give her two versions to type, and she'd sit there and be going, "Ooooh, oooh," and laughing her head off or crying her eyes out. She became our test audience.

I.Q. was all very strange. It was a little like *Mr. Baseball*, which could've been a much better film. It was more about a baseballer clomping around like an alien in a delicate cultural environment than it ended up being, and putting his American-sized fourteens into everything, mostly his own mouth. So we had lots of wonderful American-Japanese clashes, best described by a wonderful ad campaign someone did that I couldn't get 'em to use. You have three pieces of sushi, and right in the middle you have a great big sloppy hot dog drenched in mustard. Another version of that idea was having three pairs of clogs and in the middle was this filthy pair of sneakers with socks hangin' out. That's what the film should have been.

It was a very weird situation. The film was being done by Universal as if it was *Major League*. Then the studio was sold to Matsushita [in 1990], and the new owners wanted it changed away from *Major League* because they were fearful that we were being derogatory to the Japanese. That was when I came on board and brought Ed Solomon with me to write a new script. We went to Japan to do some background work before coming back and staying at the Beverly Hills Hotel where we wrote what I think is a terrific script. Then Ed said something to the executives that he shouldn't have and was off the picture.

After he left, Kevin Wade was employed to work on the script. He came over to Japan, and we were not far off shooting. But he was hired for three weeks, would only write five pages a day, and was getting into a lot of arguments with Selleck and vise-versa. After his three weeks were up, he left. And he was only about a third of the way through the script.

To add to the problems, I had final cut but didn't understand that Tom Selleck had script approval.

TR: What exactly were Selleck's objections? As we have it now, the film is a variation on the familiar ugly American story. Did he want to soften that?
FS: No, he wanted it to be more of a baseball film than we did: his character, the coach, and the players. Apart from one film, Selleck has never really been a success in movies, and he was nervous about his career.

TR: Stories have circulated about the problems created for you when members of a cast have had power or requirements that have compromised your vision for a film (Gary Busey, Tim Robbins, Selleck). Is this just the way things work in the US, or can the problems be overcome?
FS: It's not unusual unfortunately, although I've generally been very lucky really, working with people who sincerely care about the film and about how they're contributing to it. It often happens when a script is in a state of flux. Actors, and stars in particular, are always trying to protect themselves against being used incorrectly, worrying that you'll cut around things in an editing room rather than choose their best takes.

The very best of them know very quickly whether you're gonna be good, bad, or indifferent. Very quickly. If they learn to trust you, they'll be prepared to take risks. The ones who are insecure and uncertain all act as if they know everything, and they're a problem.

Some really do have something big to protect. Sylvester Stallone has always been notorious for trying to take over the pictures he's in: there's a certain image, a Sylvester Stallone stamp, that he likes to put on a movie. What I say to that is that if you're doing it for the credit and the money, then go along for the ride. But if you're trying to make a film you care about, then don't get involved in all that because one or other of you is gonna lose it.

But it's not just you dealing with it; it's the other actors too. They don't want bad behavior or insecure behavior or diva behavior, and it can be very tough on them. You try to say, "Let's all ignore this, and we'll try to find a way through it," but it does pull everything down.

TR: Is it only on the projects where you're not working with established writers and established material that this kind of thing happens?
FS: It's probably only on the projects where the writing's not as strong or as good as it could be. But when it's something like *Last Orders*, for example, which was extremely joyous from everyone's point of view, it tends not to happen. And that had a very good screenwriter on it. (laughs) To tell you the truth, I've had very few problems. I've been very lucky.

TR: I get the sense that you really like doing romantic comedies: *Roxanne, I.Q., Mr. Baseball*, even *Words and Pictures*.
FS: If they're smart, I enjoy doing 'em. There are a few that I didn't get involved in. Even Sam Cohn, who'd originally pushed me towards *Plenty*, wanted me to do *My Best Friend's Wedding* (1997). *Runaway Bride* (1999) was another. In fact, I said I liked that one, set a price on myself, and the head of Paramount at that time went in to bat for me on it.

Then, two weeks later, I woke up and said to myself, "Why am I doing this film!?" It just seemed good in the light of all the other crap I'd been reading. To me, it didn't have anything going on underneath the surface. I had to ring up Paramount, tell them that I wasn't sufficiently passionate about it and couldn't do it justice, and apologize. I think I paid for that for a few years. It was not taken kindly. On reflection, what the fuck! I should've just done it, taken the money and moved on to something else.

TR: But you didn't pursue *My Best Friend's Wedding*, which is an example of a film that goes against the grain of so much romantic comedy?
FS: Yeah, well I think that Paul (PJ) Hogan brought a lot to it. But I enjoy romantic comedies, although there're films, like *Spy* (2015), that you enjoy but that you don't necessarily want to go and make.

But I enjoyed doing comedy when I was making commercials and industrial documentaries, and I love having a good laugh. I'd tried for many years to get to do comedy features, but nobody was interested—until *Roxanne*. That broke the ice, and everybody wanted to give me comedies.

TR: And you welcomed that?
FS: So long as it had something else going on.

TR: And is that "something else" the thing that we were talking about before: a terrific collection of characters in the background?
FS: Could be. The school-bullying was really important in *Words and Pictures*. The writer, Gerald Di Pego, was a teacher, and he gave us something to get our teeth

into. But the film wasn't really a romantic comedy, even if that's how it was sold. That's not its main thrust, and if you go to see it expecting a romantic comedy, you're going to be in for a surprise. If you take the first few minutes, you might even think you've stumbled into an English lecture. But if you go to see it as something a bit different, you'll get the reward of the romantic comedy and something more as well.

And you're right about the characters in the background. In *Roxanne*, you have the front story, which we mostly played straight, just occasionally upping it a notch for comedy. But we also upped it another notch by having a chorus of comedians playing the firemen. They were actually all stand-up comedians, and each had a physical oddity of some sort.

TR: Then there are Einstein's adorably eccentric buddies in *I.Q.*
FS: Originally, I wanted Barry Humphries, Peter Ustinov, and John Cleese. But I liked the guys we ended up with [Lou Jacobi, Gene Saks, and Joseph Maher]. I don't normally imitate anything, but I always loved all the characters in *Ball of Fire* (1941). I could see something like that in *I.Q.*, and I knew I could have a lot of fun with them.

TR: Are you attracted to material that has a strong political view?
FS: People have said that I'm attracted to outsiders. There's possibly some truth in that because it's a great way of looking at society in general because they're rubbing up against it.

TR: For example, Will Smith in *Six Degrees* becomes that film's Jimmie Blacksmith.
FS: Maybe, although I wouldn't have thought of it like that. What I'm most interested in—always—is the humanity of the piece. What makes people behave the way they do.

That's what John Guare was interested in too. All those people come from his world. He's inside it, hangs around with them, and was really excited by the idea of putting it all on film. I knew that what was really important was *not* to do the Hollywood thing and spell out exactly what we're supposed to be thinking about the characters. The point that mattered was that there was an unknown quotient in this material. We had to just let it all happen. As John said, "Don't get too lost in the words. The words are the wallpaper." It was a great guide. It's what's happening under the words, between everybody, the effect the situation is having on everybody, that matters.

TR: There's a line in the film where Ouisa describes herself as "a collage of unaccounted-for brushstrokes." Is that true of all characters, or should it be?

FS: Great line. I'd forgotten it. (laughs) The Will Smith character is talking bullshit, but they're all mesmerized by him. It's totally illogical, but it's seductive. He has this panther quality. He's working them out, stalking them. And that's what I did with the camera all the time too.

TR: *The Russia House* also has a strong political edge. Its perspective on international relations and the business implications of the arms race seems especially astute—and modern. Was this part of the appeal of the project?
FS: Absolutely. The book was well written: David Cornwell doesn't write thrillers. He describes thrillers as "the furniture in the room," the setting in which he can explore human nature.

TR: I think it's one of your best films, but the critical responses at the time it was released seem to have been lukewarm. How do *you* feel about the film now, from a vantage point of twenty-five years?
FS: I like it a lot, but it did get kicked in the arse. The interesting thing about those reviews was that a lot of them accused it of being "old-fashioned" and too straightforward. I actually take that response as a compliment. It's telling us that they hadn't seen all the artifice. When we're up in the tower in Zagorsk, the city of churches with all those beautiful minarets and domes, there's five different time zones happening.

And the music is just beautiful. When Sean Connery goes down to that meeting where you think he's really going to get into trouble, he walks across the room and down the street and that music is just phenomenal. Thank you, Jerry Goldsmith.

It was a good movie. I had fantastic people to work with. When I did the session with Quentin Tarantino in Sydney, he also said that he'd wanted to do films like novels, where you can jump around in time, but that people had been telling him that you can't jump all over the place like that, that it doesn't work. Then he saw *Russia House* and said [Schepisi doing a bizarre imitation of Tarantino being enthusiastic], "You can do it; you can do it; you can do it."

TR: That's something you do quite a bit. In *Six Degrees of Separation*, *Last Orders*, *Empire Falls* . . .
FS: The key to making it work is to keep audiences focused on what's going on with characters that they're interested in. Nothing else. If you cut to the past to insert something that gives you specific information about who a character is and why they're behaving as they are, you don't need to show details about where they are and the time period. Who gives a shit anyway? It's all background material. If it matters, it'll become clear as you're going along, and you won't have distracted from the story.

TR: Why did you agree to take over *Fierce Creatures*? Was it the promise of backing for a future project?

FS: Nah. You never believe those promises. It was a comedy, John Cleese was involved, I needed some money, and I asked for and received a reasonable amount of it. And I did it as a favor.

The film had been finished, and it was a mess. The filmmaker didn't really have a sense of humor, the timing was off, and, because of the success of *A Fish Called Wanda*, everybody's fingerprints were all over it. The first thing that I did was look at all the material, and we talked about what really shouldn't be saved and what should. I thought it had all been lazily edited, and everything was too long. There was obviously an approach in that, but I didn't think it was right. I brought on a new editor, and we zipped the whole thing up and got the timing right, while all along working on the screenplay with John and his co-writers. About a third of the film is new material, particularly the last twenty-five minutes, a whole lot of new footage, a bit for here, a bit for there, just to bring characters out into the foreground, to make it richer.

We needed to set stuff up better: the characters, the opening, the idea that it's a farce. In the original version, in one of the very early scenes, you had John turning up at the zoo and immediately wanting to kill all the cuddly animals. If you've set it up at the beginning as a crazy farce, then you can get through that scene. You can take it in the spirit that's meant. But if you don't, it's pretty itchy-scratchy, even though it's John Cleese.

I could never quite convince them to do that. And there are several other confrontations that needed to be set up better, but we didn't quite manage to do the job that we were trying to do. I think the film's predecessor, *A Fish Called Wanda* (1988), did the setting-up much better, although some of *Fierce Creatures* was very funny.

Anyway, we got it all cut, went and tested it, and it tested rather badly. They said, "What do we do? What do we do?" I said that we needed to get to the zoo sooner, but making sure that you're not expecting anything other than mad from John, and that we needed to get rid of two or three more things. William Goldman was around helping out. John was always looking for the right formulas and had him around as an extra set of hands.

So we recut it and took it back out, and it tested well this time. They were really happy, so happy in fact that the producer and John decided that, since they had all this other stuff, some of it should go back in. I thought, "What the hell are you doing? You've now got a film that works. That's what you should stick with." They were insistent. I ended up saying, "Hey! It's your film. I came here to help." I think the result is funny in parts.

TR: I like the central premise: that the "fierce creatures" are the people. It makes the film appealingly dark.
FS: Yeah. But John hasn't spoken to me much since the film didn't find success. Actually, I shouldn't have put my name on it. I should have just helped out because now I get blamed for bits that I had no control over.

TR: A playful reading of the film could suggest the businessmen in the film are simply surrogates for the suits who've made life hard for you over the years. Of course, you weren't thinking of that at the time?
FS: Of course not.

TR: What exactly did you mean when you said that you shot *Empire Falls* "as a film"?
FS: Just that it's a three-hour-twenty minute film (originally a three-hour-thirty-five minute film, with a slightly different rhythm). I wasn't shooting it as a series of parts. I knew it might get split in two. I wasn't thinking of it as a four-part miniseries, or anything like that, because if I had been I would have had to have teaser climaxes.

The HBO guys thought that maybe we should put some chapters in. I thought that was a good idea because you can't just keep following an upward arc for three and a half hours. The chapter headings allow you to take a breath and then build again, although they don't break the film down into equal parts. But it was still made to be viewed in one sitting.

TR: How did you come upon the project?
FS: Sam Cohn brought it to me, although I wasn't with him any more by then. He was Paul Newman's agent, and he put me in for it. His ex-assistant, Marc Platt, was one of the producers, along with Paul.

TR: So the script was already out there.
FS: Yeah, I think it was, or maybe it was still just the book. I honestly can't remember. But Richard Russo and I did a lot of work on it. I remember one of the things I said to him was, "Do me a favor. Read your book again, but don't read the first two chapters and see how the information contained in them comes out through the rest." That became our guide to everything that followed. You learn about the characters as you go along rather than treading water for about twenty minutes.

TR: But you still have the crucial introductory section about the history of the town, about the displacement of the indigenous people.

FS: Yeah, and it's amazing to go to those towns today and see all of those giant buildings with nothing happening in them.

TR: I'm aware as we're talking that many of the questions I'm asking you, and the way I've structured them, are steering you towards my readings of the films' politics, assuming that you're coming from roughly the same place that I am. I'm wondering if I'm just imposing that view on the films and you're being agreeable, or is it actually in line with your own feelings about them?
FS: I understand what you're saying.

TR: So I'm proposing that *Empire Falls* is actually a film about America and its history, the things that have gone wrong and how it's a nation tearing itself apart.
FS: Yeah. I mean, I wouldn't do *Atlas Shrugged*, but I would do a book by Richard Russo. My leanings are more socialist, I suppose, but it isn't specifically why I'm doing my films the way I do. It's difficult to identify *all* the things that interest me about a project. What matters is a whole range of things that allow me to make something interesting. I also like to go into areas where I don't feel all that comfortable to start with and learn something in the process. The initial interests are to do with the characters and the interactions, but, as you're presenting them, that also becomes about a way of living.

I have a bug in my bonnet about people with fixed ideas, who always vote the same way in elections, leading to a polarization that simplifies the world along party lines. I find political rallies just stupid. Surely it should be about finding the right *people* to deal with what's happening now rather than this party or that one? Politics has become about just getting into power and staying there.

TR: I look at some of your films as stories in which you get to say what you've just said through a dramatic form.
FS: That's true, but it's never quite that simple. People tend to see David Hare as a political writer who's more than a bit didactic. But actually, while that might sometimes be the case, he's also brilliant at putting both sides, or three sides, of a situation. And having people argue them out. Even if he finally might come down on the side that he believes in, that's always really interesting. He's aired the lot rather than simply shoved a one-dimensional view in your face.

I saw a play on Broadway called *A Room of One's Own*—Eileen Atkins did it—about Virginia Woolf's attempts to get a room of her own, like men get, to write in. In it, she talks about how the best writing happens when the writer gets a subject that is a great idea to explore or a story to tell or a mood piece, and they just write. And through it, without ever setting out to do this, all the things the writer has ever wanted to say come out—unconsciously.

Whereas, the other way is more likely to be a problem: I can manipulate the story to show this; I can get it to show that. That doesn't mean that it's not going to be any good, but the best stuff is going to result when it all just flows through instinctively. That's exactly what happened for John Guare in *Six Degrees of Separation*: it's his world that he's writing about, and, in doing so, everything that he ever wanted to say just flows out. It's also why it has that unknown quotient that I was talking about earlier.

TR: You've made so many films set in enclosed communities or small towns . . .
FS: I have?

TR: From *The Priest* and *Devil's Playground* onwards; the romantic comedies, *Six Degrees*, *Empire Falls*, *Words and Pictures* . . .
FS: I hadn't thought of them like that. For me, with *Devil's Playground*, I was just writing about a world that I knew and trying to present a world that people probably know nothing about. But in that world, they'll probably find every character in the world that they do know. So, yes, I guess that, in that way, the settings become microcosms. Maybe it's a working method, but in the end it's about what's happening within and between the characters. A lot of it is simply your subconscious at work.

TR: And something that you only recognize in retrospect.
FS: Yeah, and it should stay that way.

Appendix

A distinctive feature of Schepisi's work has been his belief in filmmaking as the work of a team and his ongoing collaborations with, among others, cinematographer Ian Baker and composer Paul Grabowsky, both of whom lend Schepisi's films a firm foundation. In the following interviews, Baker and Grabowsky cast light on Schepisi's working methods and their ongoing relationships with the director.

Planning and Problem-Solving: An Interview with Ian Baker

Tom Ryan / 2016

Tom Ryan: How did you meet Fred?
Ian Baker: In 1968, just before Christmas, friends of mine were working for him at his film company, and he was doing a huge commercial in the Melbourne CBD. At that time, there weren't freelance film technicians, and they were looking for gofers to carry equipment around the city. I'd just finished the film course at Swinburne, so one of these friends phoned me, wondering if I'd be available to lug gear around for a few days. That included minding all the equipment out the front of Florentino's [an up-market Melbourne restaurant] while they all went in and had lunch.

At the end of the shoot, it was the day before Christmas. Eve and Fred said to me [Baker doing an approximation of Schepisi's gruff Australian accent], "We're havin' a party tonight. You wanna come along?" So I went along to this doozy party in Fitzroy, and at the end of the night Fred said to me, "What are ya doin' next year?" I had no immediate plans, so he said, "We open on the third o' January. Why doncha come in and we'll see what we can do?"

I arrived early. I remember sitting on the doorstep of The Film House for a couple of hours before anybody else arrived. But I ended up with a job that morning, as a studio gofer for the princely sum of two pounds and sixpence a week.

At that time, Fred was employing big-time cinematographers from Sydney, and, a lot of the time, when he only needed little jobs done, he'd get me to set them up because I sort of knew about cameras. So with him cuffing me around the back of the head, we'd shoot a product shot or whatever.

Then a documentary came up, *Tomorrow's Canberra*. The cinematographer who was supposed to do it became unavailable, so luck was with me. Along the way, I also shot a lot of ads for Fred before I went freelance. But, after that, I still worked for him anyway. Then came *The Priest*, the segment of the four-part feature, *Libido*, followed by his first feature, *The Devil's Playground*. And the rest is history.

TR: What do you think he saw in you that . . . ?
IB: (laughing) Cheap labor.

TR: Beyond that, though, what do you think he thought you could bring to what he was doing?
IB: I don't know. I've never really thought about that. I was always, and I still am today, fast at what I do. I don't dilly-dally, and I tend to light shots in a simple way, which is therefore quick. Maybe it's that, but I think that's probably more a question for him than me.

TR: Why has the partnership continued for so long?
IB: I think I understand Fred. I can read a script, and I'll know what he's going to do with it. So I don't have to ask him a lot of questions. I can give ideas to him in preproduction that will build on this. I think that's come out of doing so much work together. In short, we have a very established working relationship.

TR: Given that you could look at a script and have a pretty good idea about what Fred would do with it, why haven't you ever directed?
IB: There's a very simple answer to that. I am good at what I do. I am really good at what I do. I would be a mediocre director. And I don't want to be mediocre at what I do.

TR: The credits name you as Fred's cinematographer, but there are also lots of other things you do as well. Credits compartmentalize, and I'm interested in the blurry lines between the roles, where you go out to look at locations and . . .
IB: Yeah. About ten or twelve weeks before we go into production, we'll be surveying locations. I work very closely with the production designer, a collaboration that we both love. I'll take lots and lots of photographs. They'll often be in the form of little photographic essays meant to create the look we might want to give the film. I'll discuss this with Fred and make suggestions. After that, I'll give a copy to the production designer, and then later I'll go over everything with key crew and

the rigging crew so that on the day of filming everything is prepped to ensure that Fred has as much time as we can give him.

Something we don't seem to do much anymore, but that we used to do years ago, is that Fred would get a couple of movies, we'd sit down and watch them, and he would say, "That's the sort of look I'm after for this film." The other thing we'd reference was the work of old masters. He'd say things like, "Every shot should look like a Vermeer painting." You know, with that wonderful light coming through the window. You'd have "look" references like that so that when you start, hopefully, it's all been formulated in your mind.

TR: So another way of looking at what you do is to see it as problem-solving—both beforehand and then on the spot, once you're into the shoot?
IB: Yeah. With *Words and Pictures*, the problem for me on reading the script was that it was going to be mostly shot in a school. And that's all been done before. It's going to be boring, no matter what you do, although I think we did pretty well under the circumstances. But I knew from the start that I wasn't going to win any awards with that one.

TR: One of the most striking things about Fred's films is how the environments, the settings seem alive. They have a character all their own.
IB: Yeah. That's true of all the films, going back to *The Chant of Jimmie Blacksmith*—and even *Barbarosa*, which is a visually amazing film. Fred had the biggest battles to get us to where we were in Texas, virtually Mexico, to shoot it. Scant accommodation, hardly any facilities, but he wanted to be there. He didn't want to shoot the film against the same mesas and buttes out the back of Los Angeles that everybody else has used. The studio wanted him to do that, but he fought for what he wanted, and—wow!—look at the movie.

TR: This attention to the details of a setting also seems responsible for the claustrophobia of *The Priest* and *Devil's Playground*, or the way the landscape comes alive in *Jimmie Blacksmith*, the sumptuous interiors of *Six Degrees*, or the small township in *Empire Falls* . . . That must take a lot of planning?
IB: Fred's really good at working at what he wants a location to offer. Like me, he believes that locations should be an equal-billing character to the lead actors. You have to *see* where you are, and the good thing about Fred is that he'll always push for that. It's all about scale.

New York, for example, has scale. You don't want to shoot against a brownstone wall; you want to turn around and look down the street and see the river with a boat going by. You'll have an AD down there cueing you to roll because there's a boat going down the river. It's just a little detail in the picture, but it's part of the film's multilayered texture. Not many people directing films understand that.

TR: So Fred will ask you for that? He'll come to you with a particular detail he wants to use?
IB: It runs both ways. He tells me; I suggest it to him. We just do it. I'm there to execute. In *Words and Pictures*, the Juliette Binoche character's apartment was on the river. We had an AD outside all the time. We'd be ready to roll, a barge with logs on it would be coming along, and he'd cue us to start. You'd be looking at the beautiful sparkling river, and then suddenly this huge boat would go by. This is the kind of thing that's worth waiting for because it adds so much oomph and texture to the movie.

TR: Would you ever venture to say to Fred, for example, "You're ending the sequence on a wide-shot. You really need a close-up"?
IB: No. I would never say anything like that—not uninvited—because it's clearly not my area. If he was uncertain about what to do, I *would* say it. But he knows what to do. Anyway, Fred covers a sequence more than anybody else I've ever worked with. If you've got time to do it, that's fine because it gives him and the editor many more options.

TR: Are you ever involved in the editing? Does the line blur there as well?
IB: Not really. Fred will always invite me to look at cuts as we're progressing. But I would never open my trap as we're progressing and say, "Look, I think that sequence is too long." I don't consider that to be my area.

TR: At what point did you develop what, for lack of a better description, I describe as "the prowling camera" where others might deploy static set-ups? Your camera always seem to be on the move, even if ever so slightly.
IB: There *are* some positively formal, static, still images. There's a lot of them in *Plenty* and in *Russia House*. There's also a lot of movement, but the movement's there to give an edge to what you're looking at. Like in *Words and Pictures*: the night that Clive Owen comes to her apartment, the movement's there to bring a tension into the scene. Even if you're not actually conscious of it being there, that's what it'll do.

There are other reasons for moving, of course, like to shift the angle to introduce somebody else, or something, into the frame. But the creeping camera thing is just to create a tension.

TR: Who came up with that?
IB: Fred initiated that originally. It's something we both do now. If we started a movie tomorrow, I'd know exactly when he was going to want to move the camera and where and how.

TR: I think of the Vilmos Zsigmond films for Robert Altman for an extreme example of that, although he uses a telephoto lens. Is he one of the cinematographers who's left his mark on you in some way?

IB: Not especially. I'm quite often asked the question about who's influenced me. One of the early movies that inspired me and whose techniques I still use today was *Klute*. It's in widescreen, and Fred and I always shoot widescreen. It was marvelous the way that Gordon Willis used the frame. He'd have a close-up of somebody way over at the edge of the widescreen, and the rest of the frame would all be out of focus, maybe a bit of wall, almost black, so that your eye would be drawn to the character in the enclosed space. What Fred refers to as "shuttering."

With Fred, we'll, say, be looking into a room, so you start out in the hallway. You'll have a bit of wall on one side or the other or both, and you'll have an out-of-focus vase of flowers. Your eye will be focussed on looking into the room, but you'll be aware of things pressing in on it. So you're using the wide-frame but smashing in on it wherever you can. We did that kind of stuff on *Plenty* and *Russia House*. That's a technique that I borrowed from *Klute* and that I still apply today. So you can still have a full-size figure in a drastically horizontal frame, and you're looking at them and not a whole lot of other stuff.

TR: When you watched *Last Orders*, did you ever think that (for better or worse), "I would have done that differently"?

IB: Yes, I did because I could tell straight away that Fred had shot it in a different way from how he would have if I had been the DOP. Everybody has their own way of doing things and just as I've had to make adjustments to accommodate directors I haven't worked with before, Fred would have had to restructure the way he works. I was off shooting *Queen of the Damned* . . .

TR: What work that you've done with Fred most satisfies you?

IB: I think *Plenty*, *Russia House*, *Six Degrees*. And I couldn't leave *The Chant of Jimmie Blacksmith* out of the equation. The only one I really don't like is *Words and Pictures*, which was not destined to be a cinematographer's film. But it was still fun to do.

TR: What is it about the collaboration with Fred that you find so satisfying?

IB: These days, he's really pleasurable to work with. He doesn't cuff me around the back of the head so often anymore. We've both mellowed a bit since those days, and the understanding we have is the kind of thing that takes time to grow. Now, on the basis of what we know about what we're going to do, we're streets ahead when we start shooting. He's always thinking about the big picture and willing to try things out, and it's good to know from the start that it's going to be harmonious.

Key Notes: An Interview with Paul Grabowsky

Tom Ryan / 2016

Tom Ryan: Rumor has it that you heard that Fred was making *Last Orders* and offered your services. True?
Paul Grabowsky: True. Sort of. I'd known Fred for quite a long time by then.

When I was an aspiring film composer in the mid-'80s, cautiously, or incautiously, trying to find my place in that world, Fred was the foremost Melbourne filmmaker with an international reputation.

My first wife, Vera, whom I'd married while I was living in Germany, had got a job as a receptionist at The Film House. She somehow got me through the front door there with a cassette of my work in hand: the miniseries, *The Petrov Affair* (1987), a kids' series called *Dusty* (1989), and some other stuff. Fred very graciously gave me the time of day—he's like that.

I remember Mary, Fred's wife, coming down the stairs and saying [Grabowsky doing American accent], "Fred, I like that music." I thought, "Great!" I discovered very quickly that Fred had a great love of jazz music, and we talked about that. I think that was about the time that he was preparing to start work on *Evil Angels*. So for me, in the first case, it was really just a kind of reconnaissance mission.

After that, I didn't see him for a number of years. But then I got a phone call from an orchestra booker, Ron Layton, who used to look after film-scoring sessions in the '90s, looking for a jazz pianist to play on the score for *Six Degrees of Separation*, being recorded in Melbourne by Jerry Goldsmith. I was over the moon, firstly at the thought of working with Jerry and then at reestablishing contact with Fred.

That was a really fantastic experience. It was a small group: I think the total ensemble was about ten players, very unusual for Jerry. It was a classical-ish score, tango-infused with a jazz underpinning. Jerry and I got on like a house on fire: he got me to do some extra scorings for source music while we were in the studio and was very encouraging. I guess it got through to Fred that "well, this guy's not an idiot," in this particular instance, anyway. About a year later, Jerry did another score for Fred in Melbourne, this time for *I.Q.* That was a more conventional Jerry score, for which I played piano with the orchestra. I was playing a few of those gigs then, just as a session musician.

Fred and I remained friends, and, when I heard about *Last Orders*, I felt confident enough to say, "Would you consider me?" Jerry was ill and unavailable, so I knew there was the possibility that Fred would be looking for somebody. He was in London, I emailed him and said, "Why don't you give me a go?" And he said, "Okay."

TR: What do you think he saw in you that would work for him?

PG: You know, Tom, I'm really not sure. I think he might have thought that I was a kindred spirit and that I would take direction. He knew that I was very good in the recording studio, and he knew that I could think quickly on my feet because I had to do a lot of last-minute things to make the score for *Six Degrees* exactly what Jerry wanted it to be—some small but key creative decisions about individual cues.

When I formed the Australian Art Orchestra in 1993, I asked Fred to be the patron. He had come to various concerts of ours and really loved what we were doing. He was a great fan of Gil Evans, and he used to go to see Gil's band play on Monday nights in New York at Sweet Basil. There were elements of what we were doing with the Art Orchestra that really reminded him of that.

We made an album called *Ringing the Bell Backwards*, which was a collection of reimaginings that I had done of European popular music of the 1930s and '40s. There was something very cinematic about that music, albeit in an oddball kind of way. He loved that record, and I think that may have played a role in this as well.

As well, Fred had introduced me to John Irvin, who'd come to Australia to shoot the TV miniseries, *Noah's Ark* (1999), and I did the score. John was very pleased with what I did and wanted me to do *Shiner* (2000), a dark take on *King Lear*, which he was making in London with Michael Caine on the south side of the Thames. I went to London and did the movie, and John was over the moon about it. I think he then sang my praises to Fred.

So I think that all that really tipped the scales in my favor.

TR: What kind of rules do you work by with Fred?

PG: I think one of the things that's really essential for a composer in this kind of situation is that you have to be prepared to relinquish your work. You can't be precious; the industry doesn't allow it. You've got to be absolutely prepared to take direction, although you can challenge it from time to time. But, at the end of the day, you must obey; otherwise, it's chaos. And you've got to be able to think quickly.

TR: When you and Fred have a disagreement, how strongly can you argue your case?

PG: With Fred, I can argue very strongly because I know him very well. Our relationship has become far more toned over the years. I would have had less confidence to "serve it up" at the beginning. But these days, if I really have a strong view about something, I can say, "You know, I think you're wrong about that." There's now a reasonable chance that he'll go, "Okay, let's do it your way." There's always conversation, and there's always resolution. There's never a "fuck you" moment. There's never a moment where he's gone away and changed something, leaving me to go "What have you done?" He's great like that. He's very respectful of his colleagues. And he's very, very loyal too.

TR: At what stage in the production process do you enter the scene with Fred?
PG: With *Last Orders*, once he'd agreed that I was going to be on board, he sent me the script. I don't think he'd started shooting by then, but he generally likes me to think about the score ahead of time. Coincidentally, I'd already read the book.

TR: What did he say to you to guide your thinking about it?
PG: There were conversations about it being very, very English in its subject matter. I remember when I went to New York to start working on the score with him, he kept on talking about how he wanted it to have a "quirky" quality. I remember we went and bought hundreds of CDs at Tower Records and spent hundreds of hours listening to them. I started to write a draft of the score, and it had a particular kind of "quirky" sound. We'd set up this small studio next to the cutting room so that I could react on a daily basis to what Kate Williams was doing with the cut. We got the point of a rough assemblage which we looked at with the temp score, and I thought, "It's just fuckin' wrong." This "quirky" thing is not working for it. It's actually a very soulful picture, a bittersweet picture, and the music needs to reflect that.

So I went away and cleared my head. Then I came in—it was a Sunday, and they weren't working—sat down, and wrote that theme which moves between major and minor and modulates every couple of bars. It became this constantly shifting, irresolute thing between being major and minor and finally landing on a major key that's still very ambivalent. It doesn't allow you to form a very strong view about what it is suggesting.

TR: Was that where the attachment of a theme to a character began?
PG: Rather than trying to introduce the characters by themes, it was much more important to me—and Fred's always on about this anyway—to use the music to bridge, in particular, his temporal cuts. *Last Orders* is one of those Schepisi films that jump between particular time periods . . . like *Six Degrees*. The music flows over those time cuts and kind of guides you towards the correspondences.

TR: So you're looking at the rough cut; you've got the temp score. Are you involved in the editing at all?
PG: I do occasionally make a suggestion about lengthening a particular shot because it would serve my interests as the composer. But Kate and I and Fred had a really good thing going on. With Kate and Fred it was a little more fraught from time to time, but she and I always got on very well.

With *Last Orders*, the important thing for me was breaking the ice with that theme because everything else flowed from that. Jerry got in touch to say that he really liked the score, which was very nice to hear.

TR: What are the differences between working with Fred and, say, with Paul Cox, with whom you've worked at least a dozen times?
PG: With Fred, I'm usually fully involved; with Cox, I just write music, and he does what he wants with it—sometimes in a completely mysterious way. Fred is someone I'd describe as a structured filmmaker. He demands and expects an orderly roll-out of carefully prepared decisions. He has an incredible eye for detail and an amazing memory too.

I can recall when I was doing *Empire Falls*, which was a very big production—thirteen reels—that he would remember different iterations of cues that I had written and ask where the bassoon line from three versions ago was. I had made an executive decision to remove it. "Put it back." "Okay."

TR: How do you find "the right score" for something like *Empire Falls*?
PG: This is another one that Jerry would have done, but he was too sick. It was hard. None of Fred's films are straightforward. I don't often have the chance to do something big and lush. I remember his first direction was "Americana!" I thought, "Me? Americana? That's really not my thing." I ended up doing all this interesting stuff with guitars. I got Slav Grigorian and his brother and Steve Magnusson, really good guitar players. But I wanted to have this really weird thing happening too. It was a little bit like what Thomas Newman would later do, or maybe Carter Burwell: Americana, but with something weird going on at the same time.

TR: How do you introduce something "weird"? With an instrument?
PG: Yeah, electronica. We set up this Americana-sounding thing with these other discordant sounds going on in the background that you're only vaguely aware of. I'd use those to underscore the "once upon a time there was a town" narration.

TR: So when you and Fred are working on a project, there is the preliminary work: reading the script, buying CDs, discussions. What then?
PG: The spotting sessions are where the rubber really hits the road when you're composing for films, where you sit down with a notebook, and he says, "I want something that starts here, does this kind of thing, and finishes there." There's also talk about what the music's supposed to be conveying at that point. Fred hates film music that insists on telling you what you already know, what I call "pumping the movie with steroids," which most action adventure films do. It's

gone out of control now, where there's a sting or a stab on every action. It's often technically well-crafted, but it's "Do we have to?"

TR: How fully are you involved in the choice of music within the frame, the "diegetic" music?
PG: (laughs) Sometimes. There's often a music supervisor who does that, and they are mysterious beasts. In the credit sequences, their credit often comes before the composer's! (laughter) Their job is to buy licenses and make suggestions about the songs, so they're really slaves to the music publishing industry. They and composers often don't see eye to eye. Let's just put it like that.

TR: So you're not inclined to say that the film doesn't need a David Bowie song there; it needs an aria?
PG: I might have a view. These things are determined in most instances by what you can afford because you've got to buy the rights. If it's a David Bowie song, it's going to blow the budget out of the water, unless you've got a sweetheart deal.

TR: But in *Words and Pictures*, it *is* a David Bowie song.
PG: It is. But we got a sweetheart deal. And that was okay because I love David Bowie. There were other choices that I thought, "Really?" But I tell you what, and this is a really lovely moment, there's a scene in *Words and Pictures* where Juliette Binoche's character refuses to have anything to do with Clive Owen, who's disgraced himself and destroyed her painting, which had cost her so much to make. He finally resorts to sending her a piece of music in an e-mail attachment. She plays it, and there's a two-and-a-half-minute sequence where she's just listening. Originally Fred had a pretty awful piece of music selected for that very critical scene. It was going to be an arrangement of the Pavane by Faure for a jazz violin and orchestra: really cheesy. I said to him, "I know you're wedded to that piece, but I've gotta tell you, mate, it's awful. And it's not doing what you want it to do." "Ah, no. I like it."

Well, in the recording studio, I was putting the finishing touches to the score. Clive Owen's character has stolen the poem from his son. I said to Fred, "You know, I'm going to have a crack at writing a song to the poem's lyrics, and I'm going to put it on the end titles and see what you think." He agreed, and I did. A very nice little song was the result: it's sung at the end by Gian Slater, a Melbourne singer.

Just before I was about to send the musicians home, I said, "Let me try something for that bloody scene." So I quickly wrote out an arrangement of that song for piano, cello, and clarinet. I figured out how many bars it would need to be, more or less, and we ran it a couple of times. I could tell that something was going on in the control room, and Fred asked us to do another take because it wasn't quite the right length. It took three or four takes, and we got it frame-accurate. No click track; it was just by feel, like old scores, just by looking at the pictures.

They were all in tears in the control room because we'd nailed it. It wasn't source music; it was original score. But it is diegetic music because he has sent it to her. It also recurs, for people who've got an ear for it, with the closing titles. So it ties threads together, kind of a musical gag, if you like. And it's where film music can really be extraordinary. I was so grateful to Fred for giving me the rope to do it.

TR: Does he keep editing until the last minute?
PG: He has recently. During the last few weeks on *Words and Pictures*, there were a number of different cuts. That may run up until the death knell. After the music has been mixed, you can keep editing it right up to that point, although the results aren't always to the composer's liking.

TR: Who are the composers who've left their mark on you?
PG: My favorite will always be Bernard Herrmann. He's influenced me greatly and made me realize that you don't need a hundred-piece orchestra to write great film music. You just need a great musical idea and a great bunch of players.

There are others whom I appreciate too: Nino Rota, because his music never works the way you might think that film music is supposed to and is so good at creating a psychological subtext. I loved Jerry's scores for *The Planet of the Apes* (1968) and *Basic Instinct* (1992). One of the great principles of his music is the constant variation on simple ideas—and Morricone, of course. Not everything that he's done, but he has a genius ear for sound. He was an improvising musician too, a trumpet player with a free improvisation group in the '60s.

Additional Resources

V. Amiel, "Le sauvage qui n'avait pas été enfant," *Positif*, February 1983.

Chris Beck, "On the Couch: Fred Schepisi, Film Maker," *The Saturday Age*, Saturday Extra, February 8, 1997.

Michaela Boland and Michael Body, *Aussiewood*, Allen & Unwin, NSW, 2004, pp. 229–42.

Donna Brown, "Anatomy of a Deal: *The Russia House*," *Management Review*, March 1990.

Stephanie Bunbury, "Dust to Dust," *The Sunday Age*, May 12, 2002.

Rose Capp, "*It Runs in the Family*: Sons, Sins and Structural Complexity in Fred Schepisi's *Six Degrees of Separation*," *Senses of Cinema*, Issue No. 60 (October 2011).

Anthony Carew, "Homecoming and Dislocation: An Interview with Fred Schepisi," *Metro*, No. 170 (2011), pp. 14–16.

David Coltheart, "Members Act in *Evil Angels*," *Signs*, January 16, 1988, p. 12.

———, "Misperceptions—Interview with Fred Schepisi," *Signs*, August 1988, pp. 2–4.

Bob Crimeen, "Schepisi and the Chamberlain Obsession," *The Brisbane Courier Mail*, Saturday, November 12, 1998.

Sam Dallas, "Clear Skies," *Inside Film: If*, No. 146, April 2012, p. 15.

Anna Daly, "*People Make Papers*," *Senses of Cinema*, Issue 60 (October 2011).

Adrian Danks, "Across the Borderline," *Senses of Cinema*, Issue 60 (October 2011).

Glenn Donnar, "ReViewing *Jimmie*: The Critical Reception of *The Chant of Jimmie Blacksmith*," *Senses of Cinema*, Issue 60 (October 2011).

Daniel Eisenberg, "Schepisi's Celluloid Australia," *Senses of Cinema*, Issue No. 60 (October 2011).

Ryan Gilbey, "Unmade Freds," *Sight & Sound*, January 2002, pp. 12–13.

Bryce Hallett, "Right Said Fred," *The Weekend Australian*, May 13, 1995.

Peter Hamilton, "From the Dark Night: Thomas Kenneally on *Jimmie Blacksmith*," *Metro* No. 44 (Winter, 1978), pp. 22–27.

Philippa Hawker, "Fred Schepisi Paints Picture with Words and Chemistry," *The Sydney Morning Herald*, July 15, 2014, p. 11.

Frank Heimans, "Fred Schepisi: Oral History" (audio recording and transcript), National Film and Sound Archive, Canberra, Australia.

Home Box Office, "Interview with Fred Schepisi: *Empire Falls*," 2005.

Sheila Johnston, "Reeling in the Years," *The Times*, January 8, 2002, p. 21.
Pauline Kael, "A Dreamlike Requiem Mass for a Nation's Lost Honour," *The New Yorker*, September 15, 1980 (also in Albert Moran and Tom O'Regan, eds., *An Australian Film Reader*, Sydney, Currency Press, 1985, pp. 204–10).
E. Kelleher, "Schepisi Expands Varied Career via *Six Degrees*," *Film Journal* (New York), January/February 1994.
Greg King, "IQ Test," *Beat Magazine*, October 5, 1995.
Neal Koch, "Hollywood Audition Rites . . . and Wrongs," *The New York Times*, August 23, 1992.
Jeff LaBrecque, "Clive Owen and Juliette Binoche Make Love and War in *Words and Pictures*," *Entertainment Weekly*, May 15, 2014.
Neil Lawrence & Steve Bunk, eds., *The Stump Jumpers: A New Breed of Australians*, 1985, pp. 136–71 (chapter by Fred Schepisi about his career to *Plenty*).
Catharine Lumby, "The Shootist," *The Bulletin*, July 16, 2002, pp. 78–79.
Sarah Maddox, "An Underdog of Australian Cinema: Fred Schepisi," *Metro*, No. 135, 2002, pp. 60–63.
M. Magill, "Interview with Fred Schepisi," *Films in Review* (New York), January 1984.
Brian McFarlane, "The Filmmaker as Adaptor: Fred Schepisi Takes on Patrick White in *The Eye of the Storm*," *Senses of Cinema*, Issue 60 (October 2011).
———, "Giving and Taking *Last Orders*" in *Twenty British Films: A Guided Tour*, Manchester University Press, 2015, pp. 228–39.
David Melville, "Inside *The Eye of the Storm*," *Senses of Cinema*, Issue 70 (February 2014).
Oscar Moore, "Lighting the 'Dark' Side with le Carré," *The Times*, December 21, 1989, p. 21.
Henry Reynolds, "*The Chant of Jimmie Blacksmith*," Currency Press (Australian Screen Classics), Strawberry Hills, NSW, 2008.
David Roe & Scott Murray, "Fred Schepisi—Producer/Director/Scriptwriter," *Cinema Papers*, Special Cannes Issue, 1978, pp. 9–11, 101.
Tom Ryan, "Right Said Fred," *The Age*, July 12, 2002.
———, "All in the Family," *The Age*, August 22, 2003.
Barbara Samuels, "Fred Schepisi: Boom, Bust and the 'Tax Trap,'" *Cinema Canada*, February 1983, p. 23.
Fred Schepisi, "Let's Have a Moral Decision," *The Age*, Letters Page, August 15, 1997.
———, Keynote Address at the Australian Directors Guild Conference 2013.
Fred Schepisi website: http://fredschepisi.com.
Rochelle Siemienowicz, "Riding the Storm: An Interview with Fred Schepisi," AFI Blog, September 15, 2011.
Judy Stone, *Eye on the World: Conversations with International Filmmakers*, Silman-James Press, California, 1997, pp. 26–29.

David Stratton, *The Last New Wave: The Australian Film Revival*, Angus & Robertson Publishers, 1980, pp. 126–39.

Sonia Taitz, "Fred Schepisi Puts Gossip on Trial," *The New York Times*, November 6, 1988.

Christos Tsiolkas, *The Devil's Playground*, Currency Press & Screensound, Australia, 2002 (commentary on the film).

Lawrence Van Gelder, "Protests, Paeans, and *The Chant of Jimmie Blacksmith*," *The New York Times*, August 31, 1980.

Kristin Williamson, "How Streep Tempted Schepisi to Tackle the Story of Azaria Chamberlain," *Times on Sunday*, August 16, 1987, p. 29.

Peter Wilmoth, "An Eye for an Eye," *The Melbourne Weekly*, September 1, 2011.

Peter Wilshire, "Trouble in the Brotherhood: *The Devil's Playground* Revisited," *Metro*, No. 151 (2006), p. 138–42.

Index

10BA tax incentive scheme, 77–78
20th Century Fox, 28, 29, 56
2000 Weeks (1969), 6

Adams, Phillip, 23, 79, 80, 154
Adventures of Barry McKenzie, The (1972), xii
Adventures of Robin Hood, The (1938), 57, 94
Alien (1979), 50
Allen, Karen, 56
Allen, Woody, 21
All in the Family (TV series, 1971–1979), 130
Altered States (1980), 45, 58
Altman, Robert, 182
Alvin Purple (1973), xii
Andorra (novel, 1997), xvi, 153
Ann-Margret, 56
Armstrong, Gillian, viii–x, xii, xiii, xviii, xix, 8, 138
As I Lay Dying (novel, 1930), 121
Associated Film Distribution (AFD), 58
Assumption College, Kilmore, 81
Atkins, Eileen, 176
Atlas Shrugged (novel, 1957), 176
Australian Actors Equity, 38
Australian Art Orchestra, 184
Australian Broadcasting Commission (ABC), 6
Australian Experimental Film Fund, 6, 7

Australian Film, Television, and Radio School (AFTVRS), ix
Australian Film Development Corporation (AFDC), 23
Australian Film Institute (AFI), 53, 108
Australia's "film renaissance," viii–ix, xii–xiv, 6–18, 28, 61, 79–81, 86–88
Avedon, Richard, 156
Ayers Rock, 70, 111

Babe: Pig in the City (1998), 139
Backroads (1977), xii
Baker, Ian, viii, xvii, xix, 10, 19, 25, 37, 46, 49, 53, 57, 64, 70, 72, 87, 122, 128, 141, 157, 160, 178–82
Ball of Fire (1941), 172
Barker, Ian, 69
Barry Lyndon (1975), 156
Basic Instinct (1992), 188
Bazin, Andre, 158–59
Beatles, The, 5
B.E.F. Distributors (British Empire Films), xii
Beilby, Peter, 77, 121
Beresford, Bruce, xii, 28, 33, 47, 49, 61, 72, 138, 146n
Bergman, Ingmar, 4
Big Bend National Park, Texas, 89
Big Chill, The (1983), 49
Bilcock, Jill, viii
Billy Bathgate (1991), 104

INDEX

Binoche, Juliette, 160, 166, 181, 187
Bisset, Jacqueline, 47, 57, 91–92
Blair, Ron, 80
Blue Danube, The (waltz, 1866), 95
Bonfire of the Vanities, The (1990), 104
Bowie, David, 187
Boyd, Russell, 5
Brammer, Graham, 146n
"Breaker" Morant (1980), xii
Breckman, Andy, 169
Brickman, Marshall, 169
Brides of Christ (TV series, 1991), 80
Bruce Clarke's Jingle Workshop, 95
Bryson, John, 67, 68
Bryson cinema, Melbourne, 23
Buddy Holly Story, The (1978), 57
Bunuel, Luis, 21
Burke, Simon, 11–12, 15, 24
Burstall, Tim, xii, 6, 39
Burwell, Carter, 186
Busey, Gary, 42, 57, 89, 170

Caine, Michael, 114, 117, 119, 184
Cameron, Peter, 153
Canadian National Film Board, 154
Cannes Film Festival, 16, 17, 27, 28, 29, 33
Cannon Films, 98, 111
Cantrill, Arthur and Corinne, 157
Carden Advertising, Melbourne, 154
Cars That Ate Paris, The (1974), xii
Caswell, Robert, 68, 69
Catcher in the Rye, The (novel, 1951), 104
Caulfield, Michael, 15, 120
Chamberlain, Azaria, 67
Chamberlain, Lindy, 67–70, 83–85, 111, 150, 151, 162
Chamberlain, Michael, 68–70, 83–85, 111
Chamberlain, Reagan, 69
Channing, Stockard, 104, 105, 112, 151, 168

Chant of Jimmie Blacksmith, The (novel, 1972), 7, 28, 42, 108
Chauvel, Charles, xii
Christian Brothers, The (play, 1977), 80
Cinesound Productions, 4, 5, 53, 154
Clarke, Bruce, 95, 157
Cleese, John, 118, 146n, 172, 174
Cleo from 5 to 7 (1962), 157
Clouzot, Henri-Georges, 4
Cohn, Sam, 29, 72, 93, 95, 99, 110, 165, 171, 175
Colbert, Claudette, 21
Coleman, Cy, 50
Columbia Pictures, 24, 95, 146n
Connery, Sean, 72, 100, 106, 115, 173
Cook, Pam, 60
Courtenay, Tom, 114, 117, 122
Cox, Paul, xii, 186
Craven, Peter, 144
Crouse, Lindsay, 45
Cunxin, Li, 146n
Cyrano de Bergerac (play, 1897), 62, 65, 97, 102

Dance, Charles, 59, 146n, 149, 159
Dance and the Railroad, The (play, 1981), 46
Davis, Judy, xv, 138, 139, 147
Dead Heart (1996), 82
Denby, David, 91
Devil's Playground, The (TV series, 2015), 25–26
Dignam, Arthur, viii, ix, 7, 9, 24, 43, 80, 124
DiMarco, Adam, 167
Dinner with Friends (play, 1998), 128
Di Pego, Gerald, 166, 171
Dixon, Wendy, 14, 70
Douglas, Cameron, 127–29, 136
Douglas, Kirk, 38, 127, 128–29, 133
Douglas, Michael, 127–34

INDEX

Dragnet (TV series, 1951–1959), 69
Dreams of Leaving (TV film, 1980), 94
Drimmer, John, 45–46, 58, 92
Duigan, John, xii
Dusty (TV series, 1989), 183
Duvall, Shelley, 66

Einstein, Albert, xvii, 102
EMI, 57
Entertainment Media, 77
Entre Nous (1983), 49
Epworth Hospital, Melbourne, xx
Ericksen, Leon, 89
Evans, Gil, 184
Evil Angels (book, 1985), 67–68

Fat City (1972), 21
Fiddler on the Roof (1971), 58
Field, Sally, 32, 57
Fields, Freddie, 56
Fiends, The (1955), 4
Film Australia, 8
Film House, The, viii, 5, 10, 29, 53, 56, 61, 87, 107, 121, 178, 183
Finlayson, Rhonda, viii, 7, 12, 15, 24, 25, 87, 108
Firm Man, The (1975), xii
Fish Called Wanda, A (1988), 174
Fisk, Jack, 32, 47, 57
Flaherty, Robert, 155
Florentino's, Melbourne, 178
Ford, Joan Mary, 107
Ford, John, 21
Forman, Milos, 21
Forrest, Frederick, 93
Fosse, Bob, 21
Franklin, Richard, xii
Friels, Colin, 138

Gable, Clark, 21
Gaden, John, 138

Gallipoli (1981), 30
Getting of Wisdom, The (1977), xii
Ghostbusters (1984), 77
Gielgud, Sir John, 59, 149, 159
Golden Globes, 74–75
Goldman, James, 40, 91
Goldman, William, 174
Goldsmith, Jerry, xviii, 163–64, 173, 186
Gorbachev, Mikhail, 72, 100
Gosford Park (2001), 125, 126
Grabowsky, Paul, xviii, xix, 116, 133, 162, 164, 178, 183–88
Grade, Sir Lew, 57
Greater Union Organisation (GUO), xiii, 5
Grenville, Kate, 143
Grigorian, Leonard, 186
Grigorian, Slav, 186
Grumpy Old Men (1993), 136
Guare, John, xiv, 104–5, 124, 151, 164–65, 168, 172, 177
Gudgeon, Mac, 146n

Hackman, Gene, 56
Hall, Ken G., xii, 81
Hallstrom, Lasse, 146n
Hannah, Daryl, 66, 77, 112
Happy Feet (2006), 139
Hardy, Jonathan, 81
Hare, David, xiv, 51, 53, 58–60, 63, 93, 148, 164–65, 176
Harvey, Tim, 123
Haskell, Molly, 60
Hemmings, David, 114, 122
Hepburn, Katharine, 21, 57
Herrmann, Bernard, 187
Hicks, Scott, 142
Hill, George Roy, 59
Hogan, PJ (Paul), 171
Holmes, Cecil, xii
Homeland (TV series, 2011–), 167

Homesdale (1971), xii
Honeysuckle Rose (1980), 54, 91
Hoskins, Bob, 114
Humphries, Barry, 172
Hurt, William, xvii, 56, 97
Huston, John, 21
Hutton, Timothy, 45, 46, 48

ICM (ICM Partners), 95, 110
Illuminations (1976), xii
In Melbourne Tonight (TV variety show, 1957–1970, 1996–1998), 79
Inside Looking Out (1977), xii
In the Bedroom (2001), 118, 125
In the Heat of the Night (1967), 58
Irvin, John, 184
ITC, 57, 89

Jacobi, Lou, 172
Jacobs, Sue, 133
Jewison, Norman, 45, 58, 92, 104, 128, 163

Kael, Pauline, 28, 29, 91
Kangaroo (1987), 39
Kanter, Jay, 100
Kavanagh, Brian, 124, 155
Keneally, Thomas, viii, xii–xiii, 7, 12, 28, 40, 42, 53, 79–80, 108, 150, 164
Kennedy, Robert, 40
Kerkorian, Kirk, 95
Khomeini, Ayatollah, 44
King Lear (play, 1606), 184
Kirkham, Andrew, 69
Klimov, Ellen, 99
Kline, Kevin, 76
Klute (1971), 182
Koestler, Arthur, 113
Kostas (1979), xii
Koyaanisqatsi (1982), 156
Krall, Diana, 133

Kubrick, Stanley, 156
Kurosawa, Akira, 4, 21

Ladd, Alan, Jr., 99–101
Ladd Company, 99
Lambert, Verity, 68, 98, 151, 162
Lassally, Walter, 155
Layton, Ron, 183
Lazarus, Paul, 32
Lean, David, 159
le Carré, John (David Cornwell), 72, 76, 86, 99, 101, 173
Leeson, Michael, 169
Legal Eagles (1986), 77
Le Tet, Robert, 77
Lewis, Tommy, 15, 112, 150
Libido (1973), viii, xii, xiii, xixn, 7, 8, 12, 19, 23, 53, 79, 157, 158, 179
Liddle, George, 70
Lindsay, Norman, 34
Ling, Trevor, 25, 87
Lone, John, 45, 46, 48, 58, 106
Look Back in Anger (1959), 21
Luttrell, Martha, 95

Mad Dog Morgan (1976), xii
Mad Max (1979), xii
Magnusson, Steve, 186
Maher, Joseph, 172
Major League (1989), 169
Malle, Louis, 104
Mamet, David, 94
Manchurian Candidate, The (1962), 91
Man from Snowy River, The (1982), 38
Marble Arch Productions, 89
Margulies, Donald, 128
Marist Brothers' Juniorate, Macedon, 29, 50, 53, 61
Martin, Steve, ix, xiv, 65–66, 95, 97, 102, 107, 157
Maslansky, Paul, 99

INDEX

Matsushita, 169
Matthau, Walter, xvii
McCabe and Mrs. Miller (1971), 89
McCallum, Charles, 25
McKellen, Sir Ian, 112, 148
McLaren, Norman, 154
Melbourne International Film Festival (MIFF, Melbourne Film Festival, Melbourne Film Society), 4, 154
Melnick, Dan, 65, 95
Menzel, Jiri, 21
Merrick, David, 50
Metro Goldwyn Mayer (MGM), 40, 56
Michelangelo, 113
Miller, George, xii, 19, 28, 49
Miramax, 118
Mirren, Helen, 114, 119, 126
Mizoguchi, Kenji, 21
Montand, Yves, 4
Montsalvat, 6
Moon Is Blue, The (1953), 56
Moore, Julianne, 143
Mora, Philippe, xii
Morelli, Laura, 116
Morricone, Ennio, 188
Morris, Judy, 138, 139, 148
Morse, Helen, 138
Mouth to Mouth (1978), xii
Muriel (1963), 149
My Best Friend's Wedding (1997), 171
My Brilliant Career (1979), xn, xii, xiii

Nabokov, Vladimir, 41, 47
National Film and Sound Archive, Australia, xix, 157
National Liberal Club, London, 52
Negahban, Navid, 167
Neill, Sam, 68, 70, 84, 151
Nelligan, Kate, 48, 58, 59, 93, 165
Nevin, Robyn, viii, 7, 24, 80, 138
Newman, Paul, 140, 175

Newman, Thomas, 186
Newsfront (1978), xii
Newton-John, Olivia, 39, 56
Nichols, Mike, 99
Nimrod Theatre, Sydney, 24
Noah's Ark (1999), 184

Once and Again (TV series, 1999–2002), 128
One Hundred a Day (short, 1973), ix
One Summer of Happiness (1951), 4
On the Beach (1959), xii
Oscar ceremonies, xiv, 49
Other Man, The (screenplay), 56, 94
Owen, Clive, 143, 160, 166, 181, 187
Ozu, Yasujro, 21

Palmer, Patrick, 45
Papp, Joe, 63
Paris by Night (1988), 94
Partners (1982), 32, 50, 56, 91
Passer, Ivan, 21
Paton Advertising Service, 154
Patrick (1978), xii
Pearce, Guy, 146n
Peckinpah, Sam, 18
Petrov Affair, The (TV mini-series, 1987), 183
Pfeiffer, Michelle, 72, 101, 106, 115
Phillips, John, 69
Picnic at Hanging Rock (1975), xii
Planet of the Apes, The (1968), 188
Platt, Marc, 175
Pollock (2000), 125
Pressman, Edward R., 58, 59, 92, 93
Producers and Directors Guild of Australia (PDGA), 6, 7, 79
Proser, Chip, 58
Proulx, E. Annie, 146n
Purvis, Peter, 155

Queen of the Damned (2002), 122, 182
Quest for Fire (1981), 45, 46

Raggedy Man (1981), 32, 47, 57
Ragtime (1981), 52
Raimey, Bob, 90, 91
Rampling, Charlotte, xv, 138, 139, 143, 147, 148, 151
Rank Organisation (UK), xiii
Rappaport, Jerry, 99
Raucher, Herman, 56
Ray, Satyajit, 21
Rear Window (1954), 135
Redford, Robert, 77
Reid, Dana, 146n
Reynolds, Freddy, 15, 112
Ringing the Bell Backwards (music performance, 2014), 184
Road Warrior, The (*Mad Max 2*) (1981), 19
Robbins, Tim, 170
Robinson, Elisabeth, 120–23, 146n
Rocco and His Brothers (1960), 4
Roland, Gilbert, 28, 38, 58
Romantic Comedy (1983), 50
Roof Needs Mowing, The (short film, 1971), viii
Room of One's Own, A (extended essay, 1929), 176
Ross, Judith, 40, 56
Rota, Nino, 188
Rubin, Mary, 48, 60, 103, 183
Rudin, Scott, 102, 104
Runaway Bride (1999), 171
Rush, Geoffrey, xv, 138, 139, 143, 147, 148
Russo, Richard, xiv, 166, 175, 176
Rydge, Sir Norman, 5

Saigon: Year of the Cat (1983), 93
Saks, Gene, 172
Salt, Waldo, 146n
Sardi, Jan, 143, 146n

Schaffner, Franklin, 164
Scheider, Roy, ix, 47, 56, 57, 91
Schepisi, Fred: on Australian cinema, 6–18, 20–21, 38–39, 77–78, 81–83, 86–89, 142, 145–46, 157, 178–79; on his beginnings as filmmaker, xi–xiv, 6–9, 30–44, 53–54, 56–58, 61–62, 79–81, 86–89, 107–8, 153–59; on business of filmmaking, 16, 28–29, 51, 57–58, 73–75, 91, 118–19, 122–23, 124–26, 127–30, 136, 142–43; on filming in Russia, 72–73; on job of director, xvii–xix, 18–21, 37–38, 44–47, 63–66, 68–71, 72–75, 78, 89–92, 93–95, 98–100, 103–6, 108–13, 115–19, 123–24, 133, 141–42, 144–45, 148–52, 153–77, 180–82, 184–88; on music and working with composers, xix, 95, 115–17, 121, 133, 137, 155, 162–64, 173, 183–88; themes in his work, xv–xvii, 97, 100, 102–3, 106, 110–13, 116–17, 121, 130, 132–33, 144–45, 147–49, 151–52, 161, 167, 172, 175–77, 180; on working in advertising, 3–4, 5–6, 19, 36–37, 53, 79, 108, 119, 154–56; on working in Hollywood, xiv, 28–29, 30–34, 39–40, 47, 49, 52–53, 56–58, 62–63, 74–76, 89–92, 97, 145–46, 169–71; on working with actors, 15–16, 24–25, 37–38, 63–66, 70, 75–77, 89, 97, 106, 112, 139–40, 149–51, 170
Works: *Barbarosa* (1982), xv, xvi, 18, 28–38, 42–44, 45, 49–50, 51, 52, 54–55, 57–58, 60, 61, 62–63, 64–65, 86, 88–91, 92, 110, 147, 168, 180; *Bitter Sweet Love* (screenplay), 29–30, 32, 56; *The Chant of Jimmie Blacksmith* (1978), ix, xiii, xiv, xv, xvi, 12–19, 27–29, 32, 33, 36, 42, 43–44, 45, 47, 48, 49, 52, 54, 56, 57, 61, 62, 65, 81–83, 86–87, 88, 90, 102, 104, 106–7, 108, 110–11, 112,

114, 119, 144, 150, 151, 172, 180, 182; *The Consultant* (screenplay), 47, 91; *A Cry in the Dark (Evil Angels)* (1988), ix, xiv, xv, xvi, 67–71, 74–75, 83–85, 86, 88, 96, 98–99, 111, 138, 140, 143, 144, 150, 151, 162, 167, 183; *The Devil's Playground* (1976), ix, xiii, xv, xvi, 7–12, 19, 22–26, 27, 29, 42, 43, 49, 50, 52, 53–54, 58, 61, 62, 64, 65, 79, 80–81, 86–88, 99, 104, 107, 108–10, 111, 114, 123–24, 149–50, 153, 158–59, 162, 177, 179, 180; *Don Quixote* (aborted production), 118, 146n; *Double Standards (The Other Man)* (screenplay), 56; *Empire Falls* (2005), xiv, xv, xvi, 136, 144, 166, 168, 173, 175–76, 180, 186, 187; *The Eye of the Storm* (2011), ix, xv, xvi, 138–46, 147–49, 151–52; *Fierce Creatures* (1997), xv, 147, 174–75; *A Hundred Odd Years from Now* (advertisement, 1968), 155; *Iceman* (1984), 45–47, 48, 50, 51, 52, 55, 56, 57, 58, 61, 64, 91–92, 94, 96, 102, 106, 110, 111, 147, 150, 162–63, 168–69; *I.Q.* (1994), xv, xvi, xvii, 102, 122, 164, 168–70, 171, 172, 183; *It Runs in the Family* (2003), xi, xv, 127–37, 147; *I Was Amelia Earhart* (screenplay), 118; *Last Man* (screenplay), 145, 146n; *Last Orders* (2001), ix, xi, xiv, xv, xvii, 114–19, 120–26, 127, 130, 132, 141, 144, 146n, 164, 168, 171, 173, 182, 183, 185–86; *The Mandolin Man* (screenplay), 56; *Meet Me at the Melba* (screenplay), 57, 94; *The Mild One* (short, late 1950s), 154; *Misconceptions* (screenplay), 57, 95; *Mr. Baseball* (1992), xv, xvi, 102, 164, 169–71; *Party* (short film, 1970), 158–59; *People Make Papers* (documentary short, 1965), 53, 155; *Plenty* (1985), ix, xiv, xv, xvi, xvii, 48, 51, 52–53, 56, 57, 58–60, 61, 63–64, 65, 75, 92–94, 95, 111, 112, 114, 117, 140, 144, 145, 146n, 148–49, 150, 151, 153, 159, 162, 165, 171, 182; *The Priest* (1973), viii, xii, xvii, 7, 53, 79–80, 108, 153, 158, 177, 179, 180; *Roadshow* (screenplay), 50; *Roxanne* (1987), ix, xiv, xv, xvi, 62, 65–66, 74, 86, 88, 94–97, 98, 102, 104, 107, 113, 147, 151, 157, 171, 172; *The Russia House* (1990), ix, xiv, xv, xvi, 72–73, 86, 99–101, 103, 106, 111–12, 114, 115, 147, 149, 153, 159, 161, 164, 173, 181, 182; *Six Degrees of Separation* (1993), ix, xiv, xv, xvi, xvii, 104, 110, 112–13, 114, 118, 124, 144, 147, 151, 164, 173, 177, 183; *Tomorrow's Canberra* (advertisement, 1972), 155–56; *Words and Pictures* (2013), xv, xvi, 143, 160–61, 166–68, 171, 177, 180, 181, 182, 187–88

Schindler's Ark (film, 1993), 108
Schindler's Ark (novel, 1982), xiii
Scholes, Roger, viii
Secret River, The (novel, 2005), 143, 146n
Selleck, Tom, 102, 164, 170
September 11, 131
Seventh-Day Adventists, 69, 84, 102, 111
Shine (1996), 142, 146n
Shiner (2000), 184
Shipping News, The (2001), 83, 118, 122, 141, 145, 146n
Shiralee, The (1957), xii
Shteinman, Jonathan, 145
Simon, John, 128
Simon, Neil, 76
Singer and the Dancer, The (1977), xii
Slade, Bernard, 50
Slater, Gian, 187
Smeaton, Bruce, xviii, 25, 64, 68, 162–63
Smith, Frank, 155

Smith, Will, ix, xviii, 105, 106, 165, 168, 172, 173
Solomon, Ed, 169
Spacek, Sissy, 32, 47, 57
Spacey, Kevin, 146n
Spy (2015), 171
Stallone, Sylvester, 170
Steenburgen, Mary, ix
Stevens, Roy, 14
Stigwood, Robert, 39
Stitt, Alex, 154, 155, 156
Stoppard, Tom, xiv, 72, 86, 99, 164
Stork (1971), xii, 6
Streep, Meryl, xv, 48, 52, 59, 61, 63, 68–70, 72, 84, 93, 111, 140, 146n, 148, 150, 151, 159
Streisand, Barbra, 104
Sutherland, Donald, 105, 128
Sweet Basil, New York City, 184
Swift, Graham, xiv, 114, 121, 146n, 168

Takanashi, Aya, 164
Talented Mr. Ripley, The (1999), 154
Tarantino, Quentin, xviii, 167, 173
Tate, Nick, 9
Taylor, Geoff, 79
Tesich, Steve, 60, 93, 95
Thompson, Jack, 16
Three Cheers for the Paraclete (novel, 1968), xii
Three Musketeers, The (1973), 94
Thring, Frank, Snr., xii
Tinker, Tailor, Soldier, Spy (novel, 1974), 72
Toronto Film Festival, 127, 142
Tower Records, New York City, 185
Town Like Alice, A (TV mini-series, 1981), 34
Tracy, Spencer, 21, 57
Travolta, John, 118, 146n
Treasure of the Sierra Madre, The (1948), 21

Trespassers, The (1976), xii
True Story of Eskimo Nell, The (1975), xii
Tune, Tommy, 50
Twickenham Studios, xxii, 52
Two Thousand Weeks (1969), xii

Ullman, Tracey, 59
Uncertain Fate (novel, 1998), 146n
Underhill, Geoff, 79
Universal Pictures, 29, 32, 42, 45, 51, 57, 58, 90, 92, 125, 169
Ustinov, Peter, 172

Victoria College of the Arts at Melbourne University (VCA, Swinburne Film and TV School), viii, xii, 7, 8, 10, 178
Visconti, Luchino, 144

Wade, Kevin, 170
Wages of Fear, The (1952), 4
Wake in Fright (1971), 98
Walkabout (1971), 98
Warner Bros., 40, 57, 74
Weatherhead, Bruce, 156
Weaver, Sigourney, 77
Weir, Peter, xii, 28, 30, 33, 47, 49, 61, 72, 138
Wenham, David, 146n
Werribee Park Mansion, Victoria, 25, 87, 88
Wetherby (1985), 58, 60, 94
White, Patrick, xv, 138–39, 144, 147–48
Wigutow, Jesse, 128
Wild Child, The (1991), 45
Wilder, Billy, 21
Williams, Kate, 116, 122, 128, 185
Williams, Robin, 76, 118, 146n
Willis, Gordon, 182
Winger, Debra, 77
Winstone, Ray, 122

Wittliff, William, 32, 57, 89, 168
Woolf, Virginia, 176
Wyler, William, 21

Zaks, Jerry, 104
Zigmond, Vilmos, 160, 182
Zimmerman, Don, 92

www.ingramcontent.com/pod-product-compliance
Lightning Source LLC
Chambersburg PA
CBHW021839220426
43663CB00005B/326